Singapore

THE BRADT TRAVEL GUIDE

THE BRADT STORY

The first Bradt travel guide was written by Hilary and George Bradt in 1974 on a river barge floating down a tributary of the Amazon in Bolivia. From their base in Boston, Massachusetts, they went on to write and publish four other backpacking guides to the Americas and one to Africa.

In the 1980s Hilary continued to develop the Bradt list in England, and also established herself as a travel writer and tour leader. The company's publishing emphasis evolved towards broader-based guides to new destinations – usually the first to be published on those countries – complemented by hiking, rail and wildlife guides.

Since winning *The Sunday Times* Small Publisher of the Year Award in 1997, we have continued to fill the demand for detailed, well-written guides to unusual destinations, while maintaining the company's original ethos of low-impact travel.

Travel guides are by their nature continuously evolving. If you experience anything which you would like to share with us, or if you have any amendments to make to this guide, please write; all your letters are read and passed on to the author. Most importantly, do remember to travel with an open mind and to respect the customs of your hosts – it will add immeasurably to your enjoyment.

Happy travelling!

Hilary Bradt

19 High Street, Chalfont St Peter, Bucks SL9 9QE, England
Tel: 01753 893444; fax: 01753 892333
Email: info@bradt-travelguides.com
Web: www.bradt-travelguides.com

Singapore

THE BRADT TRAVEL GUIDE

John Nichol
Adrian Phillips
Isobel Dorling

Bradt Travel Guides Ltd, UK
The Globe Pequot Press Inc, USA

First published in 2002 by Bradt Travel Guides Ltd,
19 High Street, Chalfont St Peter, Bucks SL9 9QE, England
web: www.bradt-travelguides.com
Published in the USA by The Globe Pequot Press Inc, 246 Goose Lane,
PO Box 480, Guilford, Connecticut 06437-0480

Text/maps copyright © 2002 Bradt Travel Guides Ltd
Photographs © 2002 Individual photographers

British Library Cataloguing in Publication Data
A catalogue record for this book is available from the British Library

ISBN 1 84162 046 7

Library of Congress Cataloging-in-Publication Data applied for

Photographs
Front cover Henry Oakeley (Vanda Miss Joaquim orchid)
Text Veronica Garbutt (VG), David Lansdown/Sylvia Cordaiy (DL),
Jamie Marshall (JM), John Parker/Sylvia Cordaiy (JP), Neil Setchfield (NS),
Singapore Tourist Board (STB), Julian Worker/Sylvia Cordaiy (JW)

Illustrations Carole Vincer
Maps Steve Munns

Typeset from the author's disc by Wakewing
Printed and bound in Italy by Legoprint SpA, Trento

Authors

John Nichol was born in India in 1939. After World War II, he came to England with his family and attended art school where he studied theatrical design. However, his interests changed dramatically when he was given a baby cuckoo to look after, and this led to a study of zoology and two years' work in a zoo. He spent many years abroad collecting plants and animals and researching biological subjects, as well as filming. Twenty-something years ago he entered the world of television, where he became a successful producer of documentaries and light entertainment programmes. He has also written several books and has commercial interests in Singapore.

Adrian Phillips first travelled to Southeast Asia six years ago. He joined Bradt Travel Guides in 2001, after completing a PhD in English literature, and is now the assistant editor.

Isobel Dorling is a retired maths teacher who has lived in Singapore for two or three months at a time almost every year since 1994. She has explored the island thoroughly while her husband, Peter, formerly with the BBC, worked as a consultant television journalism trainer with MediaCorp, Singapore's national TV and radio station.

Contents

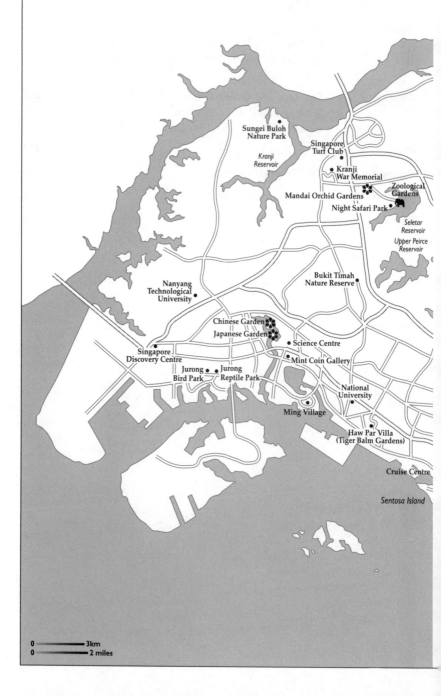

SINGAPORE ISLAND

Sungei Buloh
Nature Park

*Kranji
Reservoir*

Singapore
Turf Club

Kranji
War Memorial

Mandai Orchid Gardens

Zoological
Gardens

Night Safari Park

*Seletar
Reservoir*

*Upper Peirce
Reservoir*

Bukit Timah
Nature Reserve

Nanyang
Technological
University

Chinese Garden
Japanese Garden

Science Centre

Singapore
Discovery Centre

Mint Coin Gallery

Jurong
Bird Park

Jurong
Reptile Park

National
University

Ming Village

Haw Par Villa
(Tiger Balm Gardens)

Cruise Centre

Sentosa Island

0 — 3km
0 — 2 miles

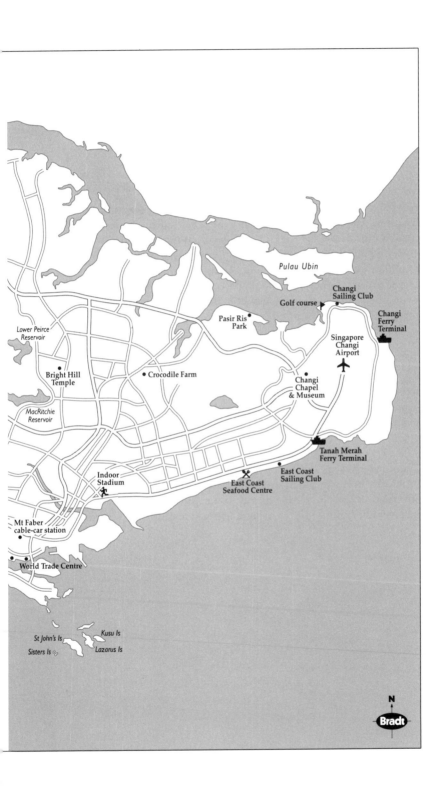

Pulau Ubin

Golf course

Changi
Sailing Club

Changi
Ferry
Terminal

Pasir Ris
Park

Lower Peirce
Reservoir

Singapore
Changi
Airport

Bright Hill
Temple

Crocodile Farm

Changi
Chapel
& Museum

MacRitchie
Reservoir

Tanah Merah
Ferry Terminal

Indoor
Stadium

East Coast
Sailing Club

East Coast
Seafood Centre

Mt Faber
cable-car station

World Trade Centre

St John's Is

Kusu Is

Sisters Is

Lazarus Is

N

Bradt

Acknowledgements

Acknowledgements in books are boring, so I will keep this section brief; however, without help from all sorts of people such a book is impossible to write. I must thank Dayne Lim and Neville at the Singapore Tourism Board, as well as Anna, Christina and Georgina, who were unbelievably patient with a million queries, and Pat Young, Wong Yew Kwan, Patsy Tayler, Sentosa Development Corporation and the Singapore Economic Development Board, whose help was invaluable. Much of the information herein came from or through them and the Singapore Tourism Board.

This is for Perse, with my love

John Nichol

My sincere thanks to Hannah Postgate, Andrew Rudd and Peter Dorling for their contributions to several sections of this guide; to my parents for their support; to Jo Scotchmer for sacrificing her social life, without complaint; and to Tricia Hayne and Hilary Bradt for the opportunity to tackle this project.

Adrian Phillips

I am indebted to our many Singaporean friends for their patience and generosity in answering numerous questions about the island and showing us around over the years. Also thanks to the Singapore Tourist Board for their help, and that of the staff of many hotels and restaurants.

Isobel Dorling

Introduction

Singapore is full of colour, laughter, fun and surprises. It is crammed with wonderful things to see and enjoy. It is vibrant, dynamic and perpetually evolving; I have been going to Singapore since the late 1950s, and each time the place has changed. Nevertheless, there are some things that remain stubbornly and satisfyingly fixed from year to year. Here you will have no difficulty communicating, as everyone speaks English. You will be safe, as there is virtually no crime. You will find that the people are immensely helpful, and will go out of their way to offer assistance. You will discover that Singapore is clean and organised, and in these ways quite different from other areas of the tropics. Transport is reliable and every part of the island readily accessible. The food is fabulous, the accommodation, at the very least, comfortable and attractive. The whole country is impressively efficient – over the years I have found that the only thing Singaporeans cannot do is make toast!

Despite all these attractions, for most tourists the country serves simply as a brief stopping – and shopping – point on the way to the Antipodes, or one short stage of a broader tour of the Far East. After a frantic three days they depart clutching Gucci watches and silk suits. And it is certainly true that Singapore is an excellent place to shop; if you are looking for designer goodies you will have no difficulty finding them, and items are invariably cheaper than at home. However, the Singapore Tourism Board has rightly been doing its best to persuade visitors to stay longer, and it is slowly getting the message across. You can easily spend an entire day wandering through the Bukit Timah Reserve without seeing more than a fraction of what is there, and a day on Sentosa Island will pass in a flash. In the middle of Singapore is a wonderful zoo (a pleasant surprise for anyone who has experienced other tropical menageries), while elsewhere one can enjoy the marine life on offer at two aquariums, the birds and reptiles in several parks, and the exotic species to be found in the Botanic Gardens and other plant nurseries. If you want to discover what exists beyond the parades of shops, leave the town centre and make for the suburbs or the tiny, hidden *katongs*, or villages, which still exist, little changed from half a century ago. Visit little corner shops and brave the malodorous *durian* – the fruit of Southeast Asia described as tasting like heaven and smelling like hell. There are still places where you can sit at chipped Formica tables on the pavement and spit the seeds into cardboard boxes on the floor. A day spent wandering through the wilder parts of the island will be well rewarded. You will encounter fascinating habitats that have grown up around abandoned farms, and flora introduced on former plantations and gardens as well as that which has always existed on the island. Alternatively, immerse yourself in the multifarious cultural events which Singapore hosts each year, and which range from art exhibitions, ballet and live theatre to food festivals and fashion shows. Or wonder at temples that look like stage sets, and spectacular, breathtaking statues.

But if you wish to relish the untamed parts of Singapore, go now. There is no doubt that the open land will in time disappear. On each trip, I discover that something else has appeared where before there was nothing. It is a sad fact that the speed of Singapore's development, the very changeability that in part makes it such an intriguing and exciting place, has also meant sacrifice. Much that used to be attractive has disappeared in the rush for an affluent future. It is becoming ever more difficult to find undisturbed pieces of the island as it used to be. Even sadder is that many Singaporeans believe this to be a good thing. Some time ago a local friend of mine looked at a monstrous construction beside the river and bemoaned the fact that it was only eight rather than 20 storeys in height. Singaporeans are proud of the progress they have made and see no merit in relics from the past. Perhaps this is even greater reason to pay the country more than a cursory glance before parts of its heritage are lost for ever.

John Nichol

FEEDBACK REQUEST

Every effort has been made to ensure that the details contained within this book are as accurate and up to date as possible. Inevitably, however, things move on – especially in a dynamic country like Singapore. Any information regarding such changes, or relating to your experiences in Singapore – good or bad – would be very gratefully received. Such feedback is priceless when compiling further editions, and in ensuring pleasant stays for future visitors.

Happy holidays!

Bradt Travel Guides Ltd, 19 High St, Chalfont St Peter, Bucks SL9 9QE
Tel: 01753 893444 Fax: 01753 892333
Email: info@bradt-travelguides.com
Web: www.bradt-travelguides.com

Part One

General Information

2

SINGAPORE AT A GLANCE

Location At the southern tip of the Malaysian peninsula
Size 650km²
Time GMT + 8 hours/BST + 7 hours
Electricity 220–240 volts, AC 50 hertz
International telephone code + 65
Currency Singapore dollar (S$)
Population Approximately four million
Language English is spoken everywhere, and is used for public notices. Other languages include Mandarin and various Chinese dialects, Malay and Tamil. The official language is Malay.
Religion Buddhism, Taoism, Islam, Christianity, Hinduism
Flag Red and white, with a crescent moon and five stars
National flower Vanda Miss Joaquim orchid
National symbol Merlion – a figure which is half-fish, half-lion (Singapura means 'Lion City')
GDP US$92.4bn
Major industries Commerce, financial services, manufacturing (electronics, chemicals), tourism

Background Information

GEOGRAPHY AND CLIMATE

Singapore is a tiny island of about the same size and shape as the Isle of Wight (off the south coast of England). It tucks into the southern tip of the Malay peninsula. Immediately to the north of it is the much larger Malaysia. Its surface area is approximately 650km², and the island measures about 42km (25 miles) east–west and 28km (14 miles) north–south. To the south are the many islands that make up Indonesia. It is only 1° 20' north of the Equator – that is, about 135km. This means that the annual temperature remains relatively constant, the daily average being 26.7°C. The difference between the hottest and the coolest months of the year is only 2°C. This close proximity to the Equator also means that the hours of daylight remain similar throughout the year. Daylight is between 07.00 and 19.00, with about 15 minutes of dusk and dawn. The country is very humid, with a daily average humidity of 84.3%. There is 400cm of rainfall annually, spread evenly throughout the year. The rain is not a problem for the visitor, even if you go during what is described as the rainy season, since showers, although heavy, are short-lived. It is lovely, after a shower, to emerge from the air-conditioned shopping mall where you have been sheltering into the humid atmosphere outside.

The sea

The Straits of Johore to the north, the South China Sea to the south and east, and the Straits of Malacca to the west – surrounding the island – remain a constant 28°C throughout the year. Typhoons, which are a menace further up the coast of Asia, do not touch Singapore.

NATURAL HISTORY

Apart from private land and an area to the very west of the island (where there is a military firing range), most of Singapore is open to exploration. If you hire a car, use it to tour the country, for the landscape varies. The northeast quarter of the island contains many abandoned agricultural premises where in years gone by there were pig farms and similar commercial operations. Nowadays Singapore does not permit the keeping of pigs or cattle, but these abandoned farms are rich in plant species and wildlife. There are an estimated 2,106 recorded species of native seed plants on Singapore, and 170 fern species. As for fauna, species of reptile, bird and amphibian are particularly prevalent. There are over two million insects and invertebrates, some 660 spiders, 24 amphibians, about 400 crabs, 40 freshwater fish, 140 reptiles (including 90 snakes), 350 recorded bird species, and around 60 mammals.

Flora

Singapore calls itself the 'garden city', and with very good reason. There is a pot-pourri of introduced and native species. Some exotics were imported, accidentally or otherwise, by early sea-traders from the Malayan archipelago, India and the Middle East, and China; others were planted in more recent times. For many years there has been a government policy to make Singapore as green a city as possible, and it has invested, and continues to invest, millions of dollars in the widespread planting of trees and shrubs. Indeed, since 1970, government agencies have planted well over five million trees and shrubs along Singapore's major roads and streets. It is estimated that by 2010 there will be 300km of green park connectors forming a 'green network' across the island. As a consequence, every footbridge across the road, every bit of undeveloped land, every block of concrete, is covered as far as possible in swathes of gloriously flamboyant **bougainvillaea**. Attractive trees are everywhere, while **hibiscus**, **jacarandas** and climbing plants like **syngonum** abound. An example of Singapore's commitment to plants (as well as an indication of the forward planning that goes into most things here) is the long straight road from Changi

Bougainvillaea

Airport into the city. It has been constructed in such a way that in the event of a national emergency it can be used as a military runway. However, in the meantime, along the extent of the central reservation are rows and rows of huge timber boxes containing so many trees and shrubs that they completely disguise the runway beneath. It must be one of the most attractive roads leading from an airport to a city in the world.

In this country there are plants wherever you go; always keep your eyes open, even in built-up areas. Many balconies and verandas have orchids and other plants growing in pots, and there are trees festooned with **ferns**, **orchids**, **mosses** and a host of other epiphytes struggling for life in their branches. Sometimes branches can have whole rows of plants growing along their lengths. Some of these, such as the bird's nest fern, grow to enormous sizes – especially by comparison with the puny specimens on our windowsills at home. Beyond the centre of the city, there are old farmsteads and other neglected buildings that are

Bird's nest fern

homes to a broad selection of species. Carnivorous **pitcher plants**, which lure and trap insects before consuming them in fluids laden with digestive enzymes, can be found in such places as the nature trails on Sentosa Island. And, of course, a trip to the Botanic Gardens (see pages 111–12) is alone worth the cost of the flight to Singapore! Keep a look out for the national flower (since 1981), the **Vanda Miss Joaquim**. This pretty pink and white orchid is a natural hybrid discovered in a local garden in 1893.

Vanda Miss Joaquim

Fauna

While there is much to interest gardeners and botanists, Singapore is also an Eden for animal enthusiasts. You will not find too many animals within the towns, but this changes as you move out to the suburbs and beyond. At first glance, the populated areas of the country seem to offer little, but in fact they heave with animal life. It is true that there is not an enormous number of mammal species; you will, nevertheless, find squirrels, tree shrews, flying squirrels, long-tailed macaques (the only wild monkeys left on the island), rodents, and many other small mammals. When it comes to birds, invertebrates, amphibians and reptiles, you will be spoilt for choice. On some evenings, conversation can be drowned out by the various sounds of frogs, cicadas, crows and sparrows. At such times you become very aware of the breadth and richness of Singapore's wildlife.

Mammals

Bats are probably Singapore's commonest mammals. They live throughout the island, although it is easy to miss them unless you keep a careful watch. The most readily spotted are the huge **flying foxes** or **fruit-bats**. They hang from branches during the day, and at dusk set off for the nearest fruiting trees. There they gorge on fruit through the hours of darkness and stream back to their trees to sleep throughout the day. Like many other species of animal, they are far less common than they were in the past, and are hunted by man. In Indonesia and Malaysia, though not in Singapore, these bats are sold live in the animal markets, and taken home for the pot. Though they are getting scarcer, however, you should still be able to spot them at dusk as they wake for the night. Ensure that you don't mistake them for birds – their silhouettes are actually quite different.

Malay fruit bat

A few generations ago, very large mammals were found in Singapore. When early colonists arrived on the island they saw a large predatory animal that was said to be a lion, after which the country is named – Singapura meaning 'Lion City'. There used to be tigers on the island, too, but they were shot out of existence. The last one was killed well into the 20th century while hiding beneath the Billiard Room at Raffles Hotel (see page 133) – although it is said that that particular animal had escaped from a circus. The largest mammals to be found now are the small-clawed otter, the long-tailed macaque, the dainty and hugely secretive mouse deer, and the remarkable pangolin.

Long-tailed macaques can be seen in large troops in Bukit Timah Nature Reserve (see pages 185–6) and in the Central Catchment Nature Reserve forests. You will hear them crashing around in the canopy, and will soon recognise their rattling call. These animals are very curious, and may follow hikers, swinging along in the trees above. Do not feed the monkeys or leave belongings unattended, or they may be subject to inquisitive scrutiny. Be especially wary of getting too close to females who are on heat or carrying babies, as you might face the wrath of protective males.

The **pangolin** is an insectivorous, strangely reptilian-looking mammal with a long nose and an even longer prehensile tail. Nocturnal, rare and extremely shy, it lives on a diet of termites and ants. It is covered in scales; sadly these are said to have a curative effect on various conditions by practitioners of Chinese medicine, and pangolins are consequently hunted wherever they are found. Of course, this faith in the curative properties of their scales is as unfounded as that in powdered rhino horn – which, incidentally, the Chinese believe is a febrifuge (a medicine that reduces fever) and not an aphrodisiac, as mistakenly understood by many in the West.

Another mammal whose numbers have been severely depleted is the **slow loris**. These are small, teddy-bear-like animals, slow-moving and nocturnal, so the chances of seeing one while you are on holiday are minimal. It is wrongly believed that their eyes have medicinal uses; in the past, lorises were hunted, and their eyes torn from them while still alive, after which the animals were put back in their trees. Unsurprisingly, they did not live long thereafter. The practice has been filmed in India, where it still continues. Elsewhere, however, they are now strictly protected, and are no longer hunted in Singapore.

The **flying squirrel** (known locally as the **flying lemur**) is a small mammal with dense, pale-grey fur like that of a chinchilla. It has flaps of skin on either side of its body, between front and rear legs, which, when it is at rest, give it an attractive, 'frilly' appearance, rather like a hovercraft's skirt. By extending these flaps, it is able to glide through the air from tree to tree. It is a frustrating animal to try to look at. As you approach, it disappears around to the far side of a tree trunk; despite your best and most stealthy efforts, it persists in scuttling out of sight.

Birds

For some time the birdlife of Singapore was in decline. However, it is now richer than ever, due in no small part to the government policy of planting

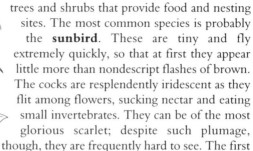

Yellow-backed sunbird

trees and shrubs that provide food and nesting sites. The most common species is probably the **sunbird**. These are tiny and fly extremely quickly, so that at first they appear little more than nondescript flashes of brown. The cocks are resplendently iridescent as they flit among flowers, sucking nectar and eating small invertebrates. They can be of the most glorious scarlet; despite such plumage, though, they are frequently hard to see. The first sign of sunbird presence is often the sound of its distinctive call. It is common for a single bird, or a small flock of half a dozen or so, to dive among the foliage of a shrub or tree in the search for insects. That is an excellent time to spot them because they are totally absorbed in what they are doing. Lie on your back on the ground looking up into the branches of a suitable tree and wait patiently. If you are lucky you will be rewarded with close views of these little gems.

Another surprisingly common species is the **tailor bird**. Like sunbirds, these are small and easy to overlook. Much of the time, they carry their tails vertically, very like wrens. They nest low down in shrubs, sewing the edges of a leaf, or sometimes two leaves, together from the underside. Once they have constructed pockets in this manner, they stuff them with fibres and lay their eggs in these secret little nests. In the story *Rikki Tikki Tavi*, Rudyard Kipling made tailor birds famous, referring to them as '*darzi*', which is what they are called in India. They are sometimes found busily attending to their nests in the Jurong Bird Park. Another, even smaller, species is the brightly coloured **flowerpecker**. Unfortunately, you are unlikely to witness one without the aid of an experienced ornithologist.

Reptiles

While snakes are common in Singapore, there is no need to be overly anxious. In the first place, you are unlikely to come across a snake by accident, both because most are small and camouflaged and because they are usually shy creatures. And, in the second, the majority of the species represent no real threat to humans. Only the **cobra** has the potential to endanger human life. The likelihood of encountering a cobra, however, either accidentally or otherwise, is extremely remote. Indeed, you are more likely to find one in a shop in nearby Indonesia, Malaysia or Thailand, where the cobra is sold as food. The meat, and especially the blood, is said to rejuvenate elderly men whose powers are flagging. Contrary to what many people think, cobras are not aggressive snakes and will disappear if they get the chance. Furthermore, they rarely bite even if cornered, although they will rear up and display their hoods, and can feint and strike with their mouths shut. If you should ever happen to be bitten, don't panic but seek medical help immediately. Once in hospital a shot of antivenin should counter the harmful effects.

Reticulate python

Pythons can be seen not infrequently swimming in the storm drains. In Jurong Bird Park, their appetite for ground-nesting birds means that they are treated as pests and trapped by the keepers. The **reticulate python** vies with the South American anaconda for the title of the world's longest snake. Although it is unusual these days to come across a reticulate python which measures more than 4m or so (these have all been made into handbags), 3m pythons are not at all rare in Singapore. I once had the privilege of watching a very large specimen being trapped by bird keepers in the walk-through aviary at Jurong Bird Park. They are beautiful animals, especially if they have recently sloughed.

Long, slender, green or brown **whip snakes** are not uncommon, though they are well hidden in the bushes. Despite the fact that they are sometimes a vivid green, their camouflage is extraordinarily effective. Though some are venomous, they are of no danger to humans. The venom is only sufficient to kill the lizards on which they prey; in any case, the fangs are located at the backs of their mouths and it is impossible to receive a toxic bite from these gentle little snakes.

Keep your eyes peeled when you are at Pasir Ris (in the east of the island; see page 196) and you might be fortunate enough to catch a glimpse of the **mangrove snake**, a handsome, nocturnal animal that grows to about 2m in length. It is black on top and bright yellow beneath, with the yellow forming vertical stripes through the black at intervals along its sides. Another you might come across in the secondary forests is the **paradise snake**. It is slim, hardly thicker than a pencil, and 1–1.3m long when adult. Its markings are exquisite, consisting of black and cream broken by a series of bright red 'flowers' along the spine. The most incredible characteristic of this species is revealed in its other name, 'flying snake'. It is able to make a hollow of its underside, which forms a long cushion of air and allows the snake to launch itself from trees and glide astonishing distances to lower branches. While strictly speaking it glides rather than flies, its method is very effective, and startling to watch. Sadly, it only 'flies' in exceptional circumstances.

There is a small and insignificant lizard that refuses to be outdone. When it is at rest it might very well be confused for any small arboreal lizard. However, revelling in the scientific name *Draco volans*, or **flying lizard**, it is able to glide from tree to tree just like its legless cousin. Its means of achieving this is equally impressive. It has very long ribs, which it spreads out at either side into two bright-red wings. Sitting motionless on the vertical surface of a tree, it will suddenly take off. After a few seconds it lands and becomes invisible once more. The speed of its actions, coupled with the fact that, like the flying squirrel, it prefers to keep a tree trunk between itself and any curious observer, make it tricky to observe closely.

You should find, though, that other lizards are less reticent about their whereabouts. Even today, when air conditioning has meant that houses and hotels are hermetically sealed from the outside world, you ought to see **geckoes**, especially in the evenings when shop-houses have their lights on. The geckoes creep out of cracks in which they spend the day, and station themselves near the lights that attract insects for the lizards to feed upon. Once you learn how to recognise it, the call of a gecko is quite distinctive and will often give its position away. All over the Orient, geckoes are known as 'chit chats' (or something similar), and this describes the sound they make very nicely. The **tokay gecko** is large, freckled with blue and red spots, and has a loud call that sounds just like its name. I have never seen one in Singapore (nor indeed have I found any reference to the animal), but I am certain that I heard its call on one occasion, and I would expect to find the species on the island since it occurs throughout the area.

If you are anywhere near a stream or a river, look out for a **monitor lizard**. These monsters, used in many of the old dinosaur movies, are more common than many people realise. They look positively prehistoric, though those that starred in the 'lost world' epics of the past usually had fins and spikes attached to give a more fearsome appearance. Though they are predators, they are unlikely to do you any harm; indeed, they will do their best to keep out of your way if they spot you. They can grow to a large size. The biggest members of the family are the Komodo dragons, from the island of Komodo in Indonesia. These can be aggressive, and are capable of tearing the carcass of a goat to pieces with their formidable teeth. The monitors in Singapore are not so dangerous. Nevertheless, they can deliver a very nasty bite to those foolish enough to handle them, locking their jaws in a vice-like grip. They are more likely, however, to lash out with their tails, catching the victim across the forearm or face, and leaving a painful weal. But leave them alone and they will leave you alone. You can watch them from bridges, looking down into the storm drains or riverbeds below. There is a healthy colony of monitors at the eastern end of the island of Sentosa (see pages 202–9); if you are travelling on the monorail, look out from the left side of the vehicle and you might see some on the muddy foreshore.

Terrapins can be found here and there. Some are native, others have been imported by dealers from the USA and are sold to devout Buddhists to release into the wild. Terrapins are hardy animals, and, given sufficient warmth and food, they thrive. The result is that American terrapins are now far more common than the native species. If you sit by the edge of a lake at the Botanic Gardens (see pages 111–12), you are certain to see many terrapins. They might not, however, look like the tiny mites seen in pet shops in the West; given the right conditions, terrapins can grow to a foot long. Terrapins are also found on Kusu ('Turtle') Island (see page 210). If you want to be sure of a sighting, and you have a strong stomach, go to the basement food market at Peoples' Park Complex in Chinatown (see page 162). Here they are packed into tiny cages, along with other wild animals, and sold for food. Avert your gaze if a sale is made – the slaughter of these animals is not for the squeamish. These terrapins are imported from other Asian countries, and appear later on Chinese menus as turtle soup.

Amphibians

You will certainly hear Singapore's amphibians in the evenings, especially after a heavy shower of rain. You might initially confuse the call of frogs with the high-pitched shriek of the omnipresent cicadas. But if you go for a walk after dark and look into water-courses and storm drains, and on grassy banks, you will begin to find frogs. And if you go further afield, and walk through a heavily vegetated area with a torch, you will discover that the place is covered with tiny amphibians. These are often **tree frogs**, with round pads on the ends of their toes, hanging on to the far sides of leaves. As you approach they will become silent, but stand quietly with your torch switched off and they will soon start to call once more. Many are smaller than a thumbnail, and few are bigger than a ten-pence piece. The volume of sound they can produce is out of all proportion to their size. Unfortunately, there are now a number of **American bullfrogs** on the island that, like the terrapins, have been introduced for release. American bullfrogs grow to be enormous and are voracious predators that quickly consume large quantities of local amphibians and fish.

CONSERVATION

Human impact upon the island's environment had begun even before Raffles arrived in 1819. Early Chinese settlers had cleared interior forest for plantations. The pace of change accelerated under British colonial rule, still more after World War II, and particularly as Singapore raced towards developed-nation prosperity in the 1970s. Today, Singaporeans enjoy clean air and water, and are surrounded by a 'greenery' of sorts. However, public education about the conservation of the country's green assets is embryonic. There are problems with waste generation and disposal – the islanders are avid consumers but lazy recyclers. And, despite an excellent public transport system and disincentives for vehicle ownership (see page 28), they remain stubbornly attached to their cars.

Singapore was once an important place in the international trade in wild animals. Furthermore, until comparatively recently – the late 1960s – it was one of the major live animal centres in the world. Shipments of livestock were flown all over the globe from the country. There are still a few legal exporters around, but modern legislation means that consignments are infinitely smaller than they used to be. These days the livestock you see in dealers' premises is primarily for local fanciers. And, with worldwide conservation legislation, the trade in wild animals is also considerably diminished.

Having said that, Singapore's conservation laws are regularly ignored by all but a few noble and dedicated people. Where there is a market there will be people to exploit it, and not many years ago there was still a very healthy illegal trade in animals from this part of the world. Bird trapping, for instance, is outlawed in Singapore, but it continues to thrive, and birds are still trapped in the isolated northern parts of the country. Taking chicks from nests and trapping birds is, and always has been, a popular pastime in the area, just as it was many generations ago in the West. As long ago as 1878, J F McNair was observing that Malays 'are very clever at catching birds by means of horsehair nooses. By this means doves and pigeons are readily taken, the juice of the *gutta* or indiarubber being sometimes used as birdlime'. Birdlime is a sticky substance used by bird catchers to trap birds on twigs so that they can be caged. Once the trapped bird is removed from the sticky branch the birdlime is removed with a little lighter fluid on a pad of cloth. The law is flouted because it is relatively ineffective; unless a person is actually caught in the act, nothing can be done to prosecute him or her. Traps and mist nets are freely available in shops throughout the country despite the fact that they have no purpose other than the capture of birds.

There are two main obstacles to effective conservation in Singapore. The first is that, unlike in many Western countries, a careful respect for, and cultivation of, the natural world is not a priority for the population; most people are unaware not only of the existence of legislation, but of the need for conservation at all. The second is that the population of Singapore is constantly growing, and this puts pressure upon a small country to meet its increasing needs. Ever since Stamford Raffles landed in 1819, the progress of 'civilisation' has steadily used up more and more of the island's natural resources. A little over a hundred years ago, Nathaniel Cantley set up the first forest reserves, and, although these were for logging, it was nevertheless the first step towards protecting parts of the countryside. Today, the only remaining area of primary rainforest, which originally covered the whole surface of the island, is the Bukit Timah Nature Reserve in the centre, which was given full protection in 1951.

The inevitable damage caused by an expanding population makes conservation more important than ever before. While it is true that there are more open areas containing shrubs, trees and wildlife than there used to be – a direct result of government policy – it is equally the case that other parts of the island are scheduled for commercial development. It concerns some that, although the government is making the right noises about conservation at the moment, there is a danger that its policies could be abandoned at a moment's notice and without a backward glance.

Perhaps this is a little unfair. There is an ever-increasing awareness of the need for conservation, and each year the country holds a 'Clean and Green Week' when citizens are actively encouraged to pick up litter, clean the streets, plant trees, and generally do 'green' things. The government has also decided to place emphasis on the life sciences, including biology, in school curricula. Three 'green groups' stand out for their long track records of good work and their sophisticated structures:

Singapore Environment Council 21 Lewin Terrace, Fort Canning Park, Singapore 179290; tel: 6337 6062; email: secnet@singnet.com.sg; web: www.sec.org.sg

Nature Society 510 Geylang Rd, #02-05 The Sunflower, Singapore 389466; tel: 6741 2036; email: natsoc@mbox2.singnet.com.sg; web: www.post1.com/hom/naturesinsingapore
Society for the Prevention of Cruelty to Animals 31 Mount Vernon Rd, Singapore 368054; tel: 6287 5355; email: spca@n3wt.com; web: www.n3wt.com/SPCA

For details of the only full-time nature tour guide, see *Local tours*, page 59.

HISTORY
Joseph Conrad called Singapore 'impalpable and ensnaring', and added that it was like 'a whispered promise of mysterious delight' when he finally came ashore after being shipwrecked and drifting in an open boat for over 13 hours. All this is still true, but it surprises many first-time visitors to discover that Singapore is not the Singapore of legend and mystery that they anticipate. Much of this tiny country could well be a tropical Manhattan. Since the place is in many ways as modern as anywhere in the world, it is easy to forget that until 1819 it was a virtually uninhabited swamp, and that until the 1950s it was much like the rest of Southeast Asia at that time. It is only in recent decades that Singapore has leapt from primitive isolation into the 21st century. It is sometimes difficult to believe that many Singaporeans were born in a British colony.

Early history
There have probably been people living on Singapore for thousands of years. Because of its location it was at the junction of many shipping routes, and, at a time when China was far more civilised than the rest of the world, there was an island at the south of the Malay peninsula known then as P'u Luo Chung. In about 230AD an expedition was sent by the Chinese emperor to the waters around what we know today as Singapore. The expedition was led by General Lu Tai. One of the remaining extracts of his writings tells of an island that is believed to refer to Singapore. He records, 'To the east of Kon Li there is the people of P'u Luo Chung, each with a tail five or six inches long. They are accustomed to cannibalism.' At that time Singapore was an island of forests and swamps, inhabited only by a small community of Bugis fishermen at the mouth of the Singapore River. These people supplemented their meagre incomes with a spot of piracy – an 'industry', incidentally, which still thrives today along the Straits of Malacca, separating Singapore from the Indonesian island of Sumatra. Later, a Malayan Buddhist empire was established in the area. It was known as Sri Vijaya. Tumasek or Tumasik ('Sea Town'), as Singapore was called in those days, became a useful centre from which ships could be sent out to levy tolls on merchants travelling along the Straits of Malacca en route to China.

In time, the Chula king, Raja Suran, arrived at Tumasek, intending to turn it into a fortified naval base from which he could attack China. If tradition is to be believed, the Chinese emperor, on hearing this, sent Raja Suran a gift of

SINGAPORE'S OLD WRITTEN TALES
One of Singapore's old tales describes how in the seas surrounding Singapore there was a fish known as the 'garfish', which would skitter across the tops of the waves, apparently while standing on its tail. There are real garfish, and the unusual method of locomotion might refer to equally real flying fish. However, according to the story these fish were large enough to attack people on the beaches. The king decided to go down to the beach on his elephant to test the validity of these rumours. As he did so, a garfish leapt at him, leaving him with torn robes. A wise little boy who had witnessed the attack asked the king why he allowed the fish to continue such attacks when he could protect his people with a barricade of banana stems planted along the beach. The king took his advice, and the garfish, attempting to storm the newly formed barricade, were impaled in their thousands. Ironically, the king, fearing that the boy's wisdom could be a threat to his position in the future, rewarded his ingenuity by having him killed.

Singapore was clearly not the place to live if you happened to be in the wrong place at the wrong time. It was not long after the events concerning the garfish that an old priest named Tun Jana Khatib was held responsible when a palm tree split down its length and fell on to the king's palace. The monarch decided that this had occurred when the old man, practising his magic outside the queen's window, had decided to indulge in a spot of royal voyeurism. This he would not tolerate, and it is said that the old man was taken 'to the place of execution, which was near a cake shop, and there they shed his blood with a stabbing blow, but his body vanished leaving only the blood on the ground'. The red blood is said to be the reason for the red soil (tanah merah) of Singapore to this day.

Enough was enough. The king packed his bags and left with his people for Malaya where he founded Malacca, later to become the richest city in the Orient, and lived there free from the torments of garfish and awkward old voyeurs.

a ship full of geriatrics and rusty needles, the implication being that it would take a very long time for him to realise his dream. As a result Raja Suran's plans for invasion were abandoned.

In the 13th century, a member of the royal family of the Buddhist empire, Sang Nila Utana or Sri Tri Buana (depending on which account you read), was looking for a site on which to build a new city. Arriving at the shores of a comparatively unexplored island, he saw a large animal that he was unable to identify. It was described as being 'very graceful, with a black head, white neck and tawny body, swift and bold, and the size of a goat.' He asked if any of his retinue could identify it; clearly the others, like him, were not destined for careers in zoology for they decided that it was a lion, using the Sanskrit name, 'Singa'. The royal personage felt that this was a good omen and resolved to build his new city here, naming it 'Singapura' – 'Lion City'. Sang Nila Utana is regarded as the first king of Singapore, and he ruled from 1299AD to 1347AD. The king brought over his adoptive mother, citizens and specialists of all sorts, and horses and elephants, and quite a large city began to develop. It is said that the city was built on a number of terraces, and there are suggestions that this was the site of what Marco Polo referred to as 'Malaiur', though he never visited it.

Little is recorded of Singapore between Sang Nila Utana's reign and the 16th century, though we do know the names of several of the subsequent rulers. However, there are some interesting tales from old writings (see box, page 13). In the 15th century, the teacher Abdullah wrote of Singapore that 'on the river banks you could see lying about on the sand some hundreds of human skulls; some were old, others were fresh, some had flesh still clinging to them. The sea gypsies said they were the skulls of the victims of pirates, Singapura being the place where the prisoners were taken to be slaughtered.'

After this, any influence Singapore had enjoyed waned. Malacca, controlled by the Portuguese, became the major port in the area. In 1602, however, the Dutch East India Company was formed and, in 1641, the Dutch attacked Malacca and took it from the Portuguese. From then on it was the Dutch who governed most of the trade in the region, until the British East India Company came along and set up shop in the early 19th century.

The 'founding' of Singapore

The British East India Company had been trading for some time in India, but once it became established there it started to look further afield. On January 28 1819, Stamford Raffles, a young entrepreneur working for the East India Company and looking for opportunities, happened to sail into Singapura (see box opposite). Raffles went ashore on February 6 and told the local leader that he wished to set up a trading centre. If allowed to do so, he promised to pay US$3,000 a year for the privilege. However, the local leader pointed out that Singapura belonged to Johore, and only the sultan could agree to such a proposal. This presented Raffles with a problem because there was a dispute going on over the legitimate Sultan of Johore. Raffles solved it by restoring the legitimate heir, Tunku Long, to the throne, and paying him US$5,000. As a consequence, Raffles had little difficulty arranging a treaty with the new sultan. To mark this occasion, Raffles declared that henceforth Singapura would be a free port – which it remains to this day.

Raffles wrote a report to the East India Company explaining that his aim was 'not territory but trade'. He saw Singapore as 'a great commercial emporium and a fulcrum whence we may extend our influence politically as circumstances may hereafter require'. The determined and daring actions of Raffles had, throughout his career, provoked anger in some quarters, and this was true after he settled in Singapore. However, the move proved such a

RAFFLES

Thomas Stamford Bingley Raffles was the son of a ship's captain. His father ran a lucrative business transporting slaves from West Africa to the West Indies, and assorted cargo thence back to England. When he died, heavily in debt, his son accepted a job with the East India Company. After ten years as a clerk, he was taken to India as the assistant to the chief secretary. Within a week, Raffles had met and married a lady named Olivia. In Madras, Raffles soon made a name for himself with his indefatigable nature, his efficiency and his good humour. Consequently, it was not long before he was sent to manage the company's business in Burma, where he was promoted to chief secretary.

At this time, the East India Company decided that the Dutch monopoly on trade in the area could not be allowed to continue; in 1811, Lord Minto was put in command of a fleet of 90 ships and sent to attack Batavia, the capital of Java. The Dutch surrendered and Raffles was appointed lieutenant-governor. It was while he held this post that his wife, Olivia, died. In 1816, Raffles was recalled to England, whereupon the Dutch promptly retook Java. At home, Raffles was taken under the wing of British society, and before long he was given a knighthood.

Raffles decided to re-marry, this time to Sophia; after the wedding, he set off for the Far East once more with his second wife. He was asked to found a new port in Malaya, but on the way there he heard that the Dutch had taken it already. He consequently altered his objectives, and wrote to a friend, 'My attention is principally directed to Johore, and you must not be surprised if my next letter to you is dated from the site of the ancient city of Singapura.' The rest, of course, is history.

Surprisingly, Raffles spent just ten months in Singapore. Some time later, he and his family suffered a series of misfortunes. Of his four children, three died, and both he and his wife became desperately ill. In October 1822, he returned home, and died, a tired and sick man, in 1826.

commercial success that the loud complaints gradually faded to muffled grumbles. The Dutch, who until now had largely controlled all shipping in the area, quickly discovered how unpopular their trade practices were as ships and traders of all nations left the Dutch harbours and sailed for Singapura. Raffles was left to get on with things.

Thereafter Singapore continued to grow and succeed. Before he died, Raffles set up a legal system based on that of Britain, oversaw the development of Singapore's commercial success, and laid out a design for the town. The plan was for a group of villages rather than a town as such, with each 'village area' being assigned to a different group. The central plain (the Padang) and the hill (Fort Canning Hill) were to be for the colonial government and the military, while the merchants were given an area known as Commercial Square south of the Singapore River. This is now the site of Raffles Place. To the north of the Padang, Beach Road – which was actually along the shoreline and now has Raffles Hotel at its southern end – was allocated for the European civilians, and the areas further north and to the east were set aside for the Arabs, the Bugis and the Sultan of Singapore's court at Kampong Glam. The land to the south of the Singapore River was given over to the Chinese and the area just north of this was where the Indian population first settled, near what is now Chulia Street. This division of racial groupings, aimed at avoiding conflict and tension, formed the foundation for the separate districts of Chinatown, Little India and the Malay quarter of the colonial sector which remain today. During Raffles' time on the island, and afterwards, Singapore continued to gain steadily in importance and prosperity.

World War II

By World War II, Singapore (together with Malaysia) was an important part of Britain's presence in the Far East, while Indonesia still belonged to the Dutch. As the war progressed, the Japanese began to extend their sphere of operations and the imperial army started to push south through the Malay peninsula. The British civilians in Malaya became alarmed and streamed south, seeking sanctuary in Singapore. No-one imagined that the Japanese were a serious threat, and, even when Malaya was abandoned to the imperial army, Singapore was thought by the British to be impregnable. However, it had always been assumed that any attack would come from the sea; the British and allied troops were themselves so encumbered by heavy equipment and unsuitable uniforms, and the considerable chains of supply necessary for such equipment, that they could not conceive of an overland offensive. All artillery was directed south towards the South China Sea. However, the Japanese understood jungles, and they travelled light, foraging for food along the way, and marching or cycling steadily towards Singapore. As a result, when the Japanese arrived from Malaya, they spread throughout Singapore in an astonishingly short time, and the British had no alternative but to surrender.

The Japanese now found themselves with a problem. As they had advanced through the Malay peninsula, they had taken British and allied prisoners. This inevitably depleted their forces because they had to leave guards at the many prisoner-of-war camps that they set up on their journey south. In Singapore they had an enormous number of prisoners to take care of, and so they built a large camp at Changi – roughly where the country's prison is today – and packed it with British and allied troops. In the last few days before the invasion, most Western women and children had left the country in a host of ships. Tragically, many of them were killed as their ships were attacked by Japanese planes and warships. Those that survived found themselves in prison

TOUCHED BY DEATH: THE HISTORY OF SAGO LANE

Although much of Singapore's heritage is disappearing in the eagerness of its people to embrace 21st-century modernity, there are still fascinating, sometimes tragic, memorials to the past to be found if you take the trouble to look for them. At the southern end of South Bridge Road, across the road and not far from the Inn of the Sixth Happiness, you will see Sago Lane in Chinatown, an unpretentious little street whose history you could never guess.

Sago Lane used to contain 'death houses', a chilling and evocative name which accurately describes the premises that existed here until fairly recently. The Chinese are gregarious people who like to live in close proximity. This proximity can become stiflingly close when large, poor families are forced to share a tiny living space. Even today, when there are strict government rules about overcrowding in HDB (Housing Development Board) homes, some families are still packed very tightly together. This causes particular problems when a family member is afflicted by serious illness. The Chinese are very superstitious and it is considered bad luck for someone to die in the home. Consequently it became the custom for sick, elderly relatives to be moved into death houses. The rest of the family paid for them to remain there until the inevitable happened. If the whole idea sounds anathema, perhaps it is worth remembering that something similar happens in the West, where old or dying relatives are often placed in homes or hospices. It is said that the death houses of Sago Lane were not gloomy, filthy dungeons, but clean and tidy, and that it was simply the air of inevitability in the face of death that made them such tragic symbols. One can see the look of hopeless blankness in the faces of the elderly today in some of the dreadful 'homes of rest' in the back-streets of seaside towns everywhere. After the death houses were abandoned, the street became the home of funeral parlours.

camps throughout Indonesia, suffering appalling hardships until the end of the war. Many of the prisoners were women, mainly nurses, and a large percentage was Australian. The conditions were awful, and it was a miracle that anyone survived. Several of those who did went on to write books chronicling the horrors of their experiences.

Malaya, too, was crowded with prison camps containing allied men, women and children who were brutally treated by the Japanese. Over the course of the war, illness and maltreatment caused many deaths, and in Singapore there are memorials to those who did not survive those terrible days. These include Changi Prison Chapel war memorial (see page 199), the Kranji Cemetery and War Memorial (see page 190), and the civilian war memorial, known as 'chopsticks', in the colonial core (see page 145). With the camp at Changi packed with prisoners, the Japanese proceeded to round up and execute those Singaporeans whom they felt had been colluding with the British. It is a testament to the Singaporean character that after the war the remaining population displayed no resentment towards the British. It would have been easy to blame them for their suffering during the war, but they retained a sense of respect and affection.

When the war finally came to an end, Singapore became crowded with ex-prisoners of both sexes who had been released not only from imprisonment in Singapore, but from camps throughout Malaya and Indonesia. Many were malnourished and ill. For a while there was utter chaos as organisations such as the Red Cross tried to return these people to their homes. Despite the confusion, the officious bureaucrats and the mountains of unnecessary red tape, everyone who wanted to be was eventually repatriated successfully.

During the occupation of Singapore, the Japanese changed the name of the country to Syonan-To, and issued their own currency and stamps. Despite this, very few signs of this occupation remain today. But that does not mean that Singapore is untouched by Japanese influence. The country is regularly visited by tourists from Japan who come here on holiday to relax and to play on the fabulous golf courses. Again, there is no residual antagonism on the part of Singaporeans. They are a pragmatic people, and recognise the importance of Japanese tourists to their economy. Nevertheless, there are those who still remember the screams of tortured prisoners issuing from the old YMCA building, not far from Orchard Road, which was the headquarters of the Kempetai (secret police) during the occupation. There are waxworks depicting both the Japanese surrender to the British and the earlier British surrender to the Japanese in the museum on Sentosa (see pages 206–7). In the north, just before the Causeway leading to Malaysia, is a cemetery for war dead, and a memorial to them, which is visited by people from all over the world seeking to remember loved ones who died in Singapore during the Japanese occupation of the island. In a country like this, where everyone looks to the future, it comes as a salutary reminder of some of the horrors of the past.

Modern Singapore

Singapore used to be a part of Malaysia, or Malaya as it was then. In 1959 it became self-governing, with Lee Kuan Yew being elected prime minister, and, in 1963, when Malaya gained independence from Britain, the British began to move out of the country and Singapore joined the Federation of Malaysia. By 1965, Britain had finally left Singapore. On August 9, Singapore was expelled from the federation and officially became an independent republic.

It is common for a country to experience a period of turmoil after such a momentous occurrence. Yet while things started to change in Singapore, they did so for the better. Within a very short time the country blossomed and grew. Today it is one of the most modern and progressive countries in the world. Without any crude oil of its own, Singapore has become the third-largest oil refiner in the world. The port is the second busiest in the world, way beyond either London or New York. Its land size has increased by ten per cent as more and more has been reclaimed from the sea. Beach Road (outside Raffles Hotel), which, as its name suggests, used to lie near the beach, is now some way inland. This tiny country has over a thousand factories that turn out goods in direct competition with the world's industrial giants. It has also become one of the world centres of finance, and the relatively new (operating since 1987) railway system – the Mass Rapid Transit (MRT) – makes the Underground of London, the Metro of Paris and the Subway of New York look very tatty and inefficient indeed.

However, it is in the sphere of 21st-century communications that Singapore has really come to the fore. The inhabitants have taken computers to their hearts, and now every stratum of society is computer-controlled and infinitely sophisticated. Singaporeans enjoy Western-style prosperity and the standard of living is as high as in Japan. There is excellent health care and little unemployment or crime; the place is unbelievably clean and in the towns one can buy almost anything from any country on the planet. The nation is truly a mini superpower, and, since politically it is more stable than anywhere along the Asian Pacific rim, it is likely to become ever more successful.

POLITICS
with Peter Dorling

Party politics in the Western sense is seen by the authorities in Singapore as an irrelevance. The ruling People's Action Party (PAP) argues that getting hung up on ideological dogma is the last thing needed to run a small, technically advanced modern state. Politics Singapore-style is seen simply as a matter of 'management'. And with a country the size and shape of the Isle of Wight, and a population approaching four million, it is indeed possible to see Singapore as one big manageable company.

The PAP has been in power ever since 1959, and all along it has viewed politics as a matter of pragmatism. If it works, do it. And whatever one thinks of the philosophy, it has been hugely successful in turning Singapore from a third-world country with no natural resources into a highly competitive first-world nation in just 40 years. The Hong Kong Political and Economic Risk Consultancy has ranked Singapore as the most stable country in Asia, both politically and socially, placing it above countries like Japan and Taiwan. Singapore is a stunningly efficient place with the most modern techniques and systems that keep it at the forefront of global business.

Most commentators acknowledge that this extraordinary success story owes a tremendous amount to the determination, courage, and far-sightedness of the country's long-serving prime minister, and now senior minister, Lee Kuan Yew. Today, President Nathan and Prime Minister Goh Chok Tong continue to run the country along the same lines as Lee Kuan Yew. Indeed, though Lee is now officially retired, few doubt that he is still a significant influence upon those in power. His 'guiding' hand was certainly behind most of the ideas, schemes, and innovations that make the garden city run like clockwork. Such schemes and innovations include measures to tackle traffic congestion, siting and overseeing the building of the country's award-winning international airport at Changi, and the scheme for purchasing apartments in the clean and brightly coloured high-rise blocks which house most of the population. (Lee Kuan Yew sets out in his memoirs his original vision for planning and setting up these amenities.) More broadly, the success of the PAP is due to the policy of encouraging foreign investment and involvement. Singapore's leaders are not suspicious of foreigners putting money into the country and running many of the biggest businesses, and will do their best to smooth away red tape and other obstructions.

This love affair with big business does not, though, mean that those citizens at the bottom of society are neglected. In his memoirs, Lee Kuan Yew tells how, right from the start, he had a vision of a multi-racial society of equal citizens, where there were opportunities for all, and a person's contribution was recognised and rewarded on merit, regardless of race, language, culture or religion. The government encourages people to help those with lower incomes and disabilities of various sorts. People who cannot work, through age, illness or disability, and who have no-one else to care for them, are able to obtain financial help through the Public Assistance scheme. The country has very little poverty, negligible unemployment, and one of the highest literacy rates in Asia (92.5%). The PAP has, in a single generation, turned the country around from an old-fashioned island with the squalid living conditions so typical of many countries in the tropics, to one with perhaps the highest standard of living in Asia. It is difficult to deny that Lee Kuan Yew has come remarkably close to realising his vision.

Alongside such resounding success stories, however, have been some policies that are less universally applauded. One area that has attracted widespread unease is the government's attitude towards population growth. The population, like that in most countries, is increasing; unlike most countries, though, there is a limited amount of available land for building upon. The fact that the birth rate is now slowing should be a cause for relief. But the government does not see it like that. A scheme has been set up to encourage young professional families to have more children and thereby maximise the country's potential for economic prosperity in the future. In the face of internal and foreign criticism about eugenics, the government is spending considerable amounts of money in its determination to get its message across. Another policy which, it could be argued, would benefit from a more balanced approach concerns the government's reaction to the effects of development upon the character of Singapore. The politicians correctly recognised that the disappearance of the country's heritage beneath a sea of concrete would be detrimental to its tourist industry, and they embarked upon an effort to save what was left. Instead of just leaving these parts alone for visitors to enjoy, however, they insisted on tidying them up and presenting sanitised shadows of what they used to be. For the most part, these changes do

Previous page Huge mask at Haw Par Villa (JW)

Above left Chilli crab (STB)

Above right Mooncakes (STB)

Right Chicken rice (STB)

Below Satay (STB)

not work. Bugis Street is an obvious example. This was the old red-light district, much frequented by transsexual prostitutes, and an area of colour and spirit during the day. But transsexual prostitutes do not suit the image that Singapore would like to project, and the street was cleared up and made distinctly bland as a result. Singaporeans cannot bear visitors seeing anything less than a perfect picture of their country.

As well as the controversy surrounding isolated policies, many will argue that the price of Singapore's success has been heavy in a more fundamental and deep-seated sense. The technique of Lee Kuan Yew's party has involved a no-nonsense authoritarian style which, among other things, has stifled internal criticism and given the country a reputation abroad for being dictatorial – albeit with benevolent intent – with a regimented populace forbidden even to think for themselves. Furthermore, it has to be said the political playing field has never been exactly level. As well as the overwhelming number of PAP MPs, would-be opposition candidates have a hard time getting publicity for their policies. Some have been harassed and even jailed. At election time the opposition parties were often boycotted by the newspapers and sidelined by television. Indeed, during election campaigns over the years there have been directives from TV bosses telling news editors to ensure they toned down their coverage of opposition rallies. But it is also true that opposition parties themselves have been pretty lacklustre in coming up with viable ideas, although they are realistic enough to admit that forming an alternative government isn't one of them. They say that their primary ambition is to ensure that there is a variety of opinions voiced in parliament, and that the PAP remains accountable to the people. And, while many of the brightest youngsters flee abroad after experiencing the relaxed life at American, British or Australian universities, most people have been far more interested in simply getting on with their lives at home and making money. For them, politics is only for the politicians.

It is far from easy to become a PAP candidate. First-class academic qualifications are called for, and preferably experience of running a high-powered company. Such candidates are wooed into public service with big salaries and prestigious posts so that, as the party often boasts, it gets only the best people. As a result, being an MP is a highly respected and much-admired calling.

Despite the PAP's control, it has had its ups and downs. For example, 1980 was undoubtedly one of its 'ups' when its share of the vote touched 77%. But it was a short-lived high point. In the following years support went into a relative decline, plunging – in 1984 – to 65%. It took 20 years to climb back into the 70s again. However, the last general election (in 2001) saw something of a sea change in Singaporean politics. All of a sudden there were thoughtful letters to the papers and key voices inside and outside parliament began speaking out about the way things were going. Issues were raised that few had dared air in public before. As usual the PAP won by a landslide, with 75% of the vote – a level of support it hadn't seen since 1980. But this time the victory was much criticised for being won at the expense of democracy, not least because in as many as two-thirds of the seats there weren't any opposition candidates, leaving many voters effectively disenfranchised. Various measures led to their poor turnout: lunchtime rallies were banned, election deposits were raised, and the campaign was pared to the absolute minimum of just eight days. All this made an already weak opposition even weaker, and gave the PAP candidates walkovers in 55 out of the 84 seats. In the constituencies that were contested, only two fell to opposition parties. As one newly elected MP concluded, 'the election wasn't fair.'

This novel outspokenness had much to do with the sudden influx of younger MPs who have proved something of a collective new broom. The major question since 2001 has concerned the future of Singaporean politics.

LEE KUAN YEW

It can be argued that Singapore's success story was due almost entirely to the efforts of a politician named Lee Kuan Yew. He trained as a lawyer in England, and returned home to become a charismatic – and utterly unscrupulous – leader of the newly independent country. There was probably no other person at the time who could have brought about Singapore's emergence as a trading country, and there is no doubt that Lee believed that what he was doing was for the good of the nation. He was fiercely determined and would brook no interference with his policies. Today he is retired, but most Singaporeans consider that he is still the power behind the throne – although few will claim that in public.

When Lee Kuan Yew started out he felt that mollycoddling was a luxury that a young, thrusting state could not afford. To the acquisitive Singaporeans, who were always more inclined to make a fortune than to share it, Lee's 'go-ahead' attitudes were enormously appealing, and everyone threw themselves behind him and his policies. Lee is an interesting man. A senior British diplomat once described him as intellectually the most impressive leader of any state. In Asia, where corruption is commonplace, there has rarely been any suggestion of impropriety on the part of either himself or any of his close associates and work colleagues. The one stain on this record occurred when a member of Lee's staff was found to have accepted a free air ticket – and for this the employee was jailed. Despite his enormous power, Lee leads a strictly modest lifestyle. He neither smokes nor drinks, and eats little. He is scrupulous about hygiene, and worked in a very plain office. His only relaxation was playing golf, when he would study each stroke carefully before playing it. This was the man who dragged Singapore out of the 19th century and into the 21st in a few short years. He left a strong country with a strong government that continues to build on his legacy.

No-one doubts the huge success of the PAP's record over the years, but this time politicians and analysts are raising other important issues. Is one-party dominance really good for modern Singapore? Is there any role at all for the opposition? If it is condemned to a life on the sidelines, will it slide slowly but surely towards total extinction? What then? It is possible to detect a gradual, creeping malaise that is common to most countries after a significant period without political change.

Senior Minister Lee Kuan Yew quickly weighed in to this debate by strongly denouncing such pessimism. 'Textbook Westminster-style democracy would not work in Singapore,' he warned. 'I work on real-life experience,' he said, arguing that the present system gives the voter a choice between the PAP and a credible opposition. He stressed that as long as the opposition could not get good men it would remain a discredited, unelectable alternative.

But there were other concerns after the 2001 election. None other than the Speaker of the House, stepping down after 13 years of service, admitted his worries about the scepticism felt by Singaporeans towards politics, and spoke of the cynicism many felt about the whole decision-making process. Newly elected MPs called on government leaders to listen more to the minority, and to learn to be magnanimous to political opponents. Others urged people to speak up, and to be openly and bravely critical of the government, without – as another MP put it – 'the fear of being hit by a big stick'. All pretty heady stuff that wouldn't have seen the light of day a very few years ago.

While the commentators ponder these political tea-leaves, others cast around for future leaders. Where are they? Might they make a difference? The present prime minister, Mr Goh Chok Tong, was the first to be hand picked (in 1990) by the second generation of PAP leaders, no doubt in the hope that he'd be a true and trustworthy bearer of the torch, but perhaps with a milder, 'people-orientated' touch. This has proved the case. But, after more than ten years, Mr Goh will himself soon be looking to a successor. Most speculation centres upon Lee Kuan Yew's eldest son, Lee Hsien Loong – currently deputy prime minister.

A highly intelligent and strong-willed politican, in the 2001 election Mr Lee unreservedly supported the PAP's unchallenged position as the dominant party. 'If the party did not represent the electorate within a small city, compact and homogeneous,' he said, 'a new team could come along and sweep the country straight away. If we didn't have the people's support we would be out overnight.' In view of his firm stand on PAP policies over the years, it used to be felt that Mr Lee's leadership might not necessarily mean a gentler, more user-friendly government. However, some now detect a mellowing of his approach; indeed, others argue that he has no choice. There is a strong feeling that if future governments fail to win the hearts and minds of the younger generation, yet more Singaporeans will simply up and leave.

A number of websites are worth checking for further information on Singapore's politics. The official website of the Singapore government can be found at www.gov.sg. There is further information about the Singapore

(Opposition) Democratic Party at www.singaporedemocrats.org. For a satirical look at the world of Singaporean politics, try www.talkingcock.com.

Public housing

Since 1959, the government has built complete towns of fairly ugly, concrete high-rise apartments. Most of the population – 75% – live in these Housing Development Board (HDB) blocks. They are the equivalents of council flats in Britain, though in Singapore there are subtle differences. Constructing these new towns costs a lot of money, and to pay for them the government takes the equivalent of 46% of a person's salary. Half of this is paid by the employer and half by the employee. This tax is known as the Central Provident Fund (CPF). The proportion of an individual's contribution that is not used to buy a flat is drawn as a pension when he or she reaches retirement age. Until then, the government uses the money to generate profits via investment, which in turn goes into the development of the country. It is an enormous sum, and is quite different from all the other taxes levied by Singapore's government.

ECONOMY

Statistics compiled in 1999 showed that the economy of Singapore was divided broadly as follows: goods producing industries brought in S$51bn; manufacturing S$37bn; construction S$11bn; utilities S$2.75bn; service industries S$97bn; wholesale and retail S$21bn; hotels and restaurants S$4bn; transport and communications S$16bn; financial services S$20bn; and business services S$18bn.

Most foodstuffs are imported, often from Australia, and only about 1.6% of the island is used for agriculture. Professional and managerial positions account for 22% of the workforce, about 30% are blue-collar workers and 18% are technicians or their equivalents. The government is committed to an education system that will produce engineers, technologists and technicians in areas that cater to today's commercial climate. Electronics comprises 50% of the manufacturing output.

While the population is happy to support such a philosophy, it does mean that there is little place for individuality in Singapore, and the government is also trying to encourage entrepreneurial thinking by introducing classes in schools and colleges. Increasingly Singaporeans gauge an individual's success by the number of 'c's – car, condominium, credit card, club and cash – that he or she has accumulated. Despite this acquisitive outlook, however – and statistics which show that inflation is among the lowest in the world, that the average annual growth of the economy is nearly 9%, and that the country's per capita GNP rose from S$1,618 in 1965 to S$38,170 in 1998 – the salaries on offer for some professions are very low by Western standards. At the end of 1998, managers were earning an average monthly salary of S$6,694 (US$3,937), clerical staff earned S$1,622 (US$954), and cleaners just S$1,027 (US$604). In addition, the conditions of employment sometimes seem draconian, with little holiday and even less compassionate leave.

Over the last 20 or 30 years, Singapore has become one of the major financial centres in Asia. Large companies from around the world operate offices here, and wherever you go you are likely to find the logos of companies with which you are familiar. The Monetary Authority of Singapore (MAS) formulates and regulates the country's monetary policies. Today there are about 200 different banks and eight international money brokers operating on the island. The country has its own stock exchange (SES) and Singapore is developing fast as an international financial centre. With Japan facing the economic troubles it is, it would not be a surprise if, in the future, Singapore were to become the most important stock market on the Asian Pacific rim.

The country's infrastructure, together with excellent hotels, shops, restaurants and business centres – and the world-renowned airport at Changi – mean that it is at the forefront of Asian convention business. Indeed, it has consistently won awards for being the best location for convention business over the last 16 years, and is one of the top-six such centres in the world, alongside London and Geneva. Each year there are hosts of conventions held throughout the country, and at any time you can be sure that some industry has a major event or trade fair.

Enormous amounts of money are spent on encouraging foreign investment. Singapore belongs to ASEAN, the Association of Southeast Asian Nations, all of whose members co-operate with each other to enhance business opportunities throughout the region. The Singapore Economic Development Board works tirelessly to promote the island as a good place to invest, and there are several good reasons to do so. About half the island has been developed for commerce and industry, and some of the 63 or so islands offshore have become important international refineries for the global petroleum companies. There are 33 industrial estates, and foreign companies wishing to set up businesses in the country have access to a broad spectrum of ready-made factories and offices. There are many tax breaks and other incentives to encourage them to come here. It is a free-enterprise economy with no restrictions on repatriating profits. The country is stable, and foreign investors are unlikely to lose their assets and profits through social or political revolution. In stark contrast to the prevarication that frequently characterises the workings of financial institutions in the West, in Singapore business decisions are made quickly. Furthermore, surveys regularly find the Singapore workforce to be the best in Asia. Most of the workers are young, dedicated, resilient and ready to learn. They are prepared to adjust their aspirations according to circumstance, and do their best to increase the profits of their companies.

The government, in its desire to retain tight control of what everyone is doing, insists that distinct parts of the island are set aside for distinct types of economic production. For instance, prawns (along with chickens and ducks) are among the few foodstuffs produced locally, and as a tourist you may suddenly come across a pocket of prawn farms (although 'farm' is a misnomer since the animals are not bred, but simply collected from the sea and kept in artificial ponds to grow). At Sembawang there is a large industrial complex building bridges, ships and roads for customers around the world. At Jurong, in the west of the island, is an estate containing small factories making and packing a variety of commodities for export. Elsewhere you might find a 'village' in which all the premises are dedicated to the commercial breeding of aquarium fish. Such fish bring in a surprisingly high amount of foreign exchange to Singapore. From the outside these places look like huge hangars such as you find in any industrial estate on the edge of any town. Inside they are enormous, light and airy factories packed with fish tanks where you can see angelfish and neon tetras. Similar 'zones' exist all over the island.

PEOPLE

The population of Singapore is 76% Chinese, 14.7% Malay, 6.4% Indian and 2.9% from other backgrounds. Interestingly, this particular mix is only comparatively recent. Until the 1950s, the majority of Singaporeans were Malays. At that time there was considerable racial tension and there were several bloody riots. After the dust had settled, an increasing number of Chinese came to Singapore, and the percentage of Malay inhabitants declined. Today, the population has grown to around four million. Of these, almost a quarter comprises foreign nationals working on contracts. The population increases at 2% a year, but the government is encouraging certain groups of the population to have three or more children (see page 20). Since the country is so small, immigration laws are strict, and immigrants must prove that they can contribute to the economy.

Over 50% of Singapore is built up, yielding one of the world's highest density ratios of almost 6,000 people per square kilometre. Most of the population live in Housing Development Board (HDB) flats, what we would call 'council flats' (but which Noel Barber less kindly referred to as 'vertical prisons'). Complete towns of concrete high-rise blocks have been built throughout the country. The aim is to provide everything that the inhabitants require: shops, eating places, markets, doctors, and even bird-singing arenas (see page 31). Singapore started building these blocks in 1965. Since then they have been erected at an average rate of one flat every four working days.

Once a person starts work, part of his or her salary goes towards buying HDB accommodation to move into after leaving the parental home. Most Singaporeans do not marry until very late by Western standards, and live with their parents until then. When they do marry, they are allocated a flat in one of the tower blocks and the money they have been 'saving' since they commenced employment goes towards the deposit. Thereafter the same contribution each month pays off the remaining cost of the flat. To own an HDB flat, the buyer must contribute 20% of the cost and the government provides the other 80%. The first owner pays 2.75% interest over either five or 20 years. If the owner stays more than ten years, he or she can upgrade to become a 'new owner' of a different, larger flat and receive further help from

BIG BROTHER
Hannah Postgate

Singapore, when you take a close look at it, is just a tiny island perched on the end of the Malay peninsula. As a modern day 'Asian Tiger', in many ways it has entirely foreign influences to thank for its success. Sir Stamford Raffles and the British navy, and later the orderly, hard-working, predominantly Chinese population, turned Singapore into the well-oiled, modern, cosmopolitan city it is today. The controlled, considered decisions of politicians and big business have ensured Singapore's place among the top five richest countries in the world – from third world to first world in merely one generation.

With less than a mile of water separating the two, how does the psyche of Singaporeans differ from that of their Malay neighbours? The relationship between the Malays and the Singaporeans has always been peppered with a keen rivalry and fervent one-upmanship.

The Malaysians frequently accuse the Singaporeans of being *kiasu* ('ashamed to lose') – meaning that they must always be one-up on their neighbours. Keeping up with the Jones's never looked so good; Singaporeans are avid trend-setters and followers of fashion. They are affluent, fashionably aware and very Westernised. They will queue for hours for the latest label or must-have accessory outside the shopping malls of Orchard Road.

Singaporeans in return accuse the Malays of being backward, corrupt and lazy. However, the sibling rivalry is all rather futile as they very much rely on one another – in fact, Singapore was briefly part of Malaysia between 1963 and 1965. Much of Singapore's water is supplied from Johore in Malaysia. The Malay economy thrives on a transitory workforce of over 100,000 making the trip across the water to find work to feed mouths at home.

Singapore is ridiculed for being a repressed society without expression or individualism, mocked for its lack of substance, but it is a multi-layered society just now beginning to find its hidden depths. With not only a history of European colonialism, but also the influences today stemming from the Chinese, Malay and Indian populations, Singapore is far from the 'Singabore' nickname it has endured until recently. There are festivals and celebrations all year round and, for an island so small, there never seems to be a shortage of things to see and do.

the government. HDB flats range in size from approximately 70m² for a single person (who must be over 35 years old), to 105m² for a family (of four or five people). In 2000, a 100m² flat cost about S$130,000.

Within their homes, many Singaporeans employ maids, who are invariably foreigners – usually Indonesians or Thais – on strictly controlled contracts.

Singaporean girls will rarely take positions as maids, both because they consider the work beneath them and because they can earn more as employees in hotels or factories. Maids are not treated particularly well, and their rooms are frequently little more than tiny box rooms. On occasions, the country has a purge of all foreign manual workers; permits are always reissued, though, because foreign labour is a vital means of filling menial jobs.

In a country without much space, cars are extremely expensive, attracting a variety of heavy taxes as well as the requisite ownership permit. A driver must obtain a certificate of entitlement (COE) before even being allowed to purchase a car. The number of COEs is limited, and they are auctioned, so prices vary; however, it would not be unusual for a certificate to cost in the region of £20,000–30,000 (S$50,000–75,000). Most cars are under ten years old – the price is higher for permission to own an older one. The cost of simply acquiring a family car and getting it on the road is about £50,000–60,000 (S$125,000–150,000). Car ownership therefore involves a considerable financial commitment that is not undertaken lightly – indeed it forms one of the 'c's by which success is measured on the island (see page 24).

In their spare time, Singaporeans like to indulge in cultivating houseplants, which often adorn the balconies of housing blocks. Aquarium fish, along with songbirds (see pages 30–3), are also popular pets since families in tower blocks are not able to keep larger animals. Beyond the home, and despite the small size of the island, there are a host of activities to keep locals occupied. Many of these are organised or sponsored by the government, and range from sports and evening classes to barbecues. The evening classes differ from those to be found in the West, however, and you are more likely to find courses on business management, computer operating or accounting than on pottery, painting or embroidery. Here everything revolves around the furthering of status and income. A Malaysian friend once said to me, 'A Malaysian will do something for fun. A Singaporean has to see a profit at the end.'

Surprisingly, this consuming obsession with monetary success does not make the Singaporean people selfish or unwelcoming. They will do everything possible to make your stay a pleasure. The only disadvantage with such hospitality is that it is frequently accompanied by a belief that Westerners are only interested in Western ways of life. On one occasion I was 'treated' to a meal by a well-intentioned Singaporean in a snack bar that could very easily have been in London or New York. On another I took a friend to a restaurant to experience the delights of a steamboat (see page 63) for the first time. Unfortunately our well-meaning host quickly replaced her chopsticks with a spoon and fork, and ordered her a pork chop instead of Chinese food. In a related sense, the people's inherent politeness can also prove frustrating at times. They are reluctant to say 'no', or to tell visitors what they think they might not want to hear, and trying to get straight answers can be like trying to knit smoke! Maddening as this can seem, however, it is worth remembering that it is a trait which stems from a pleasantness of character, an eagerness to please, rather than from any obstructionist resolve – and that, in any case, it is something you will not succeed in changing.

LANGUAGE

Although almost everyone speaks English as their first language, many people are bilingual, speaking Mandarin (or one of the other Chinese dialects), Malay or Tamil in the home, depending on their ethnic origin. Among the other languages to be found in Singapore are Chinese dialects including Hokkien, Teochew, Cantonese, Hakka, Hainanese and Foochow, and Indian languages like Punjabi, Malayalam, Telegu, Hindi and Bengali. Colloquially, most Singaporeans speak a unique, curious form of English which has become known as 'Singlish' and which is influenced by Chinese and Malay dialects and phonetics. For a guide to some of the more common Singlish phrases and idiosyncrasies that you are likely to encounter, see *Appendix 1*, pages 215–16.

Within schools, English is the preferred language in which to teach – though a pupil's mother tongue is also considered important and taught as well. In addition, students learn French, German or Japanese, all languages that are felt to be vital in the world of commerce. There is also a wide range of facilities for the children of expatriates. Of the 30 schools for the children of expats, 14 teach in English for the children of British, Canadian, American or Australian workers. The remainder cater for children from Dutch, French, German, Japanese and Korean backgrounds, while there are weekend schools teaching Finnish, Italian, Norwegian and Swedish.

RELIGION

The vast majority of Singaporeans profess to adhere to a certain faith, and in this sense it is a religious society, although the government is keen that the island should remain a secular state free from the religious tensions which could result from the mixed ethnic backgrounds of its population. The Maintenance of Religious Harmony Act of the late 1980s prohibited the mixing of politics with religion, and forbade religious teaching in schools. Over half the people follow 'Chinese religions' – primarily Buddhism and Taoism – but Islam (15%), Christianity (approximately 13%), Hinduism (about 4%) and Sikhism, are also represented, as is Judaism.

Standing as testaments to this religious diversity are some stunning and fascinating places of worship, most of which are more than happy to welcome tourists. The Chinese temples are gloriously colourful and flamboyant, and there are Muslim mosques, Hindu temples and Sikh gurdwaras in abundance. Be sure to visit the fabulous Sri Mariamman Temple (see page 169). Please remember, however, that these are active places of religious worship and expression, and should be treated with proper respect and sensitivity. In general, visitors should dress conservatively. Many require the removal of shoes before entry, and Muslim places of worship will insist that women cover their heads.

CULTURE

Because Singapore is a comparatively new country, its culture consists of a tapestry of the traditions held dear by its various ethnic groups, be they

SPECIES OF SONGBIRD

Malays and Indonesians, and some Muslim members of other races, keep only one of the five favoured species of songbird: the zebra dove (*Geopelia striata*), known locally as the *merbok*. The *merbok* is believed to imitate sounds from the Koran. These birds are now bred extensively in captivity – indeed, far more extensively than the other four species kept in Singapore. A breeder in Thailand informed me that a pair can produce up to a dozen broods each year, with usually two chicks in each brood. This breeder kept 500 pairs, which gives an idea of the scale of some of these breeders' operations.

The four species of bird favoured by the Chinese are the oriental white eye (*Zosterops palpebrosa*), known in Singapore as the *mata puteh* ('white eye'), the red-whiskered bulbul (*Pycnonotus jocosus*), called the *jambul* locally, the shama (*Copsychus malabaricus*), and the Chinese necklaced thrush, or *hwamei* (*Garrulax canorus*).

The mata puteh is tiny and active, with a wide range from India across to Malaysia. It is greenish-yellow on top and white beneath, and has a ring of white feathers around the eye, which gives the bird its name. They feed predominantly on insects, but will also eat fruit, and need some nectar in their diet if they are to thrive. They are especially sensitive to small changes in diet, though once they are established in captivity they do well.

The jambul is a little bigger than a sparrow with a longer tail, clad in brown and white with a cocky black crest and a bright red patch on each

Chinese, Malay or Indian, rather than a unified body of national heritage, beliefs and customs. Singapore is nevertheless proud of its cultural output, and each year attracts and hosts a huge range of events that include art exhibitions, ballet, and live theatre. There is even an annual film festival. For culture vultures this is very exciting, and there truly is something to interest everyone, from popular, commercial events to more specialised performances which remain incomprehensible to all but the most die-hard of followers.

Bird singing

One important part of Singaporean culture is the keeping of songbirds. While people in the West may keep birds as pets or for breeding and conservation purposes, few keep them primarily for their song. By contrast, in the Far East the keeping of singing birds is a passion that goes back a long way, and the limited space available in HDB flats makes such creatures practical in a way that larger ones are not. Such birds are not simply pets, however; they are symbols of status, and the beauty of their songs the subject of serious competition and fevered betting (see *Playing birds*, pages 32–3). Most fanciers are men, although there are an increasing number of women. Fanciers claim that once the hobby is in the blood you never get rid of it; if you sell your

white cheek. The jambul was originally a forest bird but is common today in gardens throughout its range, which is similar to that of the puteh. Jambuls feed on fruit and insects, and most of those in Singapore are imported from Thailand.

The shama is a handsome bird, intolerant of other members of the same species, with a wonderful repertoire of melodious calls. It is predominantly black, with brown undersides and a white rump. The shama again comes from across Asia, but is a shy, forest-dwelling species. It feeds almost exclusively on insects, and is very difficult to breed in captivity.

The hwamei is a drab, greenish-brown bird with a white eye ring that extends behind the eye as a streak. It is imported from China, though escapes have established themselves in Singapore. In Taiwan and Hong Kong it is used as a fighting bird, being very intolerant of others. In the days when such a sport was legal in Singapore, huge sums of money, and sometimes jade pieces, were wagered on hwamei fights. To my ear they do not have a very beautiful song; a running joke among hwamei fanciers is that, with luck, their wives will be driven from the home by the shrill calls of the birds. As with most of these singing birds, escapees have established small but thriving colonies on the island.

Each of the five species of bird kept in Singapore for singing is held in a distinct type of cage. A shama would never be put in a jambul cage, nor a puteh in that designed to house a merbok.

birds, you have only to hear a good bird sing again to be compelled to take it up once more. The hobby is so intrinsic to life on the island that new housing estates are required by law to include a bird shop and a 'void deck'. The latter is the curious name for a concrete square furnished with poles, sometimes with a grid over the top, from which bird cages can be hung. Such places are often found in conjunction with teashops, and punters can enjoy a drink while listening to their birds.

The Chinese have kept birds for thousands of years. A bronze cage from the 'Warring States' period (481–221BC) can be found in the Asia Art Museum in San Francisco.

While the Chinese kept a wide variety of species, they tended to be birds that lent themselves to competition. Particularly popular were carrier pigeons that could be raced, parrots that could be taught to talk, fighting cocks (which are still popular in nearby Indonesia and Malaysia), and fighting quail. Chinese fishermen even trained cormorants to catch fish for them – indeed they still do so in the remoter parts of China. The history of keeping songbirds also goes back a long way. There are records of senior officials keeping them at the court of the emperor during the Ch'ing dynasty from 1644 onwards.

In 1872 the *Illustrated London News* recorded that 'The Malay peninsula … is celebrated for its cockatoos and parrots. It is common for a boy, when he finishes his career as a diver, to make a new start and become a birdseller.' The same journal also reveals that by that time Singapore was 'the best place to buy birds of all kinds.' In 1881 Annie Brassey observed of a bird market in Singapore, 'The whole place is alive with birds in baskets; ... they are all very tame and very cheap.' While the British were in Singapore, many of them kept birds as pets, and came to found the Singapore Caged Birds Society. After World War II, Singaporeans continued the society, and would meet at one another's homes. Most of their birds were parrots of one species or another, together with some budgies, canaries and magpie robins.

As bird keeping blossomed, birds from local sources were no longer found in sufficient numbers to satisfy the demand, and they were imported. At the same time dealers began to explore the export market. A Malay named Haji Marip started exporting live animals to the rest of the world. In time, Rochor Road became the centre of the trade, and well into the 1960s many bird dealers in Singapore were selling hundreds of thousands of birds a year. I was once approached by a dealer who offered me a special price on spice birds on the condition that I ordered in quantities of 50,000 or more. Today the trade has declined enormously, and though there are still a few dealers around, their stock is a fraction of what it used to be. These days all the birds exported have to be brought into the country first, and stock arrives from Indonesia, Thailand, China, sometimes from India, and even from Senegal.

As well as the birds themselves, the trappings of display are also important to the keepers. The cages, feed pots and other related objects are all regarded as vital to the display of the birds, and those who make these items become respected craftsmen or artists in their own right. A really ornate cage can fetch many thousands of dollars. You can buy perches carved into the forms of dragons, or tiny ceramic pots to hold food and water. Most of the cages now to be found in Singapore have been imported from China, but there are one or two people who still make them, purely for the pleasure they get from practising their ancient craft. The imported cages are made from bamboo, but are often brought into the country in pieces that are then varnished and constructed in Singapore as good varnish is difficult to find in mainland China.

The keeping of songbirds in Singapore distresses many Westerners as the animals spend the whole of their lives isolated in tiny cages. Singaporeans argue that such concern is misplaced as every care is lavished on the birds (primarily because they can earn the owner significant sums of money), but some feel that this is small compensation for the solitary existence forced upon them.

Playing birds

A café owner will frequently capitalise on the interest in birds by erecting a grid above a suitable area from which cages can be suspended. Fanciers of all ages arrive early, proudly clutching cages covered in cloth, and hang them from the void deck; while they drink their coffee they compare notes on the quality of each other's creatures. It is all taken enormously seriously, and every posture, note and trill is carefully evaluated.

There are five main species of bird kept these days, selected for the quality of their song (although occasionally one finds someone with a parrot, bought for its speaking ability). Huge sums of money are spent on champion singing birds, which will be trained for competition. Periodically contests are held throughout the island, and once a year there is an international contest attracting fanciers from neighbouring countries. The pastime is known as 'playing birds'. Such competitions are usually held very early in the morning because it is believed that birds sing at their best at this time of the day. There is a complicated system of judging, and judges are highly respected. Points are allocated for the condition of the bird, the way it is turned out, and for each intricate phrase of the song. Around the decks where these contests are held, purveyors of cages and other bits and pieces set up their stalls for fanciers to browse as they wait for their birds to be judged. The winner will go home proudly clutching a huge trophy. On the side, bets have been placed and deals struck over the future offspring of truly successful specimens.

You can see displays of songbirds and their cages in the Jurong Bird Park, in areas of Chinatown (see page 164), and in other places all around the island. Any taxi driver will take you to a bird café, but you must be prepared to get up very early in the morning. Today the towns of Ang Mo Kio and Bedok are good areas to find people playing birds, and the mainly Malay area, Bukit Batok, is an excellent place to see *merboks* – indeed, it has been said that four out of ten people in Bukit Batok keep this species.

Pitcher plant

Practical Information

WHEN TO VISIT

Singapore can be visited throughout the year as the temperature remains fairly constant, although the rainfall varies. The hottest months are July and August, and the wettest November through until January. Temperatures average around 30°C during the afternoon, but even at dawn they are usually about 23–24°C.

HIGHLIGHTS/SUGGESTED ITINERARIES

It is a good idea on arrival in Singapore to pick up copies of the monthly *Singapore Visitor* and *Where – Singapore*, as well as *This Week – Singapore*, each of which are free to tourists and available in hotels or at the information desks in larger shopping malls. These include details of the current festivals and attractions that are worth visiting. See also *Chapter 3, Holidays, Celebrations and Events*.

Short stay

Below is a selection of recommended 'must dos' for those visiting Singapore for just a couple of days:

- Have a drink in the New Asia Rose (see page 130) bar on top of the Swissôtel, The Stamford, and watch the sun set and the lights come on in the city (although you'll have to peer through the horizontal slats of the Venetian blinds). This is the tallest hotel in the world and the bar is on the 73rd floor! You get a magnificent view; walk round and look out over Boat Quay and the Central Business District (CBD) skyscrapers from the balcony overlooking the restaurant, or have a buffet lunch or a more expensive à-la-carte dinner.
- Have lunch in the Tiffin Room (see page 134) at Raffles Hotel, where they serve a magnificent curry buffet. It is best to book.
- Take a ride on the trolley bus (see page 58), which goes around the island's main attractions. It stops at some of the bus stops in Orchard Road, and you are free to get on and off where you like. The buses run roughly twice in the morning and twice in the afternoon, but check at your hotel. It's a good way to get around if your time is limited and you want to see most things in a day. It stops at Chinatown, the Botanic Gardens, and Little India, as well as by the parliament and law buildings in the old colonial area.

- Walk around the Little India area at the foot of Serangoon Road (see pages 114–16). It is within walking distance of Orchard Road (north), or take the MRT to Little India on the new NE line (which is due to open by the end of 2002), and you'll see shops full of saris and spices. Be sure to cross the road from the new Little India shopping mall to the 'wet-market' (so called because its floors are wet, as distinct from the dry floors of supermarkets) on the opposite side of Serangoon Road. This is one of the largest of these markets and there are numerous stalls selling meat, fish, spices and a variety of strange fruits and vegetables. You should go in the morning, however, as the stalls are packed up in the early afternoon. Above this there are several floors of market stalls selling a huge number of goods at reasonable prices.
- Visit Arab Street (see pages 122–6) – only a few shops really – for Malaysian and Muslim goods and eateries, and the back-streets of Chinatown (south of the river). You can practise your bargaining skills here. Near Arab Street is the Sultan Mosque, along with several others (see page 125).
- Visit Boat Quay or Clarke Quay (see pages 159 and 158), both made up of former old-fashioned *godowns* (warehouses) which have been converted into a range of restaurants. It can be fun in the evenings to sit and eat by the river, although these places are a little 'touristy' and fairly expensive.
- Take a trip in a bumboat (a sort of ferry), which includes a brief guide to the river area as you travel along. Cruises can be caught from Clarke Quay, and cost S$10–12; alternatively, if you don't have time for a full cruise, take a bumboat from the ferry stop at the CBD end of Boat Quay up to Clarke Quay, or vice versa, for just S$1.
- Walk around the orchid terraces and the adjacent Ginger Garden at the Botanic Gardens (see pages 111–12).
- Eat at one of the hawker centres (a group of primitive-looking food stalls in the open air) or food centres (smarter versions of hawker centres, found inside). The food here is excellent value, cooked while you wait, and – despite appearances – these places are regularly inspected and the food is quite safe. For a list of some of these centres, see box, pages 64–5.
- Spend some time on Sentosa Island (see pages 202–9), opposite the World Trade Centre where the ferries to Indonesia and the cruise ships dock. Manicured and 'Disney-like', it is often referred to as a 'fantasy island' – which speaks for itself! Underwater World and the Images of Singapore exhibition, which describes events here during World War II, are worth a look.
- Shop. Browse the malls in Orchard Road. Try the basement at Tangs on the corner of Orchard Road and Scotts Road for Chinese and Japanese china rice bowls. There are reasonable-value freshwater pearls, gifts, silk shirts and blouses, and electrical goods in the Far East Plaza on Scotts Road and the Lucky Plaza on Orchard Road (you can bargain in these two malls – most of the others have fixed prices). Alternatively, go to Bugis Village, on Queen Street for goods that are a little less expensive than on Orchard Road. In the evening the stalls are open and there is more to buy

and bargain for. The mall, Parco, is Japanese-owned. Also try the Funan IT Centre on North Bridge Road (on the way to Chinatown) for computer equipment.

- Take a Chinese junk cruise (for coffee, lunch or dinner) around the southern islands. This takes you into the harbour area and then to Kusu (see page 210), a tiny island with two temples (Chinese and Indian), tortoises and a beach with swimming areas (stops for about 20 minutes), and other small islands. This costs between S$15 and S$20 during the day, depending on the length of the cruise (one hour at sunset, two-and-a-half hours for coffee or lunch), and S$36 in the evening (including dinner). You can also take a ferry from the World Trade Centre (runs more frequently at weekends) to Kusu where you can alight and catch a later ferry on to St John's Island. There are then ferries back to the World Trade Centre (but be careful not to miss the last one). This will cost about S$9 for the round trip (from the World Trade Centre to Kusu and St John's, and back again) – remember to hang on to your ticket. Ferries run Mon–Sat 10.00–13.00 (last ferry from St John's 14.45), Sun and public holidays 09.00, 11.00, 13.00, 15.00, 17.00 (last ferry from St John's at 18.15).

Longer stay

For those staying a little longer, consider some of the following attractions and excursions:

- Singapore Zoo and Night Safari (see pages 188–9). If you are feeling energetic, spend a couple of hours at the zoo in the afternoon, eat at one of the restaurants just outside the Night Safari area, and then do the Night Safari itself. The latter is a zoo visit by night (actually in the evening) which is very good. You can either tour around in a tram, listening to the accompanying commentary, or get off and walk.
- Changi Chapel and Museum (see page 199). A visit here involves a longish MRT journey to Tanah Merah station and then a bus (No 2). Open 09.30–16.30 daily. Admission free.
- The Chinese and Japanese Gardens (see pages 174–5), which offer peaceful (usually deserted) walks among water gardens and pagoda. Take the MRT to the Chinese Gardens station. Be aware that it can be uncomfortably hot in the gardens during the middle of the day.
- The Jurong Bird Park (see pages 175–6) has a very large aviary containing trees and a waterfall that you can walk through with all sorts of birds flying freely (there's a net ceiling high up above the trees!), and is particularly worth visiting. You can ride on the monorail if you find the heat too oppressive for walking. Take the MRT to Boon Lay at the western end of the island and then a bus from the bus interchange (Nos 251 or 194).
- The Singapore History Museum and the new Singapore Art Museum (housing mainly local and Asian art). The feeling at the time of writing was that the art museum's building was more interesting than its contents, but these may have improved. Both museums are at the eastern end of

Orchard Road, and best reached by bus or by walking from City Hall MRT station. See page 136.

- The many temples and mosques in Little India and Chinatown (see pages 120–1 and 168–9), some of which are stunning. Remember to remove shoes before entering them. St Andrew's Cathedral (see page 140) was modelled on Netley Abbey in Hampshire. Services are offered in both English and Chinese (one usually following the other). The cathedral is near City Hall MRT.

- Holland Village consists of a collection of older shop-houses (giving a flavour of Singapore's appearance in the past), a small wet market, a Cold Storage supermarket and some good souvenir shops in the building on the two floors above Cold Storage. Lims sells all things Chinese. There are some good restaurants in the little streets behind the wet market, as well as interesting shops selling china and basketware. Take a No 7 bus ride west from Orchard Boulevard.

- Trips into Malaysia can be organised from your hotel. There are various half- or full-day trips to Johore Bahru and elsewhere, either by coach or by taxi. Alternatively, you can get to Johore Bahru by public bus from Queen Street bus terminal, or by train from Keppel Road station which is on the south side of the island on the way to the World Trade Centre. (Note, however, that there are only a few trains a day.) The station and track are owned by Malaysia, and the trains have a tendency to run late.

- A good way to see the island is to do a complete loop on the MRT. You will see the HDB blocks, as well as the upmarket private condominiums that have more elaborate architecture, and frequently swimming pools and tennis courts. Note the lack of any agriculture of substance – in many ways Singapore is really one big building site.

TOUR OPERATORS

Most large tour operators cover Singapore, but the following smaller, specialist operators may also be worth considering:

UK

Abercrombie and Kent Travel Tel: 020 7730 9600; email: info@abercrombiekent.com
All-Ways Pacific Travel Tel: 01494 432747; email: sales@all-ways.co.uk
Asian Journeys Tel: 01604 234 855; email: mail@asianjourneys.com
Asian Explorer Tel: 01481 823417
Asia World Tel: 0870 990 8090
Destination Far East Tel: 020 7400 4573
Distant Dreams Tel: 020 8313 8019; email: info@distantdreams.co.uk
Far East Travel Tel: 020 7499 8638
Hayes and Jarvis Tel: 020 8741 9932; email: res@hayes-jarvis.com
Kuoni Travel Tel: 01306 740500
Lotus Travel Tel: 020 7962 9933
Magic of the Orient Tel: 01293 537700; email: info@magicorient.co.uk

Pearls of the Orient Tel: 020 7932 0998; email: pearls@jebsens.co.uk
Tropical Locations Tel: 020 8427 7300

Canada
Bali and Orient Tel: 1 800 665 2254
Cultural Tours Tel: 1 800 663 4160
Exotik Tours Tel: 514 861 3497
Shangrila Tours Tel: 1 800 663 9494
Tour East Holidays Tel: 1 800 667 3951

USA
Abercrombie and Kent Tel: 800 323 7308
Absolute Asia Tel: 800 736 8187
Asean Affairs Holidays Tel: 800 742 3133
Festival of Asia Tel: 800 880 ASIA
Japan and Orient Tours Inc Tel: 800 377 1080/3898
Orient Flexi-Pax Tours Tel: 800 545 5540
Pacific Bestour Inc Tel: 800 668 3288
Pacific Delight Tours Inc Tel: 800 221 7179
Pacific Holidays Tel: 800 355 8025
Pacific Protour Inc Tel: 800 776 8882
Swain Asia Tours Tel: 800 227 9346

RED TAPE
Visas
Most people entering Singapore for a social visit of no more than three months do not need a visa. In common with the majority of countries, Singapore insists that you need a passport valid for six months after your arrival, sufficient funds for your stay, and an onward or return ticket, together with any necessary permits to enter wherever you are going next. However, nationals from Afghanistan, Algeria, Bangladesh, Cambodia, the Commonwealth Independent States (which are Armenia, Azerbaijan, Belarus, Georgia, Kazakhstan, Kyrgyzstan, Moldova, Russia, India, Tajikistan, Turkmenistan, Ukraine and Uzbekistan), Iraq, Jordan, Laos, Lebanon, Libya, Myanmar, China, Syria, Tunisia, Vietnam, Yemen, Hong Kong, Macau and Palestine, and refugees from the Middle East, may need visas or other forms of documentation. Details, and the visas themselves, may be obtained from Singapore Overseas Missions.

Tourists are issued with 30-day passes on arrival. If you wish to extend your stay, apply to the Singapore Immigration and Registration department (tel: 6391 6100). Applications take at least a day to process. If you enter the country with prescription drugs necessary for your well being, take a copy of your prescription with you.

Import restrictions
You are prohibited from importing certain items without first obtaining permits. Many of these laws are common to most countries. There are

restrictions upon items ranging from cigarette lighters in the shape of pistols to chewing tobacco and tobacco substitutes, and, of all things, chewing gum. If you have any doubts, the Customs Department at the airport (tel: 6542 7058/ 6545 9122/ 6543 0755/ 6543 0754) should be able to answer your queries. Be aware, though, that permits are required for the following:

Telecommunications and radio equipment, which includes toy walkie-talkies. Contact the Telecommunications Authority (tel: 6322 1948).

Toy versions of Singaporean coins and notes. Contact the Board of Commissioners of Currency (tel: 6325 9815).

For information concerning the importation of **animals and their by-products**, and **plants with soil**, contact the Primary Production Department (tel: 1800 226 2250). To import animals, you will need to apply for a permit in advance of your arrival to the City Veterinary Centre (25 Peck Seah Street, Singapore 079315; tel: 6227 0670; fax: 6227 6403/6305; email: ava_email@ava.gov.sg). You will also require a permit in advance of importing plants with soil. Applications should be made to the Phytsanitary and Plant Quarantine Section (Lorong Chencharu, Sembawang 17km, Sembawang Field Experimental Station, Singapore 769193; tel: 6751 9843; fax: 6752 0170).

Medicines and poisons. Contact the Drug Administration Division (tel: 6325 5639). Arms and ammunition of all kinds, including swords and explosives. Contact the police (tel: 6734 4162).

Films, pre-recorded videotapes and discs. Contact the Board of Censors (tel: 6325 5639).

Books, newspapers and magazines, and pre-recorded cassettes and cartridges. Contact the Ministry of Information and Arts (tel: 1800 375 7080).

If you are importing quantities of commodities, you should be aware that there are rules governing import taxes. These do not affect tourists.

Export restrictions

There is no export duty payable on anything you take out of Singapore, but you will need permits if you want to export firearms, ammunition, explosives, gold, animals or the products of protected animals, platinum, precious stones and jewellery (except for personal jewellery), poisons and drugs. Contact the Singapore Trade Development Board (tel: 6337 6620) to enquire about any of these. Remember that if you buy anything made from parts of an animal while you are in Singapore, you might find that there are import restrictions imposed by your own country.

Duty free

If you are over 18 you can import, duty free, a litre of spirits, wine, port or beer. Alcohol is expensive in Singapore; a bottle of spirits can cost £20 (US$28) or more, and the cheapest wine on offer in a supermarket will cost £7 a bottle. It is therefore a good idea to bring your own in free of duty. There is a duty-free shop in the airport, between luggage collections and customs control. Singapore is doing its best to discourage smoking, and consequently there is no concession on importing tobacco.

Drugs

Warnings about Singapore's drug laws are printed in red on the entry permit cards filled in on arrival. The penalties for attempting to take 'recreational' drugs in or out of the country are extremely harsh. Those caught carrying even small quantities can be imprisoned for up to ten years, and those convicted of trafficking (defined as carrying as little as 15g of heroin or 200g of cannabis resin) can face the death penalty. Please do not take the risk.

EMBASSIES
In Singapore

Most embassies and foreign missions are open between 09.00 and 17.00 during the week, but do ring to check if you want to visit them. The telephone directory will list all of them, but here are the most commonly wanted:

Australia 25 Napier Rd; tel: 733 7134

Belgium 14-01, Temasek Tower, 8 Shenton Way; tel: 220 7677

Canada 15-01, IBM Towers, 80 Anson Rd; tel: 325 3200

Denmark 13-01 United Sq, 101 Thomson Rd; tel: 250 3383

France 101–103 Cluny Pk Rd; tel: 880 7800Germany 14-00 Far East Shopping **Centre**, 545 Orchard Rd; tel: 737 1355

Ireland Ireland House, 8th Floor Liat Towers, 541 Orchard Rd; tel: 238 7616

Italy 27-02 United Sq, 101 Thomson Rd; tel: 250 6022

Japan 16 Nassim Rd; tel: 235 8855

Netherlands 13-01 Liat Towers, 541 Orchard Rd; tel: 737 1155

New Zealand 15-06 Ngee Ann City, TowerA, 391A Orchard Rd; tel: 235 9966

Norway 44-01 Hong Leong Building, 16 Raffles Quay; tel: 220 7122

Sweden 05-08 PUB Building, 111 Somerset Rd; tel: 734 2771

UK 100 Tanglin Rd; tel: 473 9333

USA 27 Napier Rd; tel: 476 9100

Overseas

Australia 17 Forster Crescent, Yarralumia, ACT 2600 Canberra; tel: 06273 3944; fax: 06273 3260; email: shc.cbr@u030.gome.net.au

Belgium 198 Ave Franklin Roosevelt, 1050 Brussels; tel: 02660 2979; fax: 02660 8685; email: amb.eu@singembbru.be

France 12 Sq de l'Ave Foch, 75116 Paris; tel: 014500 3361; email: singemb@club-internet.fr

Germany Suedstrasse 133, 53175 Bonn 2; tel: 0228 951 0314; fax: 0228 31 0527; email: sing.emb.bonn@t-online.de

New Zealand 17 Kabul St, Khandallah, Wellington; tel: 04 4792 076; email: shcwlg@xtra.co.nz

Malaysia 209 Jalan Tun Razak, Kuala Lumpur, 50400; tel: 261 6277; fax: 02 03 261 6343; email: tltong@shcom.po.my

Thailand 129 South Sahorn Rd, Bangkok; tel: 02 286 2111; fax: 287 2578; email: singemb@kscll.th.com

UK 9 Wilton Crescent, London SW1X 8SA; tel: 020 7235 8315; fax: 020 7235 4557; email: schlondon@singcomm.demon.co.uk

USA 3501 International Place, NW Washington DC 20008; tel: 0202 537 3100; fax: 0202 537 0876; email: xpulo8a@prodigy.com

TOURIST INFORMATION

The airport, hotels, major tourist attractions, and the multimedia terminals along Orchard Road are all sources of information for visitors. Below are lists of Singapore Tourism Board offices on the island and abroad:

In Singapore

Singapore Visitors Centre SunTec City Mall, 01-35/37/39/41, 3 Temasek Blvd, Singapore 038983; tel: 1 800 332 5066. Open 08.00–18.30 daily.

Singapore Visitors Centre H_2O Zone, Orchard Point, 160 Orchard Rd, Singapore 238842; tel: 1 800 738 8169. Open 09.30–20.30 daily.

Singapore Visitors Centre Level 1, Liang Court Shopping Centre, 177 River Valley Rd, Singapore 179030; tel: 6336 2888. Open 10.30–21.30 daily.

STB Tourist Information Centre Tourism Court, 1 Orchard Spring Lane, Singapore 247729; tel: 1 800 736 2000. Open Sun–Fri 08.30–17.00, Sat 08.30–13.00.

Travel Café Tourist Information Centre Prinsep Place, 01-01/02/01, 50 Prinsep St, Singapore 188672; tel: 6338 9001; email: info@travelcafe-world.com. Open 11.00–21.00 Mon–Thu and public holidays, 11.00–14.00 Fri, Sat and eves of public holidays.

Overseas

Australia Level 11, AWA Building, 47 York St, Sydney NSW 2000; tel: 61-2 9290 2888/9290 2882; fax: 61-2 9290 2555; email: stb-syd@stb-syd.org.au; or, c/o Glason Marketing and Representation, Level 1, 235 Queen St, Melbourne VIC 3000; tel: 61-3 9606 0222; fax: 61-3 9606 0322; email: stbmel@compuserve.com; or, c/o Sandra Devahasdin PR and Promotions, Unit 2, 226 James St, Perth WA 6000; tel: 61-8 9228 8166; fax: 61-8 9228 8290; email: stbperth@sandrapr.iinet.net.au

Canada Suite 404, 2 Bloor St West, Toronto, Ontario M4W 3E2; tel: 1-416 363 8898; fax: 1-416 363 5752; email: AskMich@TourismSingapore.com; web: www.singapore-ca.com

China Room 1103, Shui On Plaza, 333 Huai Hai Zhong Rd, Shanghai 200021; tel: 86-21 6336 0607; fax: 86-21 6336 8565; email: stbsh@newasia-singapore.com

France Centre d'Affaires, Le Louvre, 2 Place du Palais-Royal, 75044 Paris Cedex 01; tel: 33-1 4297 1616; fax: 33-1 4297 1617; email: stbpari@worldnet.fr

Germany Hocjstrasse 35–37, 60313 Frankfurt; tel: 49-69 920 7700; fax: 49-69 297 8922; email: info@stb-germany.de; web: www.new-asia-singapore.de

Hong Kong Room 2003, Central Plaza, 18 Harbour Rd, Wanchai; tel: 852 2598 9290; fax: 852 2598 1040; email: stbhk01@hk.linkage.net; web: www.singapore.com.tw

India No 82, 8th Floor, Jolly Maker 11, Nariman Point, Mumbai 400 021; tel: 91-22 285 3004/283 4141; fax: 91-92 283 5700; email: stbindia@vsnl.com

Italy C/o Theodore Trancu and Associates, Viale Beatrice d'Este 15, 20122 Milano; tel: 39-02 5845 7080; fax: 39-02 5845 7070; email: trancu@yya.it

Malaysia C/o Edelman Public Relations Worldwide, 2nd Floor, Wisma Damansara

Jalan Semantan, Damansara Heights, 50490 Kuala Lumpur; tel: 603 225 2277/254 8957; fax: 603 255 0235; email: stc@stb-malaysia.com.my
New Zealand C/o Vivaldi World, 85B Hebron Rd, Waiake, Auckland 1311; tel: 64-9 473 8658; fax: 64-9 473 6887; email: stbauckland@xtra.co.nz
South Africa C/o Marilyn Boogaart, Boogaart House, 18 Riesling Crescent, Hurlingham Manor, Sandton, Johannesburg; tel: 27-11 886 6292; fax: 27-11 781 2491; email: Singapor@iafrica.com
Sweden C/o Airline Marketing Service, St Ericsgatan 23, 1st Floor, S-112 39 Stockholm; tel: 46-8 545 515 15; fax: 46-8 545 515 19; email: singapore@ams.a.se; web: www.newasia-singapore.nu
Switzerland Lowenstrasse 51, CH-8001 Zurich; tel: 41-1 211 7474; fax: 41-1 211 7422; email: stb@singapore.ch
The Philippines C/o Commways, 5th Floor, OAC Building, San Miguel Ave, Ortigas Center, Pasig City, Manila; tel: 632 636 2919/631 7844; fax: 632 635 9524; email: stbphils@pacific.net.ph
UK 1st Floor, Carrington House, 126–130 Regent St, London W1B 5JX; tel: 020 7437 0033 or 0800 656565 (freephone); fax: 020 7434 2191; email: info@stb.org.uk
USA Suite 510, 8484 Wilshire Blvd, Beverley Hills, California 90211; tel: 1-323 852 1901; fax: 1-323 852 0129; email: AskVince@TourismSingapore.com; web: www.singapore-usa.com; or, Suite 2615, 2 Prudential Plaza, 180 North Stetson Ave, Chicago, Illinois 60601; tel: 1-312 938 1888; fax: 1-312 938 0086; email: AskDave@TourismSingapore.com; web: www.singapore-usa.com; or, 12th Floor, 590 Fifth Ave, New York 10036; tel: 1-212 302 4861; fax: 1-212 302 4801; email: AskRoc@TourismSingapore.com; web: www.singapore-usa.com

GETTING THERE AND AWAY
By air
Most visitors enter Singapore by plane. A direct flight from London to Singapore will take approximately 13 hours – longer with stopovers. Many international airlines call at Singapore, including the excellent national carrier, Singapore International Airways. Changi Airport is the only one in the country, and all flights arrive and leave from here. If you have any queries, contact Flight Information (tel: 1800 542 4422), or the Singapore Tourism Board (tel: 1800 736 2000), which is available 24 hours a day. When you are ready to leave Singapore, you will need to confirm your onward flight. The following airlines use Changi Airport; independent travellers who have not booked through a travel agent can contact their airlines for information and confirmation of bookings.
Air China Tel: 6225 2177; fax: 6225 7546; web: www.airchina.com.sg
Air France Tel: 6737 6355; fax: 6235 8661; web: www.airfrance.com.sg
American Airlines Tel: 6839 7766; fax: 6733 9556; web: www.aa.com
British Airways Tel: 6839 7788; fax: 6235 5865; web: www.british-airways.com.sg
Cathay Pacific Airways Tel: 6533 1333; fax: 6534 1161; web: www.cathaypacific.com
China Airlines Tel: 6737 2211; fax: 6732 8627; web: www.china-airlines.com
Continental Airlines Tel: 6538 6860; fax: 6538 3183; web: www.continental.com
Emirates Tel: 6735 3535; fax: 6235 2766; web: www.emiratesairline.com

Finnair Tel: 6733 3377; fax: 6732 0214; web: www.finnair.com.sg
Garuda Airlines Tel: 6250 2888; fax: 6253 6196; web: www.indodirect.com/garuda
Indian Airlines Tel: 6225 4949; web: www.indian-airlines.nic.in
Japan Airlines Tel: 6221 0522; fax: 6224 3382; web: www.jal.com.sg
KLM Tel: 6737 7622; fax: 6235 9480; web: www.klm.nl
Korean Air Tel: 6534 2111; fax: 6538 2031; web: www.koreanair.com
Malaysia Airlines Tel: 6336 6777; fax: 6334 1891; web:
www.malaysiaairlines.com.my
Northwest Airlines Tel: 6336 3371; fax: 6339 2575; web: www.nwa.com
Qantas Tel: 6839 7788; fax: 6734 3084; web: www.qantas.com
Scandinavian Airlines Tel: 6235 2488; fax: 6235 3655
SilkAir Tel: 6225 4488; fax: 6222 7028/2221; web: www.silkair.net
Singapore Airlines Tel: 6223 8888 (reservations), 6223 6666 (fare enquiries); fax:
6229 7151; web: www.singaporeair.com
Swissair Tel: 6737 8133; web: www.swissair.com
Thai Airways Tel: 6224 9977; fax: 6223 9005; web: www.thaiair.com
United Airlines Tel: 6873 3533; fax: 6225 5753/6323 5868; web: www.ual.com.sg

Changi Airport

Changi consistently excels in surveys of international airports, and is
frequently voted the best of all. It is at the easternmost tip of the island, and
you approach it from the eastern end of the runway so that as you come in to
land you can see the whole of Singapore laid out before you.

Changi contains the usual facilities that you would expect to find in an
airport, including 108 shops (one of which is a duty-free shop between
luggage collections and customs control) and 34 restaurants. In addition, in
Terminal 1 you will find a fitness centre, a rooftop swimming pool and a
jacuzzi. There are television lounges, which are divided into different areas
so that BBC World, CNN, the local CNA, and sports channels can all be
found in separate, designated spots. There are business and internet centres
in both terminals (open 24 hours in Terminal 1, and from 07.00 to 23.00 in
Terminal 2), and also zones where businessmen can use computers with the
'wireless' system, so that there is no need for modem wire connections.
Enjoy a drink and even a live band in either one of the terminals between
19.00 and 22.00. You can get a room in one of the transit hotels while you
wait to change flights, but you are free to use the gym, the showers and the
sauna even if you are not in transit. Should you need to move from one
terminal to the other there is a Skytrain. If you are flying home, boxes of
orchids are available at the airport which can last up to five weeks, may be
carried as cabin luggage, and cost between S$15 and S$50. But if you are
stuck for more than five hours, and all this isn't enough to keep you
entertained, there are free tours of Singapore.

Terminal 2 is used by Air France, Air New Zealand, Ansett Australia,
Finnair, Lufthansa, Malaysia Airlines, Philippines Airlines, Royal Brunei
Airlines, Silk Air, Singapore Airlines and Swissair. Terminal 1 is used by all the
other carriers. Left-luggage facilities can be found in both terminals, and are

on either side of the immigration barriers so that they can be used whether or not you are in transit. Despite the fact that Singapore is not keen on smoking, there are designated smoking areas, both air-conditioned and open-air, in terminals 1 and 2.

Airport tax
There is an airport tax (or passenger service charge) of S$15, which should be included in the cost charged by your airline (although it is worth checking this). It does not apply to transit passengers staying less than 24 hours, provided they do not leave the airport.

Getting to and from the airport
It is easy to travel from the airport to the rest of the island. You can hop on a No 36 bus to Orchard Road at each terminal basement (costing S$1.50 in cash to the driver or S$1.40 using a Transit Link stored-value card – see pages 54–5), and there are plenty of ordinary taxis for hire (the fare will be S$15–17 to Orchard Road). Alternatively, you can take a Maxicab, a shuttle service between Changi and the town that will stop at most hotels along the way if requested. You can also alight from the Maxicab at MRT stations, or any other places you wish to go. These six-seater vehicles have lots of space for luggage and can take wheelchairs. They run from 06.00 until 24.00 daily, leaving at intervals of between 15 and 30 minutes, and cost S$7 for adults and S$5 for children. Tickets can be collected at the shuttle counters in airport terminals 1 and 2, but you pay the driver, who will accept cash or plastic. For more information, tel: 6553 3880.

Changi Airport is also now served by the MRT, and each train carriage has racks at either end allocated for luggage. It is the terminus of a spur on the EW line with interchanges on to the NS line at City Hall or Raffles Place, or on to the new NE line (opening autumn 2002) at Dhoby Ghaut, one stop northbound from City Hall on the NS line. The first trains leave the Changi terminal at 05.31 Mon–Sat, 05.59 Sun and public holidays. The last trains leave daily at 23.18.

The cost of any journey on the MRT is a maximum S$1.80 for a single trip or S$1.65 using a Transit Link stored-value card. Tickets can be purchased from machines at the station or from the ticket office. Transit Link cards can be obtained from Transit Link booths at the station. The latter cost S$12 and give buyers S$10-worth of travel. Unused credits can be cashed in at the end of your stay. For further information on using the Transit Link card, see pages 54–5.

By train
Mainline train services to Malaysia and beyond are operated by Keretapi Tanah Malayu (KTM), the Malaysian railway system. Trains leave from Tanjong Pagar Railway Station (30 Keppel Road, Singapore 089059; tel: 6222 5265/ 6221 3390; fax: 6227 0313), to the south of the city centre, which is Malaysian despite lying in Singapore (this arrangement was part of the agreement whereby Singapore left the Malaysian Federation in 1965; see

History, page 18). Trains to Johore Bahru leave Singapore daily at 08.00, 14.45, 18.10 and 22.10. A single fare is S$2.90, and the journey takes about half an hour. The trains are reliable (although the arrival times can be less predictable) and clean. It is worth paying extra for places on the express trains, which are considerably faster than the ordinary ones.

To travel in real luxury, take the *Eastern and Oriental Express* (tel: 6392 3500), which travels from Tanjong Pagar station and runs via Kuala Lumpur in Malaysia to Bangkok in Thailand. Leaving once daily, the journey takes a little over 40 hours. You must expect to pay for the opulence, however. A single trip (you can travel in either direction) between Singapore and Bangkok (based on sharing twin-bedded accommodation, including table d'hôte meals) is over S$2,500 for a Pullman car, over S$3,500 for state class and around S$5,000 for presidential class. The company can also organise sightseeing trips to Penang and the Kwai Railway, or travel to Butterworth, Chang Mai and Angkor Wat.

By bus

There are several bus services operating between Singapore and surrounding countries. Fares paid in Malaysia are usually cheaper than those in Singapore. It is sensible to book tickets a few days ahead if you are travelling on long-distance journeys, particularly during holiday periods. Below are companies offering transport to and from some of the more common destinations:

Pan Malaysian Express (**PME**) Tel: 6294 7034; fax: 6299 1952. Services include buses to **Malacca** (departing at 08.00, 09.00, 10.00, 11.00, 14.00, 16.00 and 17.00), which take approximately four hours and cost S$15. Buses leave from the Lavender Street Terminal or the Kallang Bahru Lorry Park.

Syarikat Sri Maju Express (**SSM**) Tel: 6293 4960/6294 8228; fax: 6299 5661. Offer services to **Butterworth** (leaving daily at 08.30), taking 11 hours at a cost of S$35, to **Ipoh** (departing at 09.00, 12.00, 15.00, and 21.45), which takes eight hours and costs S$31, and to **Penang** (leaving daily at 08.30), an 11-hour journey costing S$35. Buses leave from the Golden Mile Complex, Beach Road.

Singapore – Johore Express (**SJE**) Tel: 6292 8151; fax: 6291 5075. Services to **Johore Bahru** (leaving daily at 06.30, and every ten minutes thereafter until 12.00) take one hour and cost S$2.40. Buses leave from the Ban San Terminal at the junction of Queen Street and Arab Street.

Kuala Lumpur – Singapore Express (**KSE**) Tel: 6292 8254; fax: 6291 5075. Buses to **Kuala Lumpur** (depart Monday to Friday at 09.00, 13.00, 22.00, Saturday, Sunday and public holidays at 11.00 and 16.00) take six hours and cost S$23. They leave from the Ban San Terminal at the junction of Arab Street and Queen Street.

Malacca – Singapore Express (**MSE**) Tel: 6293 5915. Journeys to **Malacca** (depart 08.00, 09.00, 10.00, 11.00, 14.00 and 17.00) take four hours and cost S$15. Buses leave from the Lavender Street Terminal and the Kallang Bahru Lorry Park.

By sea

There are regular ferries between Singapore and Indonesia, and operators' offices are located in the Singapore Cruise Centre (in the World Trade Centre).

Penguin Ferry Services (tel: 6542 7015) offers boats to Batam, which leave at 07.30, take 45 minutes, and cost S$16 adult, S$12 child. They depart from the World Trade Centre. Note that Penguin does not operate between the months of October and March (the rainy season).

Bintan Resort Ferries (tel: 6338 3200 or 6542 4369/4379 for advance bookings) runs high-speed catamaran services to Bintan (departing Monday to Friday at 09.05, 10.50, 14.00, 17.00 and 20.00, weekends at 08.15, 09.05, 10.50, 12.00, 14.00, 16.00, 17.00 and 20.00), taking 45 minutes and costing S$32 adult, S$22 child. These leave from the Tanah Merah Ferry Terminal, on the east coast. Check-in time is 30 minutes before departure, and there is a baggage allowance of 20kg per passenger.

Channel Holidays (tel: 6272 9722) go to Tanjung Pinang (Mon–Fri 09.00, 13.00 and 17.00, weekends 09.30, 13.30 and 17.40), the crossing taking two hours at a cost of S$32 adult, S$23 child. Ferries leave from the Tanah Merah terminal.

All the quoted fares are singles. There are also ferries to Malaysia from Changi Point, which call at Tanjong Belungkor (the eastern corner of the state of Johore), before travelling on to other destinations along the east coast.

By car

Another way to visit the country is to travel overland from Malaysia. A Malaysian-registered car has to have a Vehicle Entry Permit (VEP) while it is in the country. Once the car is in Singapore, there are various charges that the driver will have to pay. Buy an Autopass card from the Woodlands checkpoint as soon as you arrive across the Causeway. This costs S$10 and contains S$4 worth of credit. It can be topped up at any ATM in Singapore, and at other outlets where you see an 'Autopass Card Top-Up' sign.

HEALTH

Singapore is a safe country, and you are unlikely to be exposed to any serious health risks. If you are, however, the country's health facilities are excellent. Ensure that you have arranged for appropriate health insurance. If outdoors, be wary of the heat, particularly during the early afternoon. Prevent dehydration by carrying bottled water with you, and use a hat (or umbrella) and sun screen if you are out in the middle of the day. Women who are more than six months pregnant should apply to the nearest Singapore Overseas Mission before going to Singapore. If you enter the country with prescription drugs necessary for your well being, ensure you have a copy of the prescription with you (or there may be complications on your arrival). Singapore's water supply is perfectly clean and you can drink from the tap. If you wish to buy bottled water, however, it is available in all supermarkets.

Most hotels have a recommended doctor on 24-hour call. Chemists, or pharmacies, are open from 09.00 until 18.00, and can dispense prescriptions or provide over-the-counter remedies. A full list of doctors and dentists can be found in the Yellow Pages. There are around 2,020 clinics of various sorts, including three mobile clinics run by the government. These cater to different medical disciplines such as gynaecology or dentistry.

Vaccinations

Vaccinations are not essential before entering Singapore, unless travelling from disease-affected areas (yellow fever and cholera certificates, for instance, are required if you have been in an endemic area within the previous six days). However, Hepatitis A, polio and tetanus vaccinations are all recommended. In Singapore, the Travellers' Health and Vaccination Clinic (Tan Tock Seng Hospital Medical Centre, Level B2, 11 Jalan Tan Tock Seng, Singapore 308433; tel: 6357 2222; fax: 6352 5661; web: www.ttsh.gov.sg/cdc) can help with any travel-related conditions and with vaccinations.

Travel clinics and health information

A full list of current travel clinic websites worldwide is available on www.istm.org/. For other journey preparation information, consult ftp://ftp.shoreland.com/pub/shorecg.rtf or www.tripprep.com.

UK

British Airways Travel Clinic and Immunisation Service There are now only three BA clinics, all in London: 156 Regent St, W1B 5LB (no appointments); 101 Cheapside, EC1V6DT (tel: 020 7606 2977); 115 Buckingham Palace Rd, SW1W 9SJ (Victoria Station; tel: 020 7233 6661); see also www.britishairways.com/travelclinics. Also sell a variety of health-related goods.

Fleet Street Travel Clinic 29 Fleet St, London EC4Y 1AA; tel: 020 7353 5678

Hospital for Tropical Diseases Travel Clinic Mortimer Market Centre, 2nd Floor, Capper St (off Tottenham Ct Rd), London WC1E 6AU; tel: 020 7388 9600; web: www.thhtd.org. Offers consultations and advice, and is able to provide all necessary drugs and vaccines for travellers. Runs a healthline (09061 337733) for country-specific information and health hazards. Also stocks nets, water purification equipment and personal protection meaures.

MASTA (Medical Advisory Service for Travellers Abroad) Keppel St, London WC1 7HT; tel: 09068 224100. This is a premium-line number, charged at 50p per minute.

NHS travel website, www.fitfortravel.scot.nhs.uk, provides country-by-country advice on immunisation and malaria, plus details of recent developments, and a list of relevant health organisations.

Nomad Travel Pharmacy and Vaccination Centre 3–4 Wellington Terrace, Turnpike Lane, London N8 0PX; tel: 020 8889 7014; email: sales@nomadtravel.co.uk; website: www.nomadtravel.co.uk. As well as dispensing health advice, Nomad stocks mosquito nets and other anti-bug devices, and an excellent range of adventure travel gear.

Thames Medical 157 Waterloo Rd, London SE1 8US; tel: 020 7902 9000. Competitively priced, one-stop travel health service. All profits go to their affiliated company, InterHealth, which provides health care for overseas workers on Christian projects.

Trailfinders Immunisation Centre 194 Kensington High St, London W8 7RG; tel: 020 7938 3999.

Travelpharm The Travelpharm website, www.travelpharm.com, offers up-to-date guidance on travel-related health and has a range of medications available through their online mini-pharmacy.

Irish Republic

Tropical Medical Bureau Grafton Street Medical Centre, Grafton Buildings, 34 Grafton St, Dublin 2; tel: 1 671 9200. Has a useful website specific to tropical destinations: www.tmb.ie

USA

Centers for Disease Control 1600 Clifton Rd, Atlanta, GA 30333; tel: 877 FYI TRIP; 800 311 3435; web: www.cdc.gov/travel. The central source of travel information in the USA. Each summer they publish the invaluable *Health Information for International Travel*, available from the Division of Quarantine at the above address.

Connaught Laboratories PO Box 187, Swiftwater, PA 18370; tel: 800 822 2463. They will send a free list of specialist tropical-medicine physicians in your state.

IAMAT (International Association for Medical Assistance to Travelers) 736 Center St, Lewiston, NY 14092; tel: 716 754 4883. A non-profit organisation that provides lists of English-speaking doctors abroad.

Canada

IAMAT (International Association for Medical Assistance to Travellers) Suite 1, 1287 St Clair Av W, Toronto, Ontario M6E 1B8; tel: 416 652 0137; web: www.sentex.net/~iamat

TMVC (Travel Doctors Group) Sulphur Springs Rd, Ancaster, Ontario; tel: 905 648 1112; web: www.tmvc.com.au

Australia, New Zealand, Thailand

TMVC Tel: 1300 65 88 44; web: www.tmvc.com.au. 20 clinics in Australia, New Zealand and Thailand, including:

Auckland Canterbury Arcade, 170 Queen Street, Auckland City; tel: 373 3531
Brisbane Dr Deborah Mills, Qantas Domestic Building, 6th floor, 247 Adelaide St, Brisbane, QLD 4000; tel: 7 3221 9066; fax: 7 3321 7076
Melbourne Dr Sonny Lau, 393 Little Bourke St, 2nd floor, Melbourne, VIC 3000; tel: 3 9602 5788; fax: 3 9670 8394
Sydney Dr Mandy Hu, Dymocks Building, 7th Floor, 428 George St, Sydney, NSW2000; tel: 2 221 7133; fax: 2 221 8401

South Africa

SAA-Netcare Travel Clinics PO Box 786692, Sandton 2146; fax: 011 883 6152; web: www.travelclinic.co.za or www.malaria.co.za. Clinics throughout South Africa.

TMVC (Travel Doctor Group) 113 DF Malan Drive, Roosevelt Park, Johannesburg; tel: 011 888 7488; web: www.tmvc.com.au. Consult the website for details of clinics in South Africa.

LONG-HAUL FLIGHTS
Dr Felicity Nicholson

There is growing evidence, albeit circumstantial, that long-haul air travel increases the risk of developing deep vein thrombosis. This condition is potentially life threatening, but it should be stressed that the danger to the average traveller is slight.

Certain risk factors specific to air travel have been identified. These include immobility, compression of the veins at the back of the knee by the edge of the seat, the decreased air pressure and slightly reduced oxygen in the cabin, and dehydration. Consuming alcohol may exacerbate the situation by increasing fluid loss and encouraging immobility.

In theory everyone is at risk, but those at highest risk are shown below:

- Passengers on journeys of longer than eight hours duration
- People over 40
- People with heart disease
- People with cancer
- People with clotting disorders
- People who have had recent surgery, especially on the legs
- Women on the pill or other oestrogen therapy
- Pregnancy
- People who are very tall (over 6ft/1.8m) or short (under 5ft/1.5m)

A deep vein thrombosis (DVT) is a clot of blood that forms in the leg veins. Symptoms include swelling and pain in the calf or thigh. The skin may feel hot to touch and becomes discoloured (light blue-red). A DVT

Switzerland
IAMAT (International Association for Medical Assistance to Travellers) 57 Voirets, 1212 Grand Lancy, Geneva; web: www.sentex.net/~iamat

Hospitals and medical centres
Open consultations are also offered at the Raffles Medical Group Centres. There are many branches of these, but the most central are located at the following addresses:

Orchard MRT Station #B1-01 Orchard Rd, Singapore 228878; tel: 6734 7355; fax: 6734 0201

182 Clemenceau Ave (24-hour care centre) #02-00, Singapore 239923; tel: 6734 7355; fax: 6331 5864

30 Raffles Place #03-01/08 Caltex House, Singapore 048622; tel: 6535 2222; fax: 6533 7811

2 Raffles Link #01-01 Marina Bayfront, Singapore 039392; tel: 6339 6644; fax: 6339 6698

Changi Airport #B16-025 Basement, Passenger Terminal 2, Singapore 819643; tel 6543 1118; fax: 6543 0717; or, #026-53 Departure Hall, Passenger Terminal 2,

is not dangerous in itself, but if a clot breaks down then it may travel to the lungs (pulmonary embolus). Symptoms of a pulmonary embolus (PE) include chest pain, shortness of breath and coughing up small amounts of blood.

Symptoms of a DVT rarely occur during the flight, and typically occur within three days of arrival, although symptoms of a DVT or PE have been reported up to two weeks later.

Anyone who suspects that they have these symptoms should see a doctor immediately as anticoagulation (blood thinning) treatment can be given.

Prevention of DVT

General measures to reduce the risk of thrombosis are shown below. This advice also applies to long train or bus journeys.

* Whilst waiting to board the plane, try to walk around rather than sit.
* During the flight drink plenty of water (at least two small glasses every hour).
* Avoid excessive tea, coffee and alcohol.
* Perform leg-stretching exercises, such as pointing the toes up and down.
* Move around the cabin when practicable.

If you fit into the high-risk category (see above) ask your doctor if it is safe to travel. Additional protective measures such as graded compression stockings, aspirin or low molecular weight heparin can be given. No matter how tall you are, where possible request a seat with extra legroom.

Singapore 819643; tel: 6543 1118; fax: 6543 0717; or, #021-36 Departure Hall, Passenger Terminal 1, Singapore 819642; tel: 6543 1113; fax: 6543 0717

There are 24 hospitals in Singapore, all of a high standard. Of these, 14 are privately owned. Should you need an **ambulance**, ring 995. Alternatively, in an emergency, contact one of the following:

Singapore General Hospital Outram Rd, Singapore 169608; tel: 6222 3322; fax: 6224 9221
Mount Elizabeth Hospital 3 Mount Elizabeth, Singapore 228510; tel: 6737 2666; fax: 6734 0518
Mount Alvernia Hospital 820 Thomson Rd, Singapore 574623; tel: 6253 4818; fax: 6290 5138
Gleneagles Hospital 6A Napier Rd, Singapore 258500; tel: 6473 7222; fax: 6475 1832

SAFETY

Singapore is one of the safer countries in the world. Crime is low, and tourists shouldn't encounter any problems. As anywhere, however, it is worth taking sensible precautions. Do not keep all your valuables together in one place, let people know where you are going and when you expect to be back, and try not to travel alone at night, particularly if female.

WHAT TO TAKE

You can afford to travel light as most items are available at reasonable prices in Singapore. You will encounter no difficulties in finding high-quality film stock, sanitary towels and tampons, deodorants or any other everyday products; frequently they will be cheaper than at home. One exception to this rule is alcohol, which is very expensive. If you enjoy a gin and tonic or a whisky in the evening, take it in with you as duty free. There is a duty-free shop at Changi Airport (see page 44) which you can enter before passing through customs. While the country is warm and humid, it is worth taking a lightweight jacket, cardigan or sweater as air-conditioned hotels and restaurants can be quite chilly. Women may find a loose cotton skirt cooler than jeans or trousers. Also be aware that most luxury hotels and restaurants operate a 'smart casual' rule, so bring a set of appropriate clothes. Female travellers should note that a backless or slipper-type sandal is not allowed in some bars or restaurants (a strap around the back of the heel is necessary). This also applies to backpacker casual sandals or trainers.

MONEY

Singaporean currency primarily comes in the form of notes, although S$1 is also produced as a coin. There are notes representing S$2, 5, 10, 20, 50, 100, 500, 1,000, and 10,000. The Singapore dollar is divided into a hundred cents, which come as coins to the value of 1, 5, 10, 20 and 50 cents. Singaporeans sometimes refer to a dollar as a buck.

You will have no difficulty exchanging cash or travellers' cheques. Money can be changed at the airport and in hotels, as well as at banks. It is possible to get a better deal, however, with the numerous licensed money-changers who can be found in shopping complexes and elsewhere. Using unlicensed changers, though, is frowned upon. Wherever you choose to change your currency, you will need to show your passport.

Credit and charge cards are readily accepted in Singapore; you can even use plastic to pay for taxis, although drivers prefer lower-value notes. If you should happen to lose your card or have any other difficulties, see the list of contact numbers below. Many places will also take American and Australian dollars, pounds sterling, yen and euros.

The current rate of exchange (July 2002) is £1 = S$2.6, US$1 = S$1.7.

Credit cards

Major credit cards are widely accepted and can be extremely convenient. The hassle caused by a lost card, however, can spoil a holiday. The following contact numbers should prove useful if you encounter any trouble:

American Express Tel: 1 800 732 2244; fax: 6295 4300
Citibank Visa Tel: 1 800 225 5225; fax: 6328 6568
Diners Card Tel: 1 800 294 4222; fax: 6294 0534

Above left Red-faced liocichia (STB)

Above right Red-tailed laughing thrush (STB)

Left Toucan (from South America)
at Jurong Bird Park (STB)

Below Flowers in the National Orchid
Garden include the heliconia from
South America (right), as well as orchids (NS)

Above Statue outside Sakaya
Muni Buddha Gaya Temple (JW)

Above right Sri Mariamman
Temple detail (NS)

Right Chinese lantern at the
Leong Sam Temple, Little India (JW)

Hong Kong Bank Visa/Mastercard Tel: 6336 5277; fax: 6338 7276
Maybank Visa Tel: 1 800 532 2604; fax: 6534 3772
OCBC Credit Card Visa/Mastercard Tel: 1 800 538 0118; fax: 6532 2179
OUB Credit Card Tel: 1 800 224 2000; fax: 6226 5181
Standard Chartered Visa Tel: 1 800 789 7662; fax: 6789 2442
UOB Card Centre Tel: 1 800 253 6888; fax: 6253 1855

Banks

Most banks are open between 09.30 and 15.00 on weekdays, and 09.30 and 12.30 on Saturday. Some banks are even open on Sunday, from 09.30 until 15.00. Please be aware that not all banks handle foreign currency at the weekend, and that you will require your passport to cash travellers' cheques. Addresses of some of the major banks are:

American Express Bank Ltd 16 Collyer Quay, Hitachi Tower, Singapore 049318; tel: 6231 8888; fax: 6532 3108
Bank of Singapore Ltd 101 Cecil St, #01-02 Tong Eng Building, Singapore 069533; tel: 6223 9266; fax: 6224 9523
Citibank NA 23 Church St, #01-01 Capital Sq, Singapore 049481; tel: 6225 5225; fax: 6328 8646
Deutsche Bank AG 6 Shenton Way, #15-08 DBS Tower 2, Singapore 068809; tel: 6224 4677; fax: 6225 9442

Tipping

On the whole, you should not tip in Singapore. Most restaurants, food outlets and hotels have a 'price + + +', which means added charges of 10% for service, a 1% government tax and a 3% goods and services tax.

GETTING AROUND

There are few places easier to travel around than Singapore. The country is compact, and everywhere easily accessible. Public transport is cheap and efficient (indeed it has to be because of the prohibitive tax on cars themselves and the cost of the necessary certificate of ownership; see *People*, page 28). The trains are clean and simple to use – the comparatively recent Mass Rapid Transit (MRT) system has been an enormous success. The buses are not clapped-out old wrecks filled to capacity as so often in the tropics. Nor is it dangerous to take the bus or the train – you can travel without fear of being the victim of muggers or con-artists. Alternatively, the small size of the island means you can ride in taxis without breaking the bank.

By taxi

There are 15,000 good, air-conditioned taxis in the country, and they are relatively cheap to use. When you are out and about, they can either be hailed or picked up at the taxi ranks to be found outside shopping malls and the larger hotels. The drivers speak English. All taxis have meters; for taxis run by Comfort and CityCab there is a fixed cost of S$2.40 for the first kilometre (S$2.20 for TIBS taxis), and thereafter a further 10 cents for each 225 metres. There are also further surcharges, however, which will not show up on the meter. You will, for instance, be charged an additional S$3 for travelling through the Central Business District during the day; S$3 for being picked up from Changi Airport, Seletar Airport or Singapore Expo; S$2–3 for booking a taxi up to 30 minutes in advance, or S$5.20–6.20 for over 30 minutes; and 50% extra between 24.00 and 06.00. The ride from Changi Airport to Orchard Road should cost S$15–17. A red destination label displayed on the windscreen means that the driver is changing shift, and prefers only to pick up passengers travelling in the direction in which he is going.

If you wish to book a cab in advance (for which there is a surcharge), your hotel will do it for you. Otherwise, try City Cab (tel: 6552 2222), Comfort Cablink (tel: 6552 1111) or TIBS (tel: 6555 8888). All these also offer more upmarket vehicles, or 'premier cabs' as they are known, as do Premier Cabs (tel: 6552 2828). Some hotels have their own taxis for the use of the guests.

Singapore now has 'road pricing', and large gantries mark entrances to the city and business areas and some parts of the expressway system. A fee is charged on entering these places during certain times of the day. Each car and taxi is fitted with a small box at the front, by the windscreen, and the driver must purchase a card to insert into the box so that the cost is automatically deducted.

By bus

Buses run from 06.00 until midnight, and are comfortable – some even entertain passengers with television screens showing local channels – and clean. Fares on air-conditioned buses range from 70 cents to S$1.50, and on others from 60 cents to S$1.20. If paying with cash, you will need the exact change for the fare. If you ask, the drivers will tell you how much to pay, but sometimes they can be difficult to understand. The main stops on Orchard Road have a list of the fare stages for each price. Alternatively, you can buy a Transit Link bus guide for S$1.40 from one of the many bookshops or from the ticket sales offices at MRT stations. This gives detailed information on fares and the route of every bus, so you can calculate your correct fare and track your journey by the bus stops.

If you would rather avoid carrying copious amounts of change in your pocket, you can purchase a Transit Link Fare Card – a stored-value card – that can also be used on the MRT. The Tourist Day ticket is available for S$10 from any of the Transit Link offices to be found in MRT stations and bus interchanges. This can be bought up to a week in advance, but you must specify the day on which you wish to use it (the date is printed on the ticket). It allows you to travel up to 12 times a day, regardless of the length of the journey, on either buses or MRT trains. A better option is to buy a S$12 card to use for the duration of your stay. This can be topped up at the Transit Link offices in MRT stations. When the credit on the card becomes low, the fare machines flash a 'top up card' instruction when you use it. Any remaining value on the card can be cashed in before you leave the country. Feed your

ON THE BUSES

The following buses and their routes should prove helpful to tourists exploring the main areas of Singapore:

Bus number	Route
36	Between Changi Airport and Orchard Road in the centre of town
190, 174	Down Orchard Road to Boat Quay, Clarke Quay and Chinatown, and back up Orchard Boulevard. Pass the Singapore Art Museum, Raffles City, and St Andrews on the way down, and the Singapore History Museum on the way back.
7	From Orchard Boulevard to Holland Village and back to Orchard Road. Passes the Botanic Gardens.
106, 111	From Orchard Road to Little India
65, 85	From Orchard Road/Orchard Boulevard to the cable car station
16, 36	From Orchard Road/Orchard Boulevard to East Coast Park
77, 167	From Orchard Road/Orchard Boulevard to Marina Promenade
65, 85, Sentosa E	From Orchard Road/Orchard Boulevard to Sentosa

card (with the arrow-bearing surface towards you) into the top slot of the machine inside the bus, key in the correct fare, and it is automatically deducted from the total on your card. The value remaining on the card is displayed before you proceed. Remember to retrieve not only your card but the ticket which is issued from the bottom slot of the machine – occasionally an inspector checks passengers' tickets. (It is amusing to watch locals who have avoided paying the correct fare leap to their feet to alight at the next stop when an inspector boards the bus.)

There is a new stored-value card, introduced in 2002, called the ez-link card, which has a deposit cost of S$5 and a maximum usage value of S$10 (which can be topped up). It can be used on the buses, MRT and LRT, and is available from the general ticketing offices at MRT and bus interchange stations. When boarding a bus, tap the card on the reader panel at the door near the driver. Initially the maximum value is deducted but, when you tap the reader again on leaving the bus, this is adjusted to the correct fare.

By MRT (local trains)

The MRT (Mass Rapid Transit) network has proved an excellent addition to Singapore's transport system. Unlike those in London, Paris and New York, MRT trains are clean, hassle-free, air-conditioned, and untroubled by beggars or thieves. The edges of underground platforms are protected by transparent screens to prevent people falling on to the lines. Outside the centre of Singapore the tracks run overland and on pillars, providing passengers with good views of the surrounding country. Trains run every few minutes between 06.00 and 24.00, and the map is easy to follow. Perhaps the only drawback is that there are significant portions of the country which are not covered by the system. Singapore is attempting to rectify this. It has recently extended the line to include Changi Airport, and a new north–east line is under construction and due for completion at the end of 2002.

MRT travel is cheap. Buy a Transit Link card (which can also be used on buses; see pages 54–5) at one of the main MRT stations for S$12. Feed the card (with the arrow-bearing surface uppermost) into one of the machines as you enter the station, and repeat the process when you reach your destination. The cost of the journey will be deducted automatically. Alternatively, purchase one of the new ez-link cards. Tap it on the reader panel mounted on top of the fare machine as you enter and leave, and the correct fare is automatically deducted. For more details on the Transit Link and ez-link cards, see *By bus*, pages 54–5).

By car

Driving is simple for the British tourist in Singapore, and pretty straightforward for other visitors, too. Road signs are in English, and Singaporeans drive on the left. Cars are modern and driving laws strictly enforced. If you plan to spend most of your time in the town, there is little point in hiring a vehicle. However, if you intend to explore more widely – and we urge you to do so – it is well worth considering. If you opt to hire a car with a chauffeur (offered by many rental companies), there is a minimum three-hour charge. If you wish to drive yourself, you will need to show a valid national driving licence or an international driving permit. You can convert these for use in Singapore at the Traffic Police Department (tel: 6547 0000). The telephone number for the Automobile Association of Singapore is 6737 2444.

There are speed restrictions all over the island, and these are monitored closely. On expressways (motorways or freeways) the speed limit is 80km/h, and elsewhere it is 50km/h. There is an abundance of speed cameras and every vehicle is fitted with a device which bleeps when you exceed the limit. Company vehicles (marked with the company name) even have lights on top that flash when the driver is speeding. The message is clear: don't speed!

There are several other regulations to bear in mind. Bus lanes are for buses only during rush hours. You will rarely find an illegally parked car. Buy a parking season ticket, pay at the time of parking in such places as shopping malls, or buy a parking coupon (S$0.45, S$0.90, S$1.80 or, for overnight parking, S$2). With the latter, scratch the coupon to reveal details of the parking payment and display it in the windscreen when you park. Never park on double yellow lines, or on red-lined areas (which are for season-ticket holders).

MRT SYSTEM

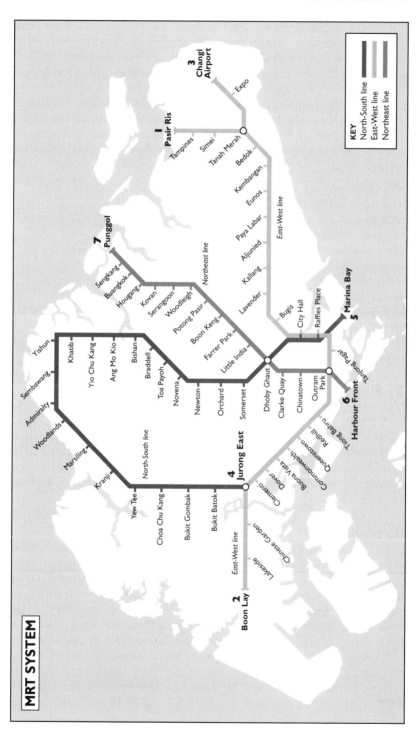

KEY
North-South line
East-West line
Northeast line

1 Pasir Ris
2 Boon Lay
3 Changi Airport
4 Jurong East
5 Marina Bay
6 Harbour Front
7 Punggol

Tampines, Simei, Tanah Merah, Expo, Bedok, Kembangan, Eunos, Paya Lebar, Aljunied, Kallang, Lavender, Bugis, City Hall, Raffles Place

East-West line

Sengkang, Buangkok, Hougang, Kovan, Serangoon, Woodleigh, Potong Pasir, Boon Keng, Farrer Park, Little India

Northeast line

Yishun, Sembawang, Admiralty, Woodlands, Marsiling, Kranji, Yew Tee, Choa Chu Kang, Bukit Gombak, Bukit Batok, Khatib, Yio Chu Kang, Ang Mo Kio, Bishan, Braddell, Toa Payoh, Novena, Newton, Orchard, Somerset

Dhoby Ghaut, Clarke Quay, Chinatown, Outram Park, Tanjong Pagar, Redhill, Tiong Bahru, Queenstown, Commonwealth, Buona Vista, Dover, Clementi

North-South line

Chinese Garden, Lakeside

East-West line

When you enter the Central Business District, an in-vehicle unit automatically deducts a charge from a card, which you can buy from petrol stations, some banks and shops, and special cash-card machines. While it sounds complicated, the system actually works very effectively. If you wish to drive across the Causeway to Malaysia, you will need to pay a toll as you leave (S$1 or S$2.50, depending on which link with Malaysia you use). In addition, you must pay for a vehicle entry permit in the form of an Autopass Card (S$10 – additional sums can be added). Cards are available at border checkpoints.

There are many rental companies to choose from, but those below are recommended:

ATS Car Rental and Tours 111 Emerald Hill Rd, Singapore 229391; tel: 6738 0003; fax: 6734 4436

AVIS Rent-A-Car 317 Outram Rd, #01-01/04, Concorde Hotel Shopping Centre, Singapore 169075; tel: 6737 1668; fax: 6235 4958

City Limo Rent-A-Car 277 Orchard Rd, #01-41, Specialist Shopping Centre, Singapore 238858; tel: 6733 8282; fax: 6733 5513

Hertz Rent-A-Car 125 Tanglin Rd, Tudor Court Shopping Gallery, Singapore 247921; tel: 1800 734 4646 (free call within Singapore); fax: 6733 0466

Lion Tourist Services 581 Orchard Rd, B1-00 Hilton Singapore, Singapore 238883; tel: 6733 9897; fax: 6733 8812

Ways Plus Services 30 East Coast Rd, #03-09/10, Paramount Hotel and Shopping Centre, Singapore 428751; tel: 6338 8863; fax: 6338 4207

By Singapore trolley

If you are sightseeing, try taking the Singapore Trolley (a bright-red, tram-like bus). This travels between Orchard Road and SunTec City, taking in all the big shops, the old colonial area, Singapore River and Raffles. The fare is S$14.90 (S$9.90 child) for a day's worth of unlimited rides, and tickets can be purchased either from the driver or from your hotel. A riverboat tour is included in this price. For further information, contact Singapore Explorer (tel: 6339 6833).

By trishaw

If you don't mind making a bit of a spectacle of yourself, you can visit the sights of Singapore aboard a rickshaw, known here as a 'trishaw'. Agree a price with the driver, and let him carry you around under his own pedal power. Trishaws can take two passengers. At one time such vehicles must have been a cheap and common means of transport. These days they are strictly for the tourists, and you can expect to pay S$25–30 for a 45-minute ride. You are most likely to be able to pick one up by the Albert Centre, off New Bugis Street.

If you cannot face haggling, or want to join a convoy of trishaws around the tourist areas, book through one of the many tour operators. These include Aananda Travel (tel: 6732 1766), East West Executive Traveller (tel: 6438 6722), Gray Line Tours (tel: 6331 8203) and Holiday Tours (tel: 6738 2622).

LOCAL TOURS
Food

There are numerous food tours on offer during the Singapore Food Festival (see *Chapter 3, Holidays, Celebrations and Events*, page 93), usually held during the months of March and April. You can find food tours – frequently referred to as '**flavours of new Asia**' – that take in the cuisine to be found in the various ethnic quarters. They usually begin at 08.00 or 09.00, last a little over three hours, and cost about S$30 adult (S$15 child). Operators include Holiday Tours (tel: 6738 2622), RMG Tours, (tel: 6220 1661), and Singapore Sightseeing Tour East (tel: 6332 3755). Tours cost about S$30 (S$15). Alternatively, you can do a crash cookery course at **Raffles Culinary Academy** (tel: 6331 1742), and impress your friends by telling them you learned to cook at Raffles. One-day courses range between about S$70 and S$140, and include lunches featuring the foods introduced during the day.

Eco-tourism

The only formally registered full-time **nature tour guide** (and birding expert) is Mr Subaraj Rajathurai (tel/fax: 6787 7048; email: serin@swiftech.com.sg). He will be able to show you the 'green' side of Singapore.

Agri-tours are another interesting eco-tourism option. You can visit working farms showcasing high-tech and intensive modern city-farming, tailored to the urban tropics. These range from **aeroponics vegetable farming** (Aerogreen Technology, Plot Lim Chu Kang 114, Neo Tiew Crescent, Singapore 718925; tel: 6792 4298; fax: 6793 6820; web: www.aerogreen.com.sg) and **endangered bird-breeding** facilities (Avifauna Breeding and Research, 2 Lim Chu Kang Lane 3A, Singapore 719842; tel: 6793 7461; fax: 6793 7910), through **goat dairy farming** (Hay Dairies, 3 Lim Chu Kang Lane 4, Singapore 718859; tel: 6792 0931; fax: 6794 1580) to **orchid** and **fish farming** (Qian Hu Fish Farm, 73 Jalan Lekar, Singapore 698950; tel: 6766 7078; fax: 6766 3995; web: www.qianhu.com). For further details, contact the Singapore Tourism Board (Tourism Court, 1 Orchard Spring Lane, Singapore 247729; tel: 1800 736 2000; web: www.newasia.singapore.com).

Several tour operators offer **agri-tours**, which explain the island's attempts to reconcile its agricultural and housing policies with an increasing sensitivity to ecological concerns. Contact Ananda Travel (tel: 6732 1766), East West Executive Traveller (tel: 6438 6722), Tour East (tel: 6238 2886) or Singapore Sightseeing Tour East (tel: 6332 3755).

Sightseeing

SIA Hop On operates **bus tours** between Orchard Road and the Botanic Gardens. Buses run every 30 minutes, from 09.00 to 18.00. Tickets are available from hotels, SIA ticket offices, or the driver, and cost S$5 adult, S$3 child.

The **Spirit of New Asia**, run by Worldlink Travel (tel: 6299 6698), is the best general sightseeing tour of the country. It sets off every morning (except Mon) at 09.00, and lasts between three and four hours. Cost S$35 adult, S$17 child.

The **Heartlands of New Asia Tour** takes customers to areas beyond the usual tourist haunts. Tours are run every weekday (RMG Tours also offers one on Sat), depart at 08.00, 13.30 and 14.00, and cost about S$30 adult, S$18 child. Operators are Holiday Tours (tel: 6738 2622), RMG Tours (tel: 6220 1661) and SH Tours (tel: 6734 9923).

Several companies offer a **city tour**, which is a good way of quickly familiarising yourself with the surroundings. They leave daily at 08.30, 09.00, 9.30, 13.30, 14.00 and 14.30, and cost around S$25 adult, S$15 child. Try Gray Line Tours (tel: 6331 8202/8203).

Two Sunday sightseeing tours are operated by Singapore Sightseeing Tour East (tel: 6332 3755). **Sunday Delights** lasts five hours and includes lunch. It leaves at 08.30 and costs S$59 adult, S$30 child. The **Round Island Tour with Tiger Balm Gardens** starts at 09.30, takes seven hours, and also includes lunch. It costs S$69 adult, S$35 child.

At night

RMG Tours (tel: 6220 1661) and Singapore Sightseeing Tours (tel: 6332 3755) each offer a **night tour**, an exciting and romantic way to see the country. The tours include dinner, last over three hours (starting at 19.00), and cost S$43–53 adult, S$22–28 child. The **Night Adventure**, with SH Tours (tel: 6734 9923) costs S$43 adult, S$23 child.

Singapore Night Scenes tours start at 18.30 or 19.00 and include a Singapore Sling (see page 133). They cost S$45–54 adult, S$23–32 child, and are run by Gray Line Tours (tel: 6331 8202/8203), Holiday Tours (tel: 6738 2622) and Singapore Sightseeing Tour East (tel: 6332 3755). Holiday Tours also offer cheaper versions, without the Singapore Sling, costing S$29–43 adult, S$15–22 child.

Possibly the best of the night tours is the **Night Safari** (at Singapore Zoo). The nocturnal displays are very well presented in landscaped enclosures without bars. Tours depart at 18.30, 19.00 and 19.15, and last about four hours. The cost of S$38–40 adult, S$20–24 child, is excellent value. Contact Gray Line Tours (tel: 6331 8202/8203, Holiday Tours (tel: 6738 2622), RMG Tours (tel: 6220 1661), SH Tours (tel: 6734 9923) or Singapore Sightseeing Tours East (tel: 6332 3755).

History

The **Milestones Tour** lasts four hours and examines Singapore's past and future. It starts at 09.00 weekdays, and costs S$28 adult, S$15 child. Contact SH Tours (tel: 6734 9923). Similar in theme is the **Footsteps of Raffles Tour** operated by Singapore Sightseeing Tour East (tel: 6332 3755). Tours begin at 09.30 every weekday (except Mon), and cost S$39 adult, S$20 child. Holiday Tours (tel: 6738 2622) runs a slightly longer version called the **Founding Footsteps of Raffles Tour**, starting 14.00 Tue–Fri, and costing S$59 adult, S$30 child.

Other

The **Tiger Brewery Tour** (Public Relations Department, Asia Pacific Breweries, 459 Jalan Ahmad Ibrahim, Singapore 639934; tel: 6860 6312/6344; fax: 6860 6324) allows visitors to look around the region's most sophisticated brewery. You must book at least two weeks in advance of your visit, and tours require a minimum of ten people.

The **Housing Development Board** (Public Affairs Section, 3451 Jalan Bukit Merah, Singapore 159459; tel: 6273 9090; fax: 6279 6097) runs a tour which traces the history of Singapore's council housing.

An excellent **Zoo Management Tour** (Marketing Department, Singapore Zoological Gardens, 80 Mandai Lake Road, Singapore 729826; tel: 6269 1411; fax: 6367 2974) is run by one of the world's first-class zoos. There are opportunities to be photographed with the animals, handle unusual species, and even breakfast with an orang-utan.

The **Painted Faces Tour** explores **opera** and **exotic theatre**. Tours take place during the evenings, and chart the significance of the flamboyant costumes and grotesque make-up that characterise Chinese opera. Contact Singapore Sightseeing Tour East (tel: 6332 3755).

The **In Harmony with Feng Shui Tour** teaches about the ancient Chinese art of self-improvement and inner peace, much practised in Singapore. Tours open at 14.00 every weekday, and cost S$33 adult, S$17 child. For information, contact SH Tours (tel: 6734 9923).

The Singaporean passion for the turf (and for gambling in general) is reflected in the **horse-racing tours**. You will need to check availability in the newspapers or with the tourist office as these only operate on race days. Setting off at 11.00 and including lunch, these last six hours and cost S$80 (adults only). Contact Gray Line Tours (tel: 6331 8202/8203 or Singapore Sightseeing Tour East (tel: 6332 3755).

CRUISES
Local

Cruising is a popular business in Singapore – indeed, the country has a S$50-million Cruise Centre that serves 14 million passengers a year – and there is a variety to choose from. Some allow customers to enjoy the sight of Singapore's skyline, frequently including a disco. Others visit some of the islands off Singapore's coast. Cruises along the Singapore River in bumboats cost S$10 adult, S$5. They are run by Singapore River Boat (tel: 6338 9205) and Singapore River Cruises (tel: 6336 6111).

Two ships, the *Superstar Virgo* and the *Superstar Gemini*, offer three-, four-, and eight-day cruises to neighbouring countries, including Malaysia and Thailand:

Three-day Keeps to local waters. Departs Friday.

Three-day Singapore to Malacca, Port Klang, and back. Departs Wednesday.

Four-day Singapore to Phuket, Langkawi, and back. Departs Sunday.

Eight-day Singapore to Port Klang, Pangkor Island, Phuket, Langkawi, Penang, Malacca, and back. Departs Sunday.

Charter

You can charter boats from the following companies:

Fantasy Cruises Tel: 6283 2182; fax: 6382 5293; web: www.fantasycruises.com.sg
Kingfisher Cruises Tel: 6275 1771; fax: 6270 1771; web: www.kingfishercruises.com
Star Cruises Tel: 6223 0002; fax: 6220 6993; web: www.starcruises.com
Watertours Tel: 6533 9811; fax: 6535 7743

ACCOMMODATION

In Singapore, tourist accommodation means 'hotels'. You will very rarely come across hostels, bed and breakfasts or schemes offering you the opportunity to stay with locals. Furthermore, cheap accommodation – of the type sought by backpackers in Malaysia and Thailand – is non-existent. Singapore is not a place for those on very tight budgets.

Singapore's hotels are rarely less than satisfactory, invariably good, and sometimes excellent. They are comfortable and clean, and the service courteous and efficient. There are few of poor quality. Hotels belonging to the international chains are luxurious but also somewhat homogeneous. Indeed, in general the hotels do not have the character one finds in those of some other countries, although there are exceptions (Raffles being the most obvious). It is worth trying some of the smaller hotels around Chinatown and Little India for a little more colour (see pages 164–6 and 116–18). Singapore values modern efficiency – with a Western flavour – and that is largely what you must expect.

The hotels listed in this guide are divided by price, and the prices refer to room rates. Rooms in super-luxury hotels cost S$300 or more; those in luxury hotels are between S$200 and S$299; moderate hotels are in the range of S$80 to S$199; budget accommodation is under S$80. (Do, however, ask for special rates, promotions or discounts when booking – these are regularly available.) Most hotels have coffee lounges where you can meet friends and have a drink. Frequently these contain musicians in evening dress playing fairly schmaltzy – and invariably irritating – tunes in the background. All super-luxury, luxury and medium-priced hotels offer air-conditioned en-suite rooms with telephone, TV, mini-bar, fridge, safe, and room and laundry services. Most have several restaurants and bars, tour desks and internet facilities (at a price!), along with swimming pools, and fitness and business centres. The individual listings in *Part Two* indicate when these are or are not on offer. Hotels outside the more central districts provide free shuttle buses to the Orchard Road area. These run several times in the morning and afternoon, but usually not later than about 19.00. Shuttle buses, where provided, are indicated in the listed information.

There are a couple of things to bear in mind regarding hotels. First, most luxury hotels (and restaurants) operate a 'smart-casual' rule. And second, all hotel bills will be higher than those quoted in advertising literature (and in this guide) because they are subject to various taxes. The more expensive the hotel, the higher the tax you will pay. In the best hotels you will be required to pay about 14% over the quoted rates. These taxes consist of a 3% goods and service tax (GST) on rooms, a 10% service charge, and a 1% government tax (known as 'cess'). These are indicated by three plus signs (+ + +), each representing one of the taxes. The taxes also apply to food outlets.

If you are an independent traveller and wish to organise accommodation before your arrival, the Singapore Hotels Association (web: www.sha.org.sg) can offer advice and help. It also has desks at Changi Airport, in the west wing (open Sun–Fri 07.00–02.00, Sat 07.00–22.30) and east wing (10.00–23.00 daily) of Terminal 1, and in the south wing (Tue–Sun 07.00–06.00, Mon 07.00–23.30) and north wing (07.00–23.00 daily) of Terminal 2.

EATING AND DRINKING

Food is taken seriously in Singapore. Every year, between the months of March and April, there is a large food festival in which food outlets all over the country participate (see page 93). There are countless demonstrations and food tours for the gourmet visitor to choose from (for operators of food tours, see page 59). Perhaps, then, it is unsurprising to learn that there is a wealth of eating places in Singapore, offering an enormous range of cuisine. You will find the burger bars and pizza parlours familiar in the West (along with the Starbucks and Coffee Bean coffee shops), and you will be able to order steak and kidney pudding or braised oxtail if they take your fancy. But more logically, within a short distance of wherever you choose to stay, there will be restaurants serving all sorts of Asian food, including Chinese, Indian, Thai, Mongolian, Vietnamese, Korean, Indonesian, and Japanese, and frequently different regional variations. Alternatively, you can eat English, American, French, Italian, Brazilian, and Lebanese. The seafood is excellent here, from barbecued stingray to sea cucumber (and chilli crab is out of this world!). The East Coast Seafood Centre will offer these dishes and many more (see page 194). Vegetarians are well catered for, as are those who eat *halal* food (look out for restaurants displaying certificates from the MUIS, the Muslim Religious Council of Singapore). There are places (including most of the larger hotels,

A STEAMBOAT

Whatever you do, ensure you try a steamboat while you are in Singapore. This sits in the middle of the dining table, with a small flame at the bottom and a chimney at the top. It is surrounded by a moat of water, which the flame keeps at simmering point. The rest of the table is filled with small dishes of raw food – pieces of prawn, strips of beef, chunks of vegetables, and more – which are picked up with chopsticks and dunked into the hot water and eaten, freshly cooked, with rice. Gradually the water is transformed into a rich soup with a flavour all of its own, and is gorgeous when spooned over the rice. In larger restaurants the raw foods are laid out buffet-style, and customers may help themselves to as much or as little as they wish. It makes for a delicious and memorable dining experience.

HAWKER CENTRES AND FOOD CENTRES

Not so very long ago, food hawkers used to wander the streets with barrows, just as they do throughout the Far East; the Singaporean government, however, decided that the system could be better controlled by restricting hawkers to designated areas. These places are known as 'hawker centres'. Refreshing, outdoor alternatives to restaurants, they are frequented by the majority of Singaporeans. Some are tourist attractions, while others are only patronised by locals, but they are all worth visiting, and the food is considerably cheaper than that served in hotels and restaurants. You can eat well for between S$2.50 and S$5 per head. There are also indoor, air-conditioned and slightly more upmarket versions known as 'food centres'.

On entering a hawker centre, find an empty table and make a note of its number. Leave one of your party to keep the table, and you are then free to wander through the stalls, each of which has a different speciality. Choose dishes from as many stalls as you wish, telling them your table number. The freshly cooked food will then be brought to you. There are stalls selling fruit; a platter of seasonal fruits, served ice-cold, sweet and crunchy, is particularly good. Try rambutans, jackfruit, mangosteens, duku and sapodillas, fruits you are unlikely to have sampled at home. As well as food stalls, there are those selling drinks, the best buys being freshly squeezed juices – including sugarcane (which you can watch being pressed) and lychee (a glass full of tinned lychees – wonderfully silly!) – or coconut milk sucked through a straw directly from the fruit. A fruit juice will set you back as little as S$2.

catering for foreigners) where you can eat at any time of day or night. As if this richness of choice was not enough, Singapore has just discovered fusion food (sometimes called 'New Asia'), a blending of Eastern and Western ingredients and cooking techniques, and restaurants are exploring it with enthusiasm. You can even eat 'herbal' food. In addition, restaurants in the better hotels offer a variety of international dishes.

There is a considerable range of prices. You can eat very well at hawker or food centres (see box above) for about S$5 a head; buffet meals (eat as much as you like) in hotels cost between S$20 and S$40 each; expect to pay anything from S$30 a head for a meal in a restaurant; and, if you fancy spending some serious money, a meal for two (including wine) in the exclusive Lighthouse Restaurant at The Fullerton Hotel could set you back S$800.

If you are not in Singapore for long, you must try a hawker centre, and eat at either Boat Quay or Clarke Quay, CHIJMES and Raffles. If your stay is longer, it shouldn't prove difficult to find places that serve the food you fancy.

Most alcoholic drinks are imported into Singapore, and are consequently very expensive. The local beer is the very palatable Tiger. The supermarkets on the basement floors of several of the shopping malls on Orchard Road (eg: Cold Storage) or in Tanglin Place Shopping Mall sell beer and other beverages

If you fancy sampling some of the wares to be found at these establishments, the following are worth a visit. Be sure to try one of the local desserts, consisting of crushed ice with a variety of toppings such as melon, sea coconut, lychees, jackfruit, and coconut milk. They look strange but are very refreshing in the heat.

Hawker centres

Boon Tat Street beside Lau Par Sat. This is open during the evenings.
Newton Circus, at the intersection of Scotts Road and Bukit Timah Road. The biggest hawker centre, although it is repeatedly threatened with closure for redevelopment. Be wary of the prices, as they tend to spot the tourist coming. King prawns are expensive.
The **Satay Club** in the street at Clarke Quay is open in the evenings.

Food centres

Scotts Picnic Centre, basement in Scotts Road.
Lau Par Sat Festival market. Open during the day.
Several food centres in the basement of **Takashimaya**, **Orchard Road**. They are a little expensive because the rents for the sites are high.
Many of the **malls in Orchard Street** now have food centres – usually in the basements.
The renovated shopping area of Little India.
Basement of Tanglin Mall.
In the evenings, **Bugis** has several food centres and street stalls.

for considerably lower prices than the hotels and restaurants. Yet, even in supermarkets, you are unlikely to find a bottle of wine for under S$17 (£7/US$10). A better idea, therefore, is to stock up in the duty-free shop at Changi Airport (see page 44) on your arrival. Unlike in many tropical countries, tap water is safe to drink.

It is worth re-iterating that the addition of tax to the bill (signalled by three plus signs; see *Accommodation*, pages 62–3, for an explanation) will come on top of the price listed in the menu. Also worth mentioning again is the smart-casual dress code operated by some restaurants and hotels (see *What to take*, page 52). You may come across the term 'F&B' used in relation to restaurants; this simply stands for 'food and beverage'. And don't forget that Muslims use only their right hands when eating; in the areas of Arab Street and Little India in particular, it is polite to observe this practice when eating food with your fingers. Most restaurants provide customers with cutlery anyway, but those that do not will happily do so on request.

Tea houses

Singaporeans are very fond of tea, and there are several tea houses to be found, mostly in the Chinatown area. Here you can taste an enormous variety of teas,

HAWKER FOOD

As you walk past the food stalls of a hawker or food centre, you will see that most have pictures of the food on sale, along with its price. Nevertheless, if you want to try ordering your meal without the aid of a pointing stick, below are the names of some of the items you are likely to come across. Note that *mee* means 'noodle' and *nasi* means 'rice'.

Ayam goreng Malay fried chicken (*goreng* means 'fried')
Assam pedas ikan Malay hot and sour fish
Bak kut the pork rib soup with garlic and Chinese herbs
Bao (or *pau*) steamed buns filled with roast pork (*char*), chicken or sweet red bean paste
Bee hoon rice vermicelli noodles
Chai tow kueh (literally 'carrot cake' – *kueh* means 'cake') steamed and fried white radishes with egg and pickled turnip. If it is 'black', it means that dark sweet soy sauce is added.
Char siew fan barbecued pork with rice (*fan* is another word for 'rice')
Congee rice porridge with fish or pork or chicken
Dosai thin Indian crêpe stuffed with potatoes or other ingredients and served with various sauces
Gado gado vegetable salad covered in a peanut-and-coconut sauce, served with prawn crackers
Goreng pisang fried banana fritters
Hainanese chicken rice rice cooked in chicken stock, with boiled white boneless chicken, light soy sauce and sesame oil. Must be served accompanied by a chilli sauce with minced garlic, ginger and lime juice
Hokkien mee thick yellow noodles and vermicelli fried with pork and prawns in a thick rich gravy
Ikan bilis dried anchovies
Kway teow thick flat rice noodles with various ingredients and sauces
Char kway teow noodles, clams, prawns, Chinese sausage and egg in a sweet black sauce

learn how to serve tea correctly in tiny cups and teapots, and watch a demonstration of a 'tea ceremony'. Every Chinese wedding has a tea ceremony, when the bride and groom serve the drink to their parents. The Ixing Xuan Tea House (30 Tanjong Pagar Road; tel: 6224 6961) offers tea appreciation talks for S$15, and talks including a *dim sum* lunch for S$25 (the latter requires a minimum party of five). As well as learning about the background to tea, you are also given samples and taught how to appreciate its different flavours. You could also try the Tea Village (45A–51A Pagoda Street; tel: 6221 7825; contact Ms Lee), where you sit in small, relaxing alcoves upstairs, the Tea Chapter (9A Neil Road; tel: 6226 1917; contact Ms Isabelle Bay), or the Chinese Theatre Circle (5 Smith Street; tel: 6328 4862; contact

Laksa spicy noodle soup made from coconut milk and chilli with chicken and prawns

Lontong vegetable-and-rice cake covered in rich coconut gravy

Mee pok fish balls and noodles

Mee rebus Malay noodle dish in thick spicy sauce

Mee siam rice vermicelli, fried with chilli and prawns in a sweet-sour gravy

Nasi Biryani masala-flavoured basmati rice with chicken or mutton covered in *daal* (lentil) curry

Nasi padang Sumatran dish of rice with a variety of meat, fish or vegetables

Popiah large spring roll stuffed with bean sprouts, peanuts, dried shrimps, stewed turnips, lettuce and hard-boiled egg, served with chilli and sweet black sauce. It is assembled while you wait, and you are likely to be asked if you would prefer the hot or medium chilli sauce (or none at all)

Rendang Indonesian curry with beef or chicken

Rojak salad of bean sprouts, white turnip, pineapple and bean curd in a spicy peanut-and-shrimp paste

Roti prata Indian crêpe – the dough is kneaded, twirled in the air and flipped until flat, before being lightly fried. Served dipped in curry, filled with egg or sprinkled with sugar. If it is filled with chicken or mutton it is called *murtabak*

Sambal balacan prawn-chilli paste

Satay strips of chicken, beef, mutton or king prawn marinated and barbecued on skewers, served with chunks of cucumber and onions and a spicy peanut sauce

Shui jiao prawn dumplings

Soto ayam spicy chicken soup with vegetables and fried potato cakes

Tahu soy bean

Tahu goreng deep-fried bean curd covered with peanut sauce

Tau hui chui soy bean milk

Yong tau foo eggplant (aubergine) and bean curd stuffed with fish paste and minced meat in a thick sauce

Mr Leslie Wong), all of which run similar events. In addition, the latter holds Chinese opera appreciation classes and Cantonese karaoke (with lunch).

NIGHTLIFE

Singapore is not geared to a sophisticated clubbing scene as found in cities like London or New York, but there is no doubt that nightclubs and bars are growing in quality to cater to the tastes of the wealthy and relatively young. Chinatown and Orchard Road have many venues to offer, and Boat Quay is always very lively. Decent live music is restricted primarily to the clubs and discos rather than the bars, however, and even here the fare is usually cover versions of more famous acts.

I'LL TRY IT IF YOU WILL...

There are some truly weird and wonderful foods to be found in Singapore. How about trying an iced *kachang*? This is a pudding the like of which you will probably never have had before, a sort of cross between a knickerbocker glory and a firework display. It consists of a mound of ice containing an unholy mixture of red beans (*kachang* means 'bean'), sweetcorn, fruit, jelly, and frequently much else besides – there are as many recipes as there are restaurants. Over the top are poured several syrups of lurid colours and sweetened condensed milk. The heap is then garnished with anything of a gaudy colour. Sounds revolting? It actually tastes considerably better than you would imagine, and children adore it.

If this doesn't take your fancy, how about a *durian*? This football-sized fruit is olive-sage green in colour, and is brought in mainly from Thailand. The outside is covered in vicious spikes; the inside contains a creamy flesh surrounding huge seeds. No-one is indifferent to *durian*. To some, its pungent smell – not unlike rotting meat – is unbearable. Hotels will not allow them under their roofs; airlines prohibit passengers from carrying them on to their planes. Others, however, are addicted to the fruit, arguing that, though it smells like hell, it tastes like heaven. Western *durian* lovers are few and far between – it seems to be an Eastern taste – but judge for yourself. Purchase a *durian* and sit in splendid isolation at a hawker centre somewhere. If you are lucky, you might even find a *durian* milk shake on offer at MacDonalds.

Most clubs close at about midnight during the week, although some will open until 03.00 at weekends. Entrance usually costs about S$30, which may include a couple of free drinks. Because the price of alcohol is high in Singapore, a single drink can cost around S$10. Clubs are usually happy to accept credit cards. You will not be allowed in unless you are fairly respectably dressed – smart-casual being the rule of thumb, as with the better hotels and restaurants. Be aware that Singaporean fashions can differ from ours, and, consequently, what might be considered suitably trendy attire in the West can be frowned upon at a nightclub in Singapore. The majority of the larger hotels have their own discos. As you would expect, most bars have a more relaxed attitude to attire. They also have extended happy hours – sometimes covering four hours or more – which is a saving grace in a country where the price of alcohol can be prohibitive.

SHOPPING

While Singapore is far more than a brief stopping point for travellers to pick up designer clothes, there is no doubt that it is nevertheless a shopper's paradise. There is a range of fashion accessories on sale, sometimes for a fraction of the price that you would pay at home (although the price advantage is considerably less than it used to be, and you may have to look hard for real bargains). Beyond

Orchard Road, however, there are fascinating stores to explore that sell the curious, the tasteless and the downright pointless. Standing within yards of office blocks, you will come across traditional Chinese medicine shops stocking dried scorpions, snakes, and deer antlers. Pick up cruet sets shaped like rotund, pink children, or glorious chinoiserie splashed with gold, red and silver in the souvenir shops in Tiger Balm Gardens, to the west of town (see pages 176–7). Browse the tacky and politically incorrect keyrings and purses made from the skins of snakes and crocodiles at the reptile parks (see pages 176 and 196). On Sentosa Island (see pages 202–9), there are large, real beetles set in clear plastic, and models of the country's national symbol, the Merlion. At Parkway Parade (80 Marine Parade Road, Katong), one of the best out-of-town shopping precincts, you can purchase furry covers for refrigerator handles, or the exquisitely fashioned bamboo prawns and bunches of lucky bananas that Singaporean drivers hang from the rear-view mirrors of their cars. How about some longevity noodles, in a packet bearing the illustration of an impossibly ancient man? Or a set of ornate toothpicks? Or, of course, a brooch made from an orchid (the national flower) dipped in gold?

If you are looking for some slightly more mundane items – sticking plasters or photographic film – the suburban supermarkets should serve you well. There are, of course, the oddities – like *durian* sausages – but also the usual tins of food that you would expect to find in supermarkets in the West. Because Singapore is a tiny island, most goods have to be imported and you will find yourself familiar with many of the brands.

For the more general shopping experience, Singaporeans have taken shopping malls to their hearts. There are malls not only in the centre of town but in many of the suburban estates. The latter are very much parts of the surrounding communities, and contain not only car parks and hawker centres, but services like doctors' and dentists' surgeries, and special areas for holding songbird contests (see *Songbirds*, pages 30–3). British and American chains are well represented, and every mall has a variety of eating places attached to it.

But for serious shopping you have to hit the centre of town. Most of the big shops are open between 10.00 and 21.00. All tourists head at some time or other for Orchard Road (see pages 101–14), a wide, attractive thoroughfare where you can buy Armani suits, Gucci watches, Prada handbags, and top-quality jewellery. There are also bookshops, and even a Marks and Spencer. Antiques from Singapore, Indonesia, Malaysia and Thailand are available, both on Orchard Road and in the Tanglin Shopping Centre (on the adjoining Tanglin Road). One of my favourite shops is Tang's Department Store, underneath the Singapore Marriott Hotel on the corner of Orchard Road and Scotts Road. This is a treasure trove of Beijing *cloisonné* – sculpted into anything from tiny birds to colossal vases. There are lovely silk blouses and ties, too, and wonderfully intricate fans.

Excellent though the shops of Orchard Road and its adjacent streets are, it is worth also looking a little further afield. Arab Street (see pages 122–6) has a couple of shops selling extraordinary basketware, and stalls selling cheap Indian jewellery. Little India (see pages 114–22) is more extensive; shops here sell fabulous saris and glorious Benares silk, embroidered with real gold and silver thread. You can buy inexpensive costume jewellery, Indian silver and flamboyant, brassy-looking gold. The pieces are set with genuine gems, and the price of all this jewellery is based on weight. You will see shops selling the most beautiful garlands, made from scarlet hibiscus blooms, glowing orange French marigolds and ivory-white lotus buds. These are used to festoon friends, colleagues and relations. Sweet-shops carry extravagant selections of sugary Indian confectionery, which give you toothache just thinking about them (see box, page 119).

Since the government embarked on its clearance programme, the majority of shops in Chinatown (see pages 162–71) are fairly sanitised affairs in air-conditioned shopping malls – which is a shame. Nevertheless, there are still a few streets of old shop-houses selling paper goods to burn at funerals, plastic lanterns for festivals, and 100-year-old eggs. You can also buy a 'chop', which is a stone animal representing one of the months of the Chinese lunar year. This is sold along with a pot of ink, and the shop will carve your name into the base so that it can be used as a stamp. Indeed, Singaporeans frequently use such stamps instead of hand-written signatures. You might find a bargain at the Under S$2 shop at Coleman Street.

While you can haggle at some of the markets and little shops beyond the usual tourist haunts, the majority of the large shops have fixed prices, and bargaining here will be regarded with disapproval. Another difference from other countries in the Orient is that you will not face repeated harassment from street sellers attempting to flog fake goods. Although you may occasionally be approached by furtive-looking individuals asking, *sotto voce*, if you are interested in replica watches, on the whole the Singaporean ethos is dismissive of false badges of success and there is not a large market for such wares. Shopping is therefore an altogether less stressful ordeal.

Don't forget to get international warranties and receipts, especially when buying watches or anything electronic or electrical. If you are having purchases sent directly home, always ask for written confirmation of your order along with any relevant delivery details. When buying electronic goods, check that the voltage and cycle is compatible with the electrical system in your own country. If not, you may need an adaptor.

Tax-free shopping

Most purchases in Singapore attract a goods and service tax (GST) of 3%. If you spend more than S$300 you can claim a refund of this tax when you leave the country. Look for the 'Tax-Free Shopping' stickers in shop windows, and ask for a Global Refund Cheque when you make your purchase. To be eligible for one, you must spend at least S$100 in one shop; you can go to one or more other shops to make up your minimum spend of S$300. When you leave the country (within two months of the purchase date), get your cheques validated at the customs counters at the airport. They will require all receipts and cheques, as well as the purchases. Once they have confirmed your eligibility, you can make your claim at the Global Refund counter. A small handling fee will be deducted – this, coupled with the fact that the refund is only 3%, means that it is probably worthwhile only for those spending a lot of money or those really counting the dollars. Finally, ensure that your refund cheque is stamped by customs before you leave. If you have any queries about the scheme, contact Global Refund (Singapore), Robinson Road Post Office, PO Box 639, Singapore 901239; tel: 225 6238; fax: 225 5773.

The Gold Circle
In Orchard Road and Marina Bay, some shops, travel agencies, shopping malls (and more) display a gold and black symbol that represents the Gold Circle mark of excellence. These places are obliged to maintain a reputation for reliability and quality. You are unlikely to receive poor service anywhere, but if you want to be sure of receiving courteous and thorough assistance, the Gold Circle is worth looking out for.

Complaints against shops
There is a government scheme in place to prevent unscrupulous dealings by shops. Any shopper who encounters less than satisfactory service from retailers can talk to the Retail Promotion Centre (Block 528, Ang Mo Kio Avenue 10, #02-2378, Singapore 560528; tel: 450 2114; fax: 458 6393), which handles complaints from tourists. Alternatively, if you have a claim against someone of less than S$10,000, you can take it up with the Small Claims Tribunal (Apollo Centre 05-00, 2 Havelock Road, Singapore 059763; tel: 6435 5937/6553 5383; fax: 6435 5994; web: www.sg/judiciary/subct). This can be done by fax or over the internet, but there is a small fee payable, and you must make your complaint within seven days. Cases brought by tourists are normally heard within 24 hours of the claim being lodged, and judgements are given instantly. If the shop is found to be at fault, its details are made public and people are warned against shopping there. As you might imagine, this is a considerable deterrent and 'errant retailers', as they are called, are few and far between.

Where to shop
There is a bewildering array of shops in Singapore. Below is a brief and rough guide to where to find what:

Orchard Road
Centrepoint Fashion, toys, furniture, household goods, Marks and Spencer, boutiques, sports goods, books, electrical and electronic goods
Delfi Orchard Pewter, Waterford crystal, china, jewellery
Far East Plaza Street-wear, accessories, precious stones, carpets, handbags
Far East Shopping Centre Souvenirs, jewellery, sports goods, antiques, fashion, bags
Forum the Shopping Mall Toys, high-street fashion, furniture, optical goods, sports, leisurewear, souvenirs, antiques
International Building Fashion
Lucky Plaza Shoes, electronic goods, sports goods, watches, clothing
Meridien Shopping Centre Fashion, accessories, lighting

Midpoint Orchard Music, art, sports and leisure
Ngee Ann City Books, luggage, Cartier, Chanel, Tiffany's, Gianni Versace, Tag Heuer
OG Building Clothes, shoes, and much else
Orchard Emerald Watches, CDs, sports goods, leisure goods
Orchard Plaza Cameras, electronic goods, hand-made shoes, jewellery, souvenirs
Orchard Point Fabrics Silks (wonderful), soft furnishings, arts and crafts
Orchard Tower Jewellery, antiques, electronic goods, tailored clothes and leather goods
Pacific Plaza (Scotts Road) Boutiques, comics and more
Palais Renaisance Haute couture, jewellery to match
Park Mall Lifestyle, home furnishings
Scotts Shopping Centre Fashions, furnishings, lifestyle
Shaw Centre Sports goods, boutiques, fashion, jewellery, shoes
Shaw House Japanese goods
Tanglin Mall Comics, beadwork, lifestyle, boutiques, Peranakan goods
Tang's Cosmetics, household goods, everyday fashion, electronic goods, fabrics, and wonderful, inexpensive pieces of Beijing *cloisonné*. One of my favourites.
The Heeren Music (HMV), make-up, and a shop that sells everything for S$1.99
The Paragon Department store, designer boutiques
The Promenade International fashion, furnishings, hair-care products, electronics, food. Closed for renovation during 2002.
Tudor Court Arts and crafts
Wheelock Place Books, and more
Wisma Atria UK high-street fashions, cosmetics

City centre and marina
Arab Street Baskets, basketware
Capitol Building Fashion, sports
City Link Underground centre on walkway between SunTec City and Raffles City. 50 shops.
Funan Centre Computers, software, accessories, games and computer information
Kampong Glam area Batik, Malay clothing, textiles, jewellery, perfumes
Marina Square Clothes, shoes, souvenirs, children's things, sports goods, watches, leather goods. At end of City Link.
Millenia Walk Lingerie and much else
Parco Bugis Junction Boutiques, speciality shops, Japanese goods, clothing, books
Raffles City Shopping Centre Tablecloths, napkins, handkerchiefs, scarves, hi-fi equipment, watches, clothing, jewellery. This mall won the 1998 Award for the Best Shopping Experience.
Raffles Hotel Arcade Jewellery, watches, leather goods, silk, *cloisonné*, carpets, pewter, antiques, Raffles merchandise
SunTec City Mall Boutiques, lifestyle, entertainment. Over 200 shops.

Singapore River
Clarke Quay Fashion, leather, cameras, watches, gems, jewellery, books, toys, furnishings, electronic goods, antiques, gifts, clogs, calligraphy, batik, beadwork, pottery, woodcraft and much else

Liang Court Japanese shoes, fashion, accessories, books, magazines
Riverside Point Host of small shops selling little bits and pieces

Chinatown
Back-streets of Chinatown You will find much that never appears in shopping malls
Chinatown Point Antiques, antique opium pipes, opera face masks, wooden clogs, waxed paper umbrellas, porcelain, jade, arts and crafts, traditional Chinese medicine
People's Park Complex Multitude of Chinese goods, including carved chops

Little India
Little India Arcade Indian handicrafts, food, spices, bangles, jewellery, cutlery, brassware, saris, Indian music
Mustafa Centre Groceries, electronics, clothing

East
Century Square Books, department stores, electrical appliances. At Tampines MRT, EW2.
Eastpoint Fish, terrapins, hamsters, birds, cats, dogs, music, clothing, shoes. Next to Simei MRT, EW3.
Tampines Mall Children's clothing, ladies clothing, electrical goods, books, magazines, Japanese shops

West
Holland Village Handicrafts, carpets, florists, supermarkets, electrical goods, sports goods. Bus No 7 from Orchard Boulevard/Orchard Road.
Jurong Point Department store, furniture, home appliances. Next to Boon Lay MRT station, EW27.
Tiong Bahru Plaza (above Tiong Bahru station) Speciality shops, food

North
Junction B Department stores and supermarkets. Near Bishan MRT station, NS17.
Loy 1 Supermarket. Caters to nearby estates. Beside Choa Chu Kang MRT station, NS4.
Northpoint Toys, department store. Near Yishun MRT station, NS13.

ARTS AND ENTERTAINMENT
Theatre
Singaporeans are great lovers of live theatre and there are invariably a range of shows being held, from well-known Western works such as *Phantom Of The Opera* to productions by local companies. Singapore's government is keen to establish the country as the centre of culture in Southeast Asia. To this end, **The Esplanade – Theatres on the Bay**, an ambitious (and expensive) flagship project, is due for completion in October 2002. With an operating annual expenditure of S$45 million, it will have outdoor performing spaces, a 2,000-seat theatre, some smaller studios, a 1,600-seat concert hall, and the inevitable

shopping mall (with about 30 outlets, all of which will have some link with the arts scene). The **Victoria Hall** stages most theatrical and dance performances.

Although Western shows frequently embark on tours of the Far East, large commercial companies in Singapore buy enormous blocks of tickets as soon as they are available as incentives and for their favoured clients. Consequently it can be difficult to get hold of tickets. Singaporeans bemoan the fact that they would love to be able to go and see the touring shows but are simply unable to book seats. Ask your travel agent to book places in advance. Be aware that when tickets are available, they can be expensive. The dress code is smart-casual.

It is far easier to obtain seats at local shows. Check newspapers or tourist literature, ask the concierge of your hotel or contact the Singapore Tourism Board for details of what is on and where. You can buy tickets for any theatrical performance through SISTIC (tel: 6348 5555; fax: 6440 6784; web: www.sistic.com.sg) or Ticketcharge (tel: 6296 2929; fax: 6296 9897; web: www.ticketcharge.com). Both these companies also have several offices.

Performance venues

Performance venues in Singapore can be found at the following addresses:

Alliance Française de Singapour Auditorium 1 Sarkies Rd, Singapore 258130; tel: 6737 8422; fax: 6733 3023; web: www.alliancefrancaise.org.sg

Caldwell Arts Pte Ltd CHIJMES, 30 Victoria St, Singapore 187996; tel: 6337 7810; fax: 6334 3801; web: www.caldwellarts.com.sg

Drama Centre 40 Canning Rise, Singapore 179870; tel: 6336 0005; fax: 6338 2430; web: www.nac.gov.sg

DBS Auditorium The Development Bank of Singapore, c/o Resma Property Services, 6 Shenton Way, DBS Building Tower 1, Singapore 068809; tel: 6228 1691; fax: 6224 1920

The Esplanade –Theatres on the Bay 60 Raffles Ave, Singapore 039800; tel: 6337 3711; fax: 6337 3633; web: www.esplanade.com.sg

Fort Canning Park and Centre Cox Terrace, Fort Canning Pk, Singapore 179618; tel: 6332 1200; fax: 6339 9715

Harbour Pavilion 1 Maritime Sq, Ground Floor, World Trade Centre, Singapore 099253; tel: 6321 2516; fax: 6274 0721

Jubilee Hall Raffles Hotel, 1 Beach Rd, Singapore 189673; tel: 6337 1886; fax: 6337 0778

Kreta Ayer People's Theatre 30-A Kreta Ayer Rd, Singapore 088997; tel: 6222 3971

Kallang Theatre Stadium Walk, Singapore 397688; tel: 6345 8488; fax: 6344 2340; web: www.nac.gov.sg

Singapore Indoor Stadium (opposite the National Stadium) 2 Stadium Walk, Singapore 397691; tel: 6344 2660; fax: 6344 5903

Singapore International Convention and Exhibition Centre 1 Raffles Blvd, SunTec City, Singapore 039593; tel: 6337 2888; fax: 6825 2222; web: www.sicec.com

SP Auditorium Singapore Power, 111 Somerset Rd, Singapore 238164; tel: 6823 8848; fax: 6823 8822

Stamford Arts Centre 155 Waterloo St, #03-06, Singapore 187692; tel: 6336 1929; fax: 6337 1706

The Substation 45 Armenian St, Singapore 179936; tel: 6337 7535; fax: 6337 2729; web: www.substation.org

SunTec City 3 Temasek Blvd, Singapore 038983; tel: 6295 2888; fax: 6294 0880/ 6334 5495; web: www.sunteccity.com.sg

University Cultural Centre National University of Singapore, 10 Kent Ridge Crescent, Singapore 119260; tel: 6874 3940; fax: 6778 1956

Victoria Concert Hall 11 Empress Place, Victoria Memorial Hall, Singapore 179558; tel: 6338 1230; fax: 6336 6382; web: www.sso.org.sg

Victoria Theatre 9 Empress Place, Singapore 179556; tel: 6338 8283; fax: 6274 0721; web: www.nac.gov.sg

WTC Auditorium 11th Floor, World Trade Centre, 1 Maritime Sq, Singapore 099253; tel: 6321 2536; fax: 6274 0721

Music

Many of the hotels host live music, primarily involving house bands playing covers of older tracks. They will also usually have house discos (see *Nightlife*, pages 67–8). Some of the clubs and bars based around Orchard Road, the colonial area, Singapore River and Holland Village have live groups. Classical music is on offer at the Victoria Hall, often featuring the Singapore Symphony Orchestra. Performance dates and times can be found in the *Straits Times*. The Nanyang Academy of Fine Arts (tel: 6337 6636) organises Chinese classical music events.

Cinema

There are over 50 cinemas in Singapore, showing the latest Western and Asian films. Major Hollywood films are usually available shortly after their release in the US. Tickets cost about S$7, and there are performances during the day and late showings at the weekends. The *Straits Times* contains listings.

Museums and galleries

The Art Galleries Association of Singapore (tel: 6338 8337; fax: 6735 6495; web: www.agas.org.sg) publishes a free map and guide to the island's galleries. Details of the galleries themselves are given in entries under individual areas in *Part Two*.

MEDIA
with Peter Dorling
It would be a mistake simply to compare the Singapore media with its Western counterparts. They do things differently in Asia, and Singapore is different again. From a casual reading of the newspapers or watching a bit of television in the hotel bedroom, one gets an impression of a lively, young, vibrant (and, where television's concerned, American-orientated), hard-working and happy society. But control – albeit subtle – there is, though probably not to a degree any first-time visitor would notice. The whole media environment is actually tightly regulated, and censorship is common.

FAMILY VALUES
Hannah Postgate

Going to the cinema is certainly an experience anywhere in Asia. Sharing front-row seats with a large, beady-eyed rat may not be what you'd find at home, but cinema is often at the centre of Asian cultures, and Singapore is no different.

Moving pictures brought entertainment and news to hundreds of thousands of Singaporeans in the 1920s. The Shaw family were responsible for introducing the first silent movies to Singapore. Because they were 'silent', the films enjoyed instant success in a polyglot society such as Singapore. Many of the films were re-makes of popular Chinese stage plays from Shanghai. In the early 1930s, the Shaws began to produce homegrown local films to satisfy not only the entertainment-starved thirst of Singaporeans, but also the Malay and Indonesian markets further afield.

The family developed their interests to include amusement parks and fairgrounds, all of which had huge cinemas, dance halls and cabaret clubs. Big bands like the American Dance Band and D'Souza's entertained the crowds with the latest Western tunes. They were even able to attract the likes of Charlie Chaplin.

By 1939 the Shaw family owned and operated a chain of 139 cinemas across Singapore, Malaya, Thailand, Indonesia and Indo-China. The Alhambra became the first Singapore cinema to have air conditioning and played films like Errol Flynn's *Robin Hood* to packed audiences.

When World War II hit Southeast Asia, business stopped abruptly. During the Japanese occupation of Singapore from 1942–5, the Shaw family were forced to operate under the strict Japanese occupation monopoly, showing only propaganda films. After the war, business soon began to boom again. The Shaw empire has gone from strength to strength ever since. Now an international force behind Asia-Pacific film production and distribution, the family has been instrumental in carving out recognition for one of the largest film and television sectors worldwide.

Still one of the most influential Singaporean families, the Shaw Organisation has 40 cinemas around the city. Many of these are Cineplex centres, with shopping, restaurants, and even bowling alleys to keep the punters entertained. Well worth a visit is the Lido Cineplex in Shaw House on Orchard Road.

A company called Singapore Press Holdings, which has close links with the ruling People's Action Party, manages almost all 12 **newspapers** in all four official languages and is the only newspaper chain in Singapore. The upbeat, positive feel to almost everything the papers publish is deliberate and part of the overall plan. Anything the least bit politically controversial has to be searched for with the proverbial fine-tooth comb. The principal English-language newspapers are the *Straits Times* (and the *Sunday Times*), the *Business Times*, *Today* and the *New Paper* (tabloid). The *Straits Times* (web: http://straitstimes.asia1.com.sg) is the leading one of these, and has a long and interesting history. It is widely read and attractively produced. Its coverage of world news, and particularly of neighbouring countries in Asia, is comprehensive, trustworthy, and often imaginative. But when it comes to Singaporean affairs, things are different. Look a little closer: its front page will often carry a rallying speech by a senior government figure – but it is printed verbatim. The report will rarely include any elaboration, explanation or comment by the paper itself about the significance – or otherwise – of the event, or the relevance or context of the minister's words. Occasional outspoken comments – printed, say, in letters to the paper – are usually followed the next day by dusty answers from the ministries concerned. Rarely will serious criticism of the government be initiated by one of the paper's own correspondents.

The situation is similar with **television**. There are several English-language channels on the hotel TV set. Principal among them are MediaCorp TV's Channel 5 (popular entertainment; web: www.mediacorptv.com), Channel NewsAsia (news and current affairs; web: http://channelnewsasia.com), and Channel i (one of Singapore Press Holdings' TV channels; web: www.sphmediaworks.com). It may also be possible to see BBC World TV, CNN, and other channels familiar to cable/satellite viewers in the West. Many – like the very popular Channel 5 – come from the main local broadcaster, MediaCorp TV. They carry programmes varying from US-type light entertainment shows to more serious news and documentaries. There are also English-language programmes beamed into the country from neighbouring Malaysia. The Singapore-based all-news station, MediaCorp's Channel NewsAsia, broadcasts throughout Southeast Asia, and further afield to countries as scattered as India, the Philippines, China and Japan. The channel has its own correspondents in many countries in the region, reporting on a wide range of news and current affairs from the countries they cover. But Channel NewsAsia claims a different agenda from other broadcasters like CNN or the BBC, and their presentation of events; Channel NewsAsia's remit is for 'an Asian perspective' to its reporting, although this is sometimes hard to detect.

Again, however, it's the local broadcasting, from stations like MediaCorp's Channel 5, where the difference lies. Although such locally produced programming is undeniably popular, there is a subtext to much of it. For example, there's plenty of cajoling of Singaporeans to be better citizens. There are frequent 'do-gooding' TV campaigns of one sort or another, from promoting racial harmony to how to speak better English, or explanations of why positive family values are so important. But there's no challenging questioning of people in the news by intrepid interviewers, or lively no-holds-barred discussions with senior MPs. Where news and current affairs are concerned, this deference inevitably produces a lot of bland television, and a

MAKING THE BEST OF YOUR TRAVEL PHOTOGRAPHS
Nick Garbutt and John R Jones

Subject, composition and lighting

As a general rule, if it doesn't look good through the viewfinder, it will never look good as a picture. Don't take photographs for the sake of taking them; film is far too expensive.

People

There's nothing like a wonderful face to stimulate interest. Travelling to distant corners of the world provides the opportunity for exotic photographs of colourful minorities, intriguing lifestyles and special evocative shots which capture the very essence of a culture. A superb photograph should have an instant gut impact and be capable of saying more than a thousand words.

Photographing people is never easy and it requires a fair share of luck. Zooming in on that special moment requires sharp instinct, conditioned photographic eyes and the ability to handle light both aesthetically and technically.

- If you want to take a portrait shot, it is always best to ask first. Make a bold but friendly approach; never be tentative.
- Focus on the eyes of your subject since they are the most powerful ingredient of any portrait.
- The best portraits are obtained in the early morning and late evening light. In harsh light, photograph without flash in the shadows.
- Respect people's wishes and customs. Remember that, in some countries, candid snooping can lead to serious trouble.
- Never photograph military subjects unless you have definite permission.

Landscapes

Landscapes are forever changing, even on a daily basis. Good landscape photography is all about good light and capturing mood. Generally the first and last two hours of daylight are best, or when peculiar climatic conditions add drama or emphasise distinctive features. Never place the horizon in the centre – in your mind's eye divide the frame into thirds and either exaggerate the land or the sky.

Cameras

- Keep things simple: cameras which are light, reliable and simple will reduce hassle. High humidity in many tropical places, in particular rainforests, can play havoc with electronics.
- For keen photographers, a single-lens reflex (SLR) camera should be at the heart of your outfit. Remember you are buying into a whole photographic system, so look for a model with the option of a range of different lenses and other accessories.
- Totally mechanical cameras which do not rely on batteries will work even under the most extreme conditions. Combine one with an exposure meter which doesn't require batteries and you have the perfect match. One of the best and most indestructible cameras available is the FM2 Nikon.
- Compact cameras are generally excellent, but because of restricted focal ranges they have severe limitations for wildlife.
- Automatic cameras are often noisy when winding on, and loading or unloading film.
- Flashy camera bags or colourful clothing can draw unwelcome attention to your kit.

Lenses

The lens is the most important part of the camera, with the greatest influence on the final result. Always choose the best you can afford – the type of lens will be dictated by the subject and the type of photograph you wish to take.

For people
- The lens should ideally should have a focal length of 90 or 105mm.
- If you are not intimidated by getting in close, buy one with a macro facility which will allow close focusing.
- If you want to take candid photographs, a 70–210 zoom lens is ideal.
- A fast lens (one with a maximum aperture of around f2.8) will allow you to use faster shutter speeds which will mean sharper photographs. Distracting backgrounds will be thrown out of focus so improving the images' aesthetic appeal.

For landscape
- In tight situations, for example inside forests, wide-angle lenses (ie: 35mm or less) are ideal for taking habitat shots. These lenses are also an excellent alternative for close ups, as they offer the facility of being able to show the subject within the context of its environment.
- For other landscapes and scenic photographs, try using medium telephoto lenses (100mm–300mm) to pick out the interesting aspects of the vista and compress the perspective.

Film
Two types of film are available: prints (negatives) and transparencies (colour reversal). Prints are instantly accessible, ideal for showing to family and friends and putting into albums. However, if you want to share your experiences with a wider audience, through lectures or in publication, then the extra quality offered by transparency film is necessary.

Film speed (ISO number) indicates the sensitivity of the film to light. The lower the number, the less sensitive the film, but the better quality the final image. For general print film, ISO 100 or 200 fit the bill perfectly. If you are using transparencies just for lectures then again ISO 100 or 200 film is fine. However, if you want to get your work published, the superior quality of ISO 25 to 100 film is best.
- Try to keep your film cool. Never leave it in direct sunlight.
- Do not allow fast film (ISO 800 and above) to pass through X-ray machines.
- Under weak light conditions use a faster film (ISO 200 or 400).

For people
- For very accurate results there is nothing better than Kodachrome 64 because of its warmth, mellowness and superb gentle gradation of contrast.
- Reliable skin tones can also be recorded with Fuji Astia 100.
- If you want to jazz up your portraits, use Fuji Velvia (50 ISO) or Provia (100 ISO), but remember that you will have to pay extra for the processing.
- If cost is your priority, stick to process-paid Fuji films such as Sensia 11.
- Black-and-white people shots can be extremely evocative, so include in your kit bag a few rolls of Kodax T Max or Fuji Neopan.

For landscapes and wildlife
- For natural subjects, where greens are a feature, Fujicolour Reala (prints) and Fujichrome Velvia and Provia (transparencies) cannot be bettered.

Nick Garbutt is a professional photographer, writer, artist and expedition leader, specialising in natural history. He is co-author and contributory photographer to 'Madagascar Wildlife', published by Bradt Travel Guides. In 1996, he was a winner in the BBC Wildlife Photographer of the Year Competition.

John R Jones is a professional travel photographer specialising in minority people. He is the author of the Bradt guide to Vietnam, and several photographic books.

feeling that nothing of substance has been said. Part of the local news programming, for example, is often little more than an uncritical shop window for the latest government initiatives. If challenged over their upbeat, positive approach, however, Singapore's TV bosses, nursing their hurt pride, would argue that they are attempting to find a consensus of views. They would contrast this approach with the Western media's obsession with controversy and conflict.

The official reason for this heavy-handedness – some would say 'the official excuse' – is that Singapore is a young country and is still in its nation-building stage. Many remember its traumatic birth, when there was serious rioting in the streets and people were killed. The authorities still call for vigilance in the media, and indeed few need reminding, since the terrorist attacks on the United States in 2001, that they live in a dangerous corner of the world. The prime minister himself has spoken of 'the real threat' from extremists among Singapore's mainly Muslim neighbours. It is therefore seen as only reasonable and prudent that the press and television should support – and certainly not undermine – what the government is trying to do. Any reporting that would seem to sow doubts about what it's up to would be almost treasonable.

Workings within the media itself provide a classic reflection of Singapore's constant eagerness to ratchet up competition wherever it can (even where one would have thought it almost unsustainable in such a small country). So now the newspaper chain Singapore Press Holdings runs its own television channels and MediaCorp TV produces a daily newspaper (*Today*).

Of course the great internet revolution represents the other side of the coin when it comes to controlling news. In fact it has transformed Singapore's media. Its citizens can now read all sorts of outspoken views about their country that would have been unheard of – literally – a few years ago. For example, in the mid-1990s the conviction for murder and subsequent hanging of a Filipino maid while working in Singapore caused outrage in the Philippines and rioting on the streets of its capital, Manila. But very few of the dramatic TV pictures shown around the world were seen in Singapore. Such a clampdown would be impossible today (although private satellite dishes still aren't allowed). Having embraced the internet from the start, and more wholeheartedly than many countries in the West, Singapore is probably the most technologically advanced city on earth. As well as the workplace, almost every home in the land – be it a private apartment or a couple of rooms in a huge HDB block – is wired up with broadband internet access. And where e-commerce is concerned, the government keenly promotes the country as the 'information hub' of Southeast Asia. But there's a tiny catch: the internet service providers are controlled by the ever-watchful Singapore Broadcasting Authority. Although it regulates the internet with what it calls 'a light touch', in a crisis it could, in theory, still pull the plug on the whole network.

While critics argue that such control of the media is unnecessary, and unworthy of a mature society, the ruling People's Action Party says it's still important to sacrifice some personal freedom for the greater good – and, in truth, few see it as much of a sacrifice.

There are many English-language FM radio stations, including the BBC World Service (on 88.9 FM).

COMMUNICATIONS
Post
There are over 1,300 post offices in Singapore, open from 08.30 to 17.00 on weekdays, and 08.30 until 13.00 on Saturday. Post offices are efficient and offer all the services they do back home. Most hotels will look after normal tourist post for you. There is a post office at the airport, open every day between 08.00 and 20.00, and a host of couriers all over the town. Local postal rates start at 22 cents. Letters and postcards sent abroad cost S$1 and 50 cents respectively, and should take between five and seven days to reach the UK, although they can take longer. **Poste Restante** services are available at Singapore Post (Robinson Road Branch, 71 Robinson Road #01-00, Singapore 068895; tel: 6222 8899; fax: 6225 7785; web: www.singpost.com.sg), which is open 08.30–18.00 weekdays, and 08.30–14.00 Sat. It is closed Sun and public holidays.

Telephone
Telephones are modern and efficient. Public payphones are numerous and simple to use. There is a minimum charge of ten cents for three minutes. Buy pre-paid phone cards for S$3, 5, 10, 20 or 50 from post offices, supermarkets and newsagents. If you are phoning abroad, dial 001 and then your country code and phone number. Local and international calls from hotels are free of any surcharge. Singapore has three mobile phone networks (CDMA, GSM900 and GSM1800) and three mobile phone providers (Singtel, M1 and Starhub).

The international dialling code is + 65. In emergencies, call the police on 999 or the ambulance service on 995.

Internet access
While there are internet terminals in shopping malls and hotels, it is worth scouting around for internet cafés, which are very much cheaper. Note also that these are cheaper still (as well as less crowded) during the day, when local children are at school. Because Singapore is so technologically advanced, you should have no difficulty finding such cafés. A few are listed below:

CyberArena 11 Stamford Rd, #01-09 Capitol Building, Singapore 178884; tel: 6334 1260. Open 09.00–23.45.

Cyber@net Fans 133 New Bridge Rd, #02-16 Chinatown Point, Singapore 059413; tel: 6535 9829; fax: 6535 9772

Cybertrak Internet Café Pte Ltd Airport Blvd 036-20-01, Changi Airport, Passenger Terminal 1, Singapore 819642; tel: 6546 9084; fax: 6256 6420

e-station 3 Temasek Blvd, #03-029 SunTec City Mall, Singapore 038983; tel: 6733 2722; fax: 6735 2722

Netshock 8 Grange Rd, #05-02 Cineleisure Orchard, Singapore 239695; tel: 6738 6861; fax: 6738 8897

@Netwave Cybercafé 501 Orchard Rd, #02-08 Wheelock Place, Singapore 238880; tel: 6887 1078; fax: 6887 0278

PI@Ngee Ann City #04-2OU Ngee Ann City, Singapore 238874; tel: 6733 8528; fax: 6733 8485

Pi@Suntec 3 Temasek Blvd, #02-066 SunTec City Mall, Singapore 038983; tel: 6337 1155; fax: 6334 1221

Surf@Café 227 Orchard Rd, #01-23 Hotel Phoenix, Singapore 238858; tel: 6737 4901

ELECTRICITY

Singapore's supply is 220–240 volts, AC 50 hertz. Sockets take three-pin plugs, so tourists from Britain will not require adaptors.

CULTURAL DOS AND DON'TS

Singapore is a clean and ordered country, which makes it an ideal holiday destination. Travellers – including female visitors – have little reason to feel unsafe. In part, though, the reason for the country's low level of crime is its intolerance and harsh punishment of anti-social behaviour. In many ways, this is to be applauded, yet it can also leave an unsavoury taste in the mouths of citizens from more liberal regimes. The island's legal and punitive system may appear draconian to those from the West. People are flogged (and often scarred) for relatively minor offences, and the courts still mete out capital punishment – indeed, Singapore has the highest number of executions per capita in the world. At a lower level, and in a way that is far more likely to impact upon the foreign visitor, the government monitors every aspect of a citizen's life. It governs according to the Confucian philosophy that a respectful child makes an obedient citizen; it is easy, however, to wrongly interpret fear as respect. Certainly there is a 'Big Brother' feel to the place, and there are several restrictions of which you should be aware.

Drugs Penalties for the possession or trafficking of illegal drugs are particularly harsh. There are warnings printed in red on the entry permit cards issued to tourists on arrival. Those caught carrying even small quantities can be imprisoned for up to ten years, and those convicted of trafficking (defined as carrying as little as 15g of heroin or 200g of cannabis resin) can face the death penalty.

Pornography Even the mildest of erotica is banned.

Smoking This is strongly discouraged. It is forbidden to smoke in public-service vehicles (including buses, trains and taxis), museums, libraries, lifts, theatres, cinemas, air-conditioned restaurants, hair salons, shopping malls, supermarkets, department stores and government offices, though you can smoke in some air-conditioned pubs, discos, karaoke bars and nightspots. You can be fined up to S$1,000 for smoking in a prohibited area.

Litter Drop any rubbish and you can be fined S$1,000 for a first offence; do it again, and the fine is double, and you can be forced to do a stint of corrective cleaning-up of public places.

Chewing gum There is a widespread misconception that you cannot chew gum in Singapore; in fact, carrying and chewing it is acceptable. Selling it, however, carries a S$2,000 penalty. In 1992, the government implemented a ban on the importation, sale and manufacture of chewing gum after it was claimed discarded gum was affecting the running of MRT trains. It was also proving unsightly and expensive to remove from streets.

Crossing the road There are numerous pedestrian crossings controlled by lights, and public footbridges across roads. Always use these as jaywalking is frowned upon, and can incur a fine.

Spitting This is considered to be hugely offensive, and should be avoided.

ACTIVITIES
Sport
Singaporeans are fiercely competitive, so it is not surprising to find that most sports are catered for on the island. International events are hosted here in sports ranging from rugby and cricket to badminton and pool (see box, pages 84–5). Football is very popular, and local matches attract enthusiastic crowds. The *Straits Times* carries details. Many Singaporeans are avid followers of the English Premier League, and taxi drivers often enjoy discussing their favourite teams. In a more recreational sense, there are numerous cycling paths, and places to hire bikes at Sentosa, Pasir Ris, East Coast Park, Pulau Ubin and Bishan. Below is a selection of some of the main sports on offer. If you would like further details of these or any other sports activities, contact the Singapore Sports Council (National Stadium, Kallang, Singapore 397188; tel: 6345 7111; fax: 6340 9573).

Horse racing
The island's racecourse is at Kranji (opened in 1999), in the north of the island, and just a short walk from Kranji MRT station (on the NS line). Indeed, the magnificent stadium, which can accommodate 30,000 racegoers, is visible from the train. Here the Singapore Airlines International Cup is held in May, one of the richest races in the world. The Queen Elizabeth Cup is run in August and the Singapore Gold Cup in October. Admission costs S$3 for areas without air conditioning, S$7 for an air-conditioned area open to the general public, and S$20 for a place in the air-conditioned Hibiscus Room (where you will have to show your passport). There is a strict dress code (smart-casual) for entrance to the latter, while even in the public stands shorts, vests, T-shirts and casual footwear like flip-flops are expressly forbidden. Meetings are held under floodlights on Friday evenings (first race at 19.00), and in the afternoons on Saturdays and Sundays (starting at 14.30). Contact the Singapore Turf Club (1 Turf Club Avenue, Singapore Racecourse, Singapore 738078; tel: 6879 1000; fax: 6879 1010) for information concerning forthcoming races.

Golf
Singapore contains some world-class golf courses, which are generally open between 07.00 and 19.00 (although you can play on some until 23.00). As a

SINGAPORE'S SPORTING EVENTS

Singapore holds its fair share of annual international sporting events. The following are the main ones. Dates vary from year to year, but information can be obtained from your hotel concierge or the Singapore Tourism Board.

Asian Nine Ball Pool Championships Fifteen Asian countries take part in this annual tournament, although it is not always held in Singapore.
Mobil Marathon The gruelling 26-mile route starts at Stadium Boulevard, winds its way to Changi Road, returns via Orchard Road, and finishes back at the stadium.
MI/Motorola Champions (tennis) This is a major tournament and attracts many big names of the international game.
Singapore Airlines International Cup (horse racing) One of the richest races in the horse-racing world, with prize money of S$3 million. Held at the Singapore Turf Club at Kranji, usually in May.
Singapore Challenge (cricket) A five-day international organised by the Singapore Cricket Association. Each year three countries are invited to participate.
Singapore Cricket Club Hockey 6s International Tournament This attracts players from a host of Asian countries, and is played in a light-hearted spirit of fun.
Singapore Cricket Club Rugby 7s International Tournament Teams drawn from many rugby-playing nations around the globe.

visitor, you will usually be able to purchase a special day ticket for between S$50 and S$200. It is very expensive to join one of the clubs as a permanent member. A bucket of 50 balls at a driving range will cost about S$2. Be aware that it can be difficult to get a game at the weekend, and many clubs require visitors to hold a proficiency certificate or a proof of handicap from a recognised golf club. Contact one of the following:

Changi Golf Club 20 Netheravon Rd, Singapore 508505; tel: 6545 5133; fax: 6545 2531. 9-hole course.
Jurong Country Club 9 Science Centre Rd; Singapore 609078; tel: 6560 5655/7370; fax: 6567 1900
Keppel Club Bukit Chermin Rd, Singapore 109918; tel: 6273 5522; fax: 6278 1448
Orchid Country Club 1 Orchid Club Rd, Singapore 769162; tel: 6750 6726; fax: 6755 7972
Parkland 920 East Coast Parkway, Singapore 449875; tel: 6440 6726; fax: 6345 2138. Driving range only.
Raffles Country Club 450 Jalam Ahmad Ibrahim, Singapore 639932; tel: 6861 7655; fax: 6861 5563
Sembawang Country Club 249 Sembawang Rd, Singapore 758352; tel: 6257 0642; fax: 6755 8418
Sentosa Golf Club 27 Bukit Manis Rd, Singapore 099892; tel: 6275 0022; fax: 6275 0005

Singapore Cricket Club Soccer 7s International Tournament Another popular international tournament.
Singapore International Badminton Open Over 20 top international players compete at the Singapore Badminton Hall and the Singapore Indoor Stadium for prize money worth US$170,000. Usually held in August. For information, tel: 6344 1773.
Singapore International Marathon Both experienced runners and amateurs take part in this event, which takes place in crippling temperatures. It follows the same route as the Mobil Marathon. Take your place at a point along the route, or catch a special bus to the National Stadium to watch the runners finish. Usually held in December.
Singapore Masters (golf) With prize money of US$850,000, this is one of Asia's biggest golf tournaments. For information, call 6226 4646 or visit www.asianpgatour.com. Usually held in February.
Singapore Masters Cup (bowling) Featuring male and female bowlers from throughout Southeast Asia.
Singapore River Regatta Over 100 local teams race in dragon boats and canoes along the Singapore River. Usually held in November. Call 6440 9763 for further details.
Tiger 5s Futsal Players from many countries compete in this event, which is usually held in late November and early December at the Singapore Indoor Stadium. Futsal is a version of five-a-side football. For information, call 6488 6500.

Singapore Gary Player Academy C/o Jurong Country Club, 9 Science Centre Rd, Singapore 609078; tel: 6568 5118; fax: 6563 2455
Singapore Island Country Club 240 Sime Rd, Singapore 288303; tel: 6466 2244; fax: 6466 9707; or, 180 Island Club Rd, Singapore 578774; tel: 6459 2222
Singapore Turf Club – Green Fairways 60 Fairway Dr, Singapore 286966; tel: 6468 7233/7043; fax: 6468 7047
Superbowl Golf and Country Club 6 Marina Green, Singapore 019799; tel: 6221 2811; fax: 6221 7171. Driving range only.
Warren Golf Club 23 Folkestone Rd, Singapore 139599; tel: 6777 6533; fax: 6778 5502. 9-hole course.

Tennis
There are tennis courts at the Yio Chu Kang Squash and Tennis Centre (200 Ang Mo Kio, Avenue 9, Singapore 569770; tel: 6482 4980; fax: 6483 2653), the West Coast Recreation Centre (12 West Coast Walk, Singapore 127157; tel: 6778 8966; fax: 6774 1048), the Farrer Park Tennis Courts (Rutland Road; tel: 6299 4166) and the Singapore Tennis Centre (1020 East Coast Parkway; tel: 6442 5966).

Watersports
Scuba diving is becoming ever popular and the local diving schools run courses accepted by NAUI, SSI and PADI which cost from S$400. The more

experienced can go day and night diving around Singapore and Malaysia. Contact one of the following:

Club Adventures and Incentive Planners 10 Anson Rd, #02-02 International Plaza, Singapore 079903; tel: 6447 8797; fax: 6241 5186; email: info@touradventure.net; web: www.touradventure.net
SDA Dive Travel 61-B Pagoda St, Singapore 059220; tel: 6226 5187; fax: 6226 5197; email: scubada@scubada.com
SEA Dive Adventures Room 105, Metropolitan YMCA, 60 Stevens Rd, Singapore 257854; tel: 6734 7730; fax: 6737 4289; email: seadive@singnet.com.sg

Water-skiing is available on the Kallang River, where world championships have been held, and at Sembawang on the north coast. It costs S$65–85 an hour, and is offered 09.00–17.30 daily. Try:

Bernatt Boating and Skiing/Williams Water Sports 60 Jalan Mempurong (off Sembawang Rd), Singapore 759056; tel: 6257 5859; fax: 6753 7318
Singapore Water Ski Federation/Cowabunga Ski Centre Ski Site Office, 10 Stadium Lane, Singapore 397774; tel: 6344 8813; fax: 6346 1780; email: cowabunga@Pacific.net.sg; web: www.cowabunga.com.sg

You can also try your hand at windsurfing and sailing. Windsurfing costs S$20 for two hours (plus a deposit of S$10) at the Sea Sports Centre (tel: 6449 5118; open 09.30–18.30 every day) and S$13–18 an hour (plus deposit) at SAFRA Resort and Country Club (tel: 6546 5880; 09.00–17.30 daily). The hire of sailing boats costs up to S$20 per hour, together with a deposit of about S$30 and, sometimes, a guest fee.

Bowling

There are many tenpin bowling alleys, both indoors and outdoors. A few of these are listed below. Centres open at 09.00 and play can continue until 02.00. There are also a few centres around Marina South that are open 24 hours. Games cost between S$2 and $3.80 (although the price rises at weekends), and you must hire shoes. For further details, contact the Singapore Tenpin Bowling Congress (tel: 6440 7388).

Cathay Bowl 1018 East Coast Parkway, #02-01 Leisure Court, Singapore 449877; tel: 6444 0118; fax: 6444 2213
Jackie's Bowl 542B East Coast Rd, Singapore 458971; tel: 6241 6519; fax: 6441 2538
Superbowl Marina South 15 Marina Grove, Singapore 019598; tel: 6221 1010; fax: 6225 3882
Superbowl Marina Square 6 Raffles Blvd, #03-200 Marina Sq, Singapore 039594; tel: 6334 1000; fax: 6334 3498
Victor's Superbowl 7 Marina Grove, Singapore 019597; tel: 6223 7998; fax: 6223 1998

Pampering yourself

The worldwide explosion of interest in health clubs and spas has had its impact on Singapore, which has a good range of places where you can be pampered and pummelled. The following are a few companies offering services such as massage, aromatherapy, manicure and pedicure:

Cosmoprof International 1 Selegie Rd, #02-10/11/12 Paradiz Centre, Singapore 188306; tel: 6339 9118; fax: 6339 2884; email: enquiries@cosmoprofinternational.com; web: www.spacareinternational.com

Esthetica 391 Orchard Rd, #04-17/18 Takashimaya Shopping Centre, Singapore 238873; tel: 6733 7000; fax: 6466 4778

Estheva 442 Orchard Rd, #02-28 Orchard Hotel Shopping Arcade, Singapore 238879; tel: 6733 8200; fax: 6276 5168/ 6733 9218; email: spa@estheva.com; web: www.estheva.com

Kenko Healthy Family Foot Reflexology Centre 6 Raffles Blvd, #02-254-256 Marina Square Shopping Centre, Singapore 039594; tel: 6339 1711; fax: 6339 7077

My Foot 176 Orchard Rd, #03-30 Centrepoint, Singapore 238843; tel: 6736 2562

Spa Discoveries 81 Clemenceau Ave, #04-15/16 UE Shopping Mall, Singapore 239918; tel: 6735 5665; fax: 6735 5175

Spa Valley 391 Orchard Rd, #05-19 Ngee Ann City, Singapore 238873; tel: 6738 0889; fax: 6235 5076; email: spamail@singnet.com.sg; web: www.spavalley.com

St Gregory Spa 7500A Beach Rd, #04-302 The Plaza, Singapore 199591; tel: 6298 0011; fax: 6297 3591; email: plazahtl@singnet.com.sg; web: www.hpl.com.sg/spa

Yi Loong Foot Therapy 220 Orchard Rd, #02-11B Midpoint Orchard, Singapore 238852; tel: 6250 2969; fax: 6737 2790

Yellow-backed sunbird

Holidays, Celebrations and Events

Whatever time of year you choose to visit Singapore, there is likely to be a selection of festivals or events to experience. Many of these (in particular the religious festivals) are based upon ancient – frequently Chinese – traditions, although they generally take on distinctly Singaporean aspects. Even if the Singapore Federation of Chinese Clan Associations is correct in feeling that the young are increasingly disinterested in such traditions, there are enough people of older generations to guarantee that these festivals will continue in their present forms at least in the medium-term future. It is to be hoped that this is the case because they are vivid, colourful and fascinating affairs. Please remember, however, that they nevertheless represent moments of religious devotion. If you enter temples, ensure you are suitably attired and respect the established etiquette. You will be required to remove your shoes before entering most temples.

Chinese religious festivals differ greatly from those in the West. Western celebrations usually focus upon a particular, fixed date. Christmas Day, for example, always falls on December 25. In the Chinese calendar, by contrast, festivals are based on the lunar calendar and the dates of festivals alter each year. Furthermore, festivals of the Chinese lunar calendar span several days (rather than a single day), so that the first day of the Chinese New Year is simply the first day of an extended period of celebration. The lengthy duration of many festivals – and the range of cultures and religions (and thus festivals) – means that the visitor is unlikely to miss out altogether.

Some Chinese festivities date back to early rural, peasant activities, and consequently revolve around harvest and fertility rites. Others are centred upon the many gods of Chinese theology, which play a part in everyday life and must be properly worshipped and appeased. On occasions there are linguistic variations between rituals depending upon the dialect spoken in the area of China from which they stem. In addition, respect for the family is an integral part of Chinese culture; filial piety and the honouring of ancestors are both important. Considering Singaporeans live with their families until they marry, it is perhaps unsurprising that this particular feature of Chinese culture remains strong.

The following celebrations, events and holidays all occur annually. As explained above, however, the vast majority of dates change from year to year. Those given below are for 2002, but you should obtain a revised calendar from the tourist board (web: www.newasia-singapore.com) for trips during subsequent years. Sporting events are listed separately (see pages 84–5).

JANUARY

Celebration Singapore November 10 2001–February 26 2002. A hundred days of spectacular events, from carnivals to fireworks, which take place at various venues around the country. Celebration of national identity and achievement. Visit www.celebrationsingapore.com.sg for further details.

Christmas Light-Up November 16 2001–5 January 2002. At this time of the year Orchard Road takes on the appearance of fairyland, which seems an unlikely thing to say about a commercial centre. It is spectacular, and compares very favourably with the festive lights in other major cities of the world.

Celebration Tree @ Orchard December 7 2001–January 1 2002. A large Christmas tree at Orchard Road. There are nightly renditions of carols and other music.

New Year's Day January 1 2002 (fixed public holiday).

Harvest Festival (Pongal) January 14 2002 (date changes). A festival celebrated by southern Hindus at temples such as the Sri Srinivasa Perumal Temple (see pages 120–1). For four days you can watch the noisy, colourful ceremonies which start at 06.30, and include the beating of drums and the ringing of bells. Between January 7 and 14 there is also a street bazaar in Campbell Lane, Little India, where you can buy traditional Pongal items. Open 11.00–21.00; admission free.

Flower Garden Fair January 26–February 11 2002 (dates change). An exhibition at the Albert Mall that will appeal to bird lovers and horticulturists alike. You can also buy plants and flowers, listen to bird-singing contests, and attend flower-arranging displays. For information, tel: 6538 2998. Open 11.30–20.00 daily. Admission free.

Lunar New Year Light-Up January 26–February 26 2002 (dates alter). This is what Singapore is all about. Visit Chinatown and find the place ablaze with light and colour, and the street full of decorations and traditional delicacies.

Lord Murugan's Birthday (Thaipusam) January 28 2002 (date varies). At the Sri Srinivasa Perumal Temple (Serangoon Road) and the Sri Thandayuthapani Temple (Tank Road) you can watch as Hindus celebrate the birthday of Lord Murugan, a deity embodying youth, strength and virtue. This ceremony is not for the squeamish; devotees pierce their bodies with sharp instruments from which they hang weights or attach harnesses to pull carts. These pious Hindus shed no blood, and it is said that they feel no pain as they make the three-kilometre walk in a trance-like state from one temple to the other. This will make you think twice about complaining when you next get a headache.

Chinese New Year Celebrations January 28–11 February 2002 (dates change yearly). Part of the Lunar New Year celebrations, these last just over a fortnight (leading up to Chinese New Year itself) and include a range of special events in Chinatown, the centre of the Orchard Road area, and in many of the out-of-town shopping malls. There are bright street decorations, entertainment and food on offer. Stalls are usually open between 11.00 and 21.00.

FEBRUARY

Celebration Singapore See opposite.

Flower Garden Fair See opposite.

Lunar New Year Light-Up See opposite.

Chinese New Year Celebrations See opposite.

Singapore River Raft Race February 2–3 2002 (dates vary). Organised by the Singapore Polytechnic, this is typical of a university RAG event. There is

CHINESE NEW YEAR (CHUN JIE)

Chun jie literally means 'spring festival' and represents a time of rebirth. Chinese New Year is traditionally celebrated for a period of 15 days commencing on the first day of the first month of the lunar calendar. Families come together and exchange gifts. All debts should have been paid by the lunar new year so that a fresh start can be made, and towards the same end each house is cleaned thoroughly during the run up to the festival.

The Mandarin for 'Happy New Year' is *Gong Xi Fa Chai*, though a more literal translation is 'Good Fortune and Long Life'. In the hope of encouraging good wishes throughout the coming year, families may hang pieces of red paper decorated with phrases believed to bring luck. The importance of red to these customs derives from a legend in which a monster was scared away from a village by bright lights and the colour red. The colour therefore came to signify long life. Relatives give 'good fortune' presents to one another, encased in red packets and known as *hong baos*. The gifts inside are often sums of money or oranges (the Cantonese word for orange – *gam* – is the same as that for gold), but are always given in even numbers (which are supposed to bring fortune). Custom demands that a recipient of a gift offer a gift in return.

Outside the home, restaurants serve special New Year menus – a particular favourite being 'lucky raw fish' (*yu sheng*) – and businessmen pay for lion dances outside their properties to bring prosperity. Streets are decorated with lights and banners, and models of whichever one of the 12 animals of the Chinese zodiac represents that particular year. In the past firecrackers were also lit, but it was felt that these were dangerous and so now, disappointingly, these have been replaced by pictures of firecrackers. The whole festival is vibrant and colourful, so Chinese New Year is an exciting time to visit Singapore. On the other hand, shops and restaurants may be closed for several days, and some tourist attractions will be very crowded.

the usual collection of Heath Robinson crafts constructed from car tyres and plastic containers. Races start at 10.00. Admission free. For further information, call 6772 1147.

Singapore River Hong Bao February 8–17 2002 (dates change). This annual carnival celebrates the year's animal of the Chinese zodiac – in this case, the horse. There are nightly performances from Taiwan and China, as well as arts and crafts, and palm readings. Events centre on the Marina Promenade.

Chinese New Year (Chun Jie) February 12–13 2002 (public holiday; date varies). See box, page 91, for details.

Chingay Singapore February 16 2002 (date changes from year to year). Part of the Chinese New Year celebrations. It takes the form of a carnival procession, with costumes and illuminated floats. It is spectacular, but has suffered in the past from some of the problems with law and order that have dogged other carnivals around the world. Do not be surprised by long and inexplicable gaps in the procession. The route becomes very crowded with spectators, so get there early if you want a good view. Takes place on the roads between City Hall and SunTec City.

Hari Raya Haji February 23 2002 (public holiday; date varies). A day to commemorate the holy pilgrimage to Mecca and to honour those returning from the long journey. Falls on the tenth day of the 12th month of the Muslim calendar. Devout Muslims spend much of the day in prayer, and sheep and goats are ritually sacrificed – the squeamish should beware. The meat is divided among the poor.

MARCH

Singapore International Drama/Arts Festival March 17–April 8 2002 (dates change). This alternates each year between arts and drama. The festival this year focuses upon comedy, and acts include performers from the Edinburgh Festival, Montreal's Just For Laughs and the Melbourne International Comedy Festival. For information, call 6348 5555 or visit www.sistic.com.sg.

Fashion Festival March 16–31 2002 (dates alter). If you are interested in fashion, this is for you. Some of the world's most desirable clothes are on display at various venues. For information call 6228 8830 or visit www.fashion-festival.com.

Birthday of Lao Zhi March 25–31 2002 (date varies). Taoists celebrate this important festival on the 15th day of the second lunar month in temples throughout the country. If you would like to see the devotions, go to the open field in front of Aljunied MRT station where there is a display of Taoist artefacts and musical and literary events as well as religious ceremonies. If you want to know more, ring 6841 3691 for information.

Good Friday March 29 2002 (public holiday; date varies).

Singapore Food Festival March 29–April 30 2002 (dates vary). Even the most ardent and demanding of gourmets will revel in the dishes on offer during these few weeks. There are opportunities to sample a large range of international cuisine at places all over the island. You can also watch a chef preparing a meal or join a food tour. Visit www.singaporefoodfestival.com for further details, and see *Local tours*, page 59, for information on tours.

APRIL
Singapore International Drama/Arts Festival See opposite.

Singapore Food Festival See above.

Singapore International Film Festival April 4–20 2002 (dates change). Features a broad spectrum of films from over 40 countries, shown at Golden Village and United Artists Cinemas.

World Gourmet Summit April 7–13 2002 (dates vary). Chefs from around the world spend seven days in Singapore and demonstrate the very best of today's cuisine at several hotels and restaurants. Call 6270 1254 or visit www.worldgourmetsummit.com.

All Souls Day (**Qing Ming Jie**) April 12 2002 (date varies). A time when the Chinese honour their dead ancestors, sometimes by visits to the graves of relatives. As it is a quiet, family affair, the casual visitor will probably be unaware of this festival. Ceremonies can be observed, however, in Kong Meng San Phor Kark See Temple on Sin Ming Road.

Ballet Under the Stars April 19–21 and 26–28 2002 (dates to be confirmed; change yearly). Enjoy a picnic while watching an outdoor performance of ballet by the Singapore Dance Theatre at Fort Canning Green. Picnics start at 17.00, performances at 19.30. Free seating on grass. For further information, call 6348 5555 or visit www.sistic.com.sg.

MAY
Labour Day May 1 2002 (fixed public holiday).

Ballet Under the Stars May 17–19 and 24–26 2002. See above for details.

The Great Singapore Sale May 24–July 7 2002 (dates change). Wherever you go you will find astonishing reductions on a wide variety of goods, sometimes by as much as 90%. To these are added a variety of promotions, freebies and entertainment to encourage shoppers to spend their money. For more information, visit www.greatsingaporesale.com.sg.

Sentosa Sandsation May 25–June 23 2002 (dates change). A truly fun event held on Siloso Beach, Sentosa. Colossal sand sculptures are built and judged, and the outcome is eagerly contested. You can participate in the family sculpting competitions, and even help to knock all the castles down at the end. Call 6736 8672 or visit www.sentosa.com.sg.

Vesak Day May 26 2002 (public holiday; date varies).

JUNE

The Great Singapore Sale See page 93.

Sentosa Sandsation See page 93.

Singapore Arts Festival June 1–25 2002 (dates change). A celebration of all sorts of art forms – Eastern and Western, traditional and modern. There are some interesting fringe events, too. Exhibitions at various venues. Call 6270 0722.

Bak Chang (Rice Dumpling) Festival June 13–25 2002 (dates to be confirmed). Taste many differently flavoured rice dumplings in the Chinese Garden (see page 174). Locals also enter competitions. Call 6261 3632.

Singapore Dragon Boat Festival (Duan Wu Jie) June 15–16 2002 (dates movable). Held at the Marina Promenade, these races feature international and local teams. A drummer sits in the bow of each boat, beating a rhythm for the rowers. The races are fiercely competitive. The races themselves commemorate the death centuries ago of Qu Yuan, a poet and wise man who lived in China. His virtue and efficiency attracted envy at court, and he eventually committed suicide by drowning. When news arrived of his death, a fleet of fishing boats was launched to search for his body (from which the race derives). It is said that when the body could not be found, people threw rice into the water to prevent the fish from eating it. Today it is traditional to eat rice dumplings wrapped in leaves.

JULY

Ballet Under the Stars July 19–21 and 26–28 2002. See page 93 for details.

The Great Singapore Sale See page 93.

AUGUST

National Day Parade August 9 2002 (fixed public holiday). This is an event held in the National Stadium and greeted with island-wide enthusiasm by the population of Singapore. It celebrates the anniversary of independence in 1965, and includes much military ceremony, flag waving, fireworks and speeches. It can be rather tedious for the outsider.

Festival of the Hungry Ghosts (Zhong Yuan Jie) August 9–September 6 2002 (dates change). The Taoist festival itself falls on the 15th day of the seventh month of the Chinese lunar calendar, though celebrations extend considerably beyond this day. This is a time when the gates of hell are said to open, and people make offerings to placate the hungry and unhappy ghosts who roam the earth. These offerings include 'hell money' (fake currency), sticks of incense, and banquets of cake and fruit on the streets. There are also Chinese street operas (*wayangs*) to entertain them. In residential areas, so many joss papers are burned that frequently special bins for burning them are found on HDB estates.

WOMAD (World of Music, Arts and Dance) Singapore August 30–September 1 2002 (dates change). Fort Canning Park (see pages 136–7) hosts international artists performing some of the world's best musical traditions. For information, call 6734 5910.

SEPTEMBER

Festival of the Hungry Ghosts See opposite.

WOMAD Singapore See above.

The Mid-Autumn Festival (Zhong Qiu Jie) September 14–21 2002 (dates vary). Held during the Chinese eighth moon. This festival is characterised by processions of people carrying flamboyant plastic or paper lanterns, usually with small candles inside, and by the giving and eating of 'mooncakes' (hence its more common name, the Mooncake Festival). Since the festival falls on the 15th day of the eighth month, the full moon is especially bright and the occasion has always been associated with moon-appreciation parties.

Originally the Mooncake Festival was probably a harvest celebration, but it has evolved. Folklore relates the tale of an archer named Hou Yi who stole the elixir of life. His wife drank it and became the lady in the moon, to whom young women would pray during the festival. In the 14th century, there was a plot to overthrow the Yuan dynasty. Rebels hid messages detailing their plots in mooncakes so they could be passed around without being detected. Today the festival continues to be a celebration of the overthrow of the Mongolians by the Han people.

Lantern Festival Dates to be confirmed. A display of lanterns in the Chinese Garden (see page 174). For details, call 6261 3632.

Birthday of the Monkey God (Hanuman Puja) September 22 2002 (date varies). This bloody celebration of Hanuman, the Monkey God, involves devotees leading a procession while slashing themselves with fearsome knives. A sedan chair is carried, supposedly occupied by Hanuman. This god is predominantly worshipped in western India, and there is a species of monkey, the Hanuman Langur, named after him. Witness the ceremony at the Monkey God Temple.

OCTOBER

Nine Emperor Gods Festival October 6–14 2002 (dates change). These gods are thought to cure infirmities and give good luck. Priests write charms using their own blood as ink, and there is a parade by Chinese believers at the Nine Emperor Gods Temple.

Pilgrimage to Kusu Island October 6–November 3 2002 (dates change). Taoists travel to the Tua Pekong Temple (see page 210) to pray. The pilgrimage is based on the legend that a turtle rescued two sailors from drowning by transforming itself into an island on which they were able to take refuge.

Deepavali Light-Up October 19–November 16 2002 (dates vary). The build-up to the main Deepavali Festival. Hindus celebrate the victory of light over darkness with the Festival of Lights, decorating the streets of Little India with illuminations.

Sentosa Hell 'O' Ween October 26–27 2002. Despite the odd name, this is a good old-fashioned Halloween celebration at Parade Square, Sentosa, with lots of gore, ghoulies, ghosties and things that go bump in the night. Suitable for children of all ages. For information, call 6736 8672 or visit www.sentosa.com.sg.

Three Goddesses Festival (Navarathiri) Date to be confirmed (varies). Celebration in honour of three Hindu goddesses (Dhurga, Lakshmi and Saraswathi), which can be observed at either the Sri Mariamman Temple (see page 169) or the Sri Thandayuthapani Temple (see page 112) on Tank Road. Festivities continue for nine days, and on the tenth night there is a spectacular procession whose centrepiece is a magnificent silver horse. You can also join the celebrations at other temples, and in the evenings there are performances of classical Indian dance and music (between 19.30 and 22.00).

Fire-Walking Festival (Thimithi) Date to be confirmed (movable). Devout Hindus walk barefooted across beds of live coals apparently without suffering any ill effects. Celebrations start at the Sri Srinivasa Perumal Temple (see page 120) at 02.00. The fire walking can be seen at the Sri Mariamman Temple (see page 169).

On the eve of Thimithi, there is a procession from Sri Mariamman Temple to Little India. This procession, with its towering silver chariot, starts at 19.00. You will find a considerable (but always good-humoured) crowd.

NOVEMBER

Celebration Singapore See page 90.

Christmas Light-Up See page 90.

Pilgrimage to Kusu Island See page 95.

Deepavali Light-Up See above.

Hari-Raya Light-Up November 2–December 14 2002 (dates alter). This is a sort of Shrove Tuesday before the month of Ramadan, during which Muslims fast during the hours of daylight throughout the month. The focus of the celebrations is at Geylang Serai (see pages 197–9), where there are street decorations, stalls and a fairground. There is fun and food, and children are welcome.

Hindu New Year (Deepavali) November 3 2002 (variable public holiday; date to be confirmed). This joyful celebration of the Hindu New Year is also known as Diwali. Little India is bedecked with lights to encourage the goddess of prosperity, Lakshmi, to visit during the following year. Hindus don new clothes, clean their houses, and settle their debts in preparation for the new year ahead. Watch it in Serangoon Road, which is ablaze with colour. Buy a variety of wares at the myriad stalls of the street bazaar in Campbell Street, or enjoy the cultural shows on offer.

Ramadan November 6–December 5 2002 (dates change). Observed every ninth month of the Muslim calendar. Muslims fast during the day, and at night make up for their abstinence with prayers and celebrations in the island's mosques.

Singapore River Buskers' Festival November 16–24 2002 (dates change). Along the bank of the river you can watch a wide variety of street entertainers, including singers, jugglers and mime artists. Enjoy the show while having an alfresco meal at one of the many eating places.

The Great Singapore Duck Race Date to be confirmed (varies). Thousands of plastic ducks – all sporting sunglasses – are raced along the Singapore River. You can sponsor a duck to win and the money goes to charity. The whole thing is wonderfully silly. While you are waiting for your duck to come in, amuse yourself with the numerous shows and carnival events. For information, call 6220 8180.

DECEMBER

Christmas Light-Up See page 90.

Celebration Singapore See page 90.

Celebration Tree @ Orchard See page 90.

Ramadan See above.

Hari-Raya Light-Up See opposite.

Hari Raya Puasa December 6 2002 (public holiday; date varies). A form of rebirth which comes at the end of the month of Ramadan. Takes place in Geylang Serai (see pages 197–9). In the morning, Muslim males purify themselves and pray, after which there are celebrations and feasting.

Christmas Day December 25 2002 (fixed public holiday). Christians celebrate with services on Christmas Eve and Christmas Day in churches all over Singapore. There are decorations in all stores (including Christmas trees, snow and reindeer), and lights along Orchard Road. Many hotels and restaurants also organise celebratory activities.

Part Two

The Guide

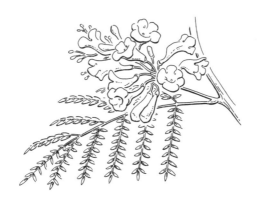

Reticulate python

Central Singapore

ORCHARD ROAD

This tree-lined road, which is so well known for its shopping malls and where tourists and locals can 'shop till they drop', has an interesting history. Orchard Road's name derives from the nutmeg plantations and pepper farms in the area in the 1840s, while the original European plantation owners like Scott, Cairnie (Cairnhill), Oxley and Cuppage are commemorated in the names of the surrounding streets. However, in the early 1900s disease spread through the nutmeg plantations and within a year most of them had closed.

At the eastern end of Orchard Road is **Dhoby Ghaut**. This name means the 'area of the washermen'. In the 19th century, the Dhobies – who were immigrants from the Bengal and Madras regions in India – washed the local residents' clothes in the stream which ran down the length of the road and dried them on the banks and open land where the YMCA building now stands. The road was subject to flooding until the Stamford Canal was widened and deepened in 1965. Part of the canal now runs under the pedestrian mall in front of the Wisma Atria shopping centre beside Orchard MRT.

The railway line linking mainland Malaya to Singapore, which began in 1903 and started at Tank Road Station, once crossed a bridge over Orchard Road where Centrepoint is today. Apparently, for several years after the bridge was built all road traffic stopped when a train passed over because people believed that bad luck would strike if they were caught under a moving train! The line continued to where Newton Circus Hawker Centre now stands, and then on via Bukit Timah to Woodlands. When Keppel Road Railway Station was built in 1932, the bridge was demolished and the railway line re-routed away from Orchard Road through Queenstown and then along Holland Road to rejoin the old track at Bukit Timah.

The 1846 town plan of Singapore shows that there were a Chinese burial ground and a Joss House near the Mandarin Hotel and a Bencoolenese burial ground where the Grand Central Hotel now stands. The 26-storey Mandarin Hotel, with its revolving restaurant at the top, was built in Chinese-style by *samsui* women from Guangdong in 1973, and was the first modern skyscraper hotel built in Singapore.

Centrepoint Shopping Centre is the site of the original 1917 **Singapore Cold Storage Company** depot in Orchard Road. The company, one of the

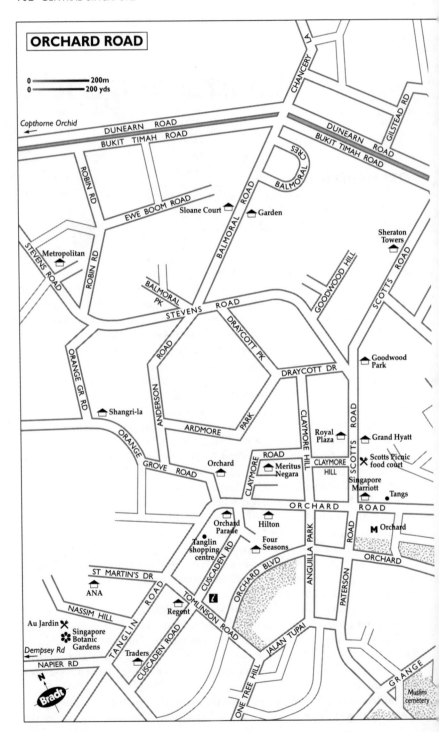

ORCHARD ROAD

0 ——— 200m
0 ——— 200 yds

Copthorne Orchid

DUNEARN ROAD

BUKIT TIMAH ROAD

DUNEARN ROAD

BUKIT TIMAH ROAD

GILSTEAD RD

CHANCERY LA

BALMORAL CRES

ROBIN RD

EWE BOOM ROAD

Sloane Court

Garden

BALMORAL ROAD

Sheraton Towers

STEVENS ROAD

Metropolitan

ROBIN RD

BALMORAL PK

STEVENS ROAD

GOODWOOD HILL

SCOTTS ROAD

ORANGE GR RD

Shangri-la

ANDERSON ROAD

DRAYCOTT PK

DRAYCOTT DR

Goodwood Park

ARDMORE PARK

ORANGE GROVE ROAD

Orchard

CLAYMORE ROAD

Meritus Negara

CLAYMORE HILL

Royal Plaza

CLAYMORE HILL

SCOTTS ROAD

Grand Hyatt

Scotts Picnic food court

Singapore Marriott

Tangs

ORCHARD ROAD

Orchard Parade

Hilton

M Orchard

Tanglin shopping centre

CUSCADEN RD

Four Seasons

ANGUILLA PARK

ROAD

ORCHARD

ST MARTIN'S DR

ANA

TANGLIN ROAD

TOMLINSON ROAD

Regent

ORCHARD BLVD

PATERSON

NASSIM HILL

Au Jardin

Singapore Botanic Gardens

Dempsey Rd

CUSCADEN ROAD

Traders

JALAN TUPAI

ONE TREE HILL

GRANGE

Muslim cemetery

NAPIER RD

N

Bradt

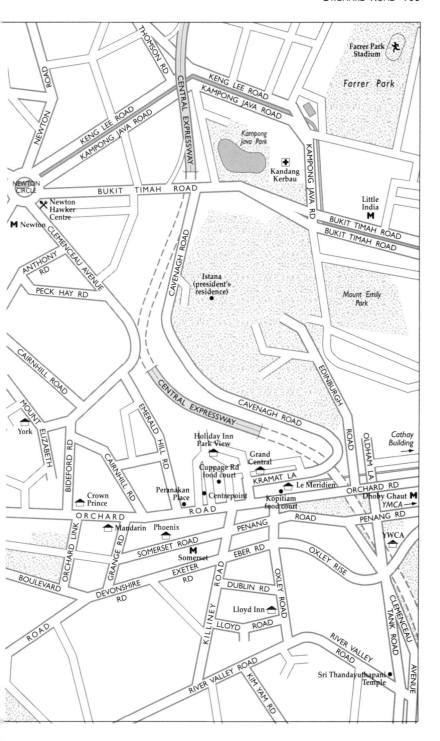

oldest in the area, started in 1903 and pioneered the processing and distribution of hygienic food supplies in Malaya. It made the first ice-cream in Singapore in 1923, started a pig farm in 1926 and a dairy farm at Bukit Timah in 1929, and had introduced a grocery department by 1933 (with vegetables from the Cameron Highlands, meat from New Zealand, fruit from South Africa and the United States, and groceries from Europe). Today, Cold Storage supermarkets can be found in the basements of several Orchard Road shopping malls and many shopping centres throughout the island, and still stock familiar foods from around the world.

Another interesting local business is **C K Tang's** department store at the corner of Scotts Road and Orchard Road. This was started in 1958 by Choon Keng Tang, a former lace-peddlar from the Chinese province of Swatow, and when the old building was replaced in 1982 they kept the distinctive green-tiled roof and red pillars. At Tang's you will discover an open-air terrace café where you can rest weary feet, enjoy a cake and an iced *kachang*, and watch the world go by. The store itself is a treasure trove of Beijing *cloisonné*, from enormous enamel vases to minute figurines, along with beautiful silk garments and wonderfully intricate fans.

Orchard Road is one of the first ports of call for tourists visiting Singapore. It is a wide, attractive thoroughfare with shops offering Armani suits, Gucci watches, Prada handbags, and the very best jewellery. Halfway along the street is a fascinating complex called **Peranakan Place** (see below, page 112). Here you can sit in a (modernised) old-fashioned village, the like of which can no longer be found anywhere else on the island, and sample Peranakan food, admire the ancient buildings, and buy Peranakan artefacts. Elsewhere on the road are a wide variety of stores. Alongside the boutiques, you will find bookshops and a Marks and Spencer. In Tanglin Road, which joins the end of Orchard Road, is the **Tanglin Shopping Centre** which is packed with a host of antiques shops, selling goods not only from Singapore but from nearby Indonesia, Malaysia and Thailand. (Lovers of antiques should also pay a visit to **Dempsey Road**, a ten-minute drive away, where the warehouse-like buildings used to hold an army barracks, but are now home to antique dealers.) For a list of shopping malls in Orchard Road, and guidance on what they sell, see *Shopping*, pages 71–2.

Getting there
Take the MRT to Orchard Road, Somerset, or Dhoby Ghaut stations. Most buses, particularly travelling from the hotels, will pass along Orchard Road.

Where to stay
Super-luxury
ANA Hotel 16 Nassim Hill, Singapore 258467; tel: 6732 1222; fax: 6732 2222; email: roomrsvn@anahotel.com.sg. Set off the western end of Orchard Rd, about 20 minutes' walk from MRT and main shopping area. Ugly exterior, but spacious and well-designed lobby. Pool, fitness and business centres. Excellent Japanese restaurant. 457 rooms. Single S$300–60, double S$300–60, suite S$400–2,000. *Nearest MRT* Orchard (NS line)

Shangri-la Hotel 22 Orange Grove Rd, Singapore 258350; tel: 6737 3644; fax: 6737 3257/6733 1029; email: sls@shangri-la.com. One of the best. Large hotel built in wings (rather than as a high-rise) and set in beautiful, landscaped gardens surrounding a delightful pool area. Good fitness centre and business facilities, often used for conferences. One wing is separate and can be secured so that it is suitable for important visitors and their entourages. Runs shuttle bus to Orchard Rd and SunTec City. Restaurants: Blu (top floor, Californian), Nadamon (Japanese), Shang Palace (local and *dim sum*). 760 rooms. Single S$420–550, double S$480–610, suite S$1,000–3,200. Recommended. *Nearest MRT* Orchard (NS line)

The Regent Hotel 1 Cuscaden Rd, Singapore 249715; tel: 6753 8888; fax; 6732 8838; email: regent3@magix.com.sg. Set in quiet street off western end of Orchard Rd, near Tanglin Mall and Botanic Gardens. Impressive lobby with full-height atrium, water fountains and flowers. Comfortable and spacious rooms with marble bathrooms. Pool in landscaped garden, good fitness and business centres. Restaurants include Summer Palace (Cantonese), Capers (Asian and Western, Sunday champagne brunch), lobby café serving typically British afternoon tea of scones and cakes. 441 rooms. Single S$370, double S$390; suite S$570. Recommended. *Nearest MRT* Orchard (NS line)

Four Seasons Hotel 190 Orchard Blvd, Singapore 248646; tel: 6734 1110; fax: 6733 0669; email: serene.law@fourseasons.com. Set at the quieter end of Orchard Blvd, but a short walk to Orchard Rd, this excellent select hotel offers a very personal service (more like a gentleman's club) and displays many Asian artworks. Has 2 pools, and the only air-conditioned tennis courts in Singapore. Good fitness centre and business facilities. Restaurants serving Cantonese and American food. 254 rooms. Single S$325–75, double S$365–415, suite S$505–705. Recommended. *Nearest MRT* Orchard (NS line)

Meritus Negara Singapore 10 Claymore Rd, Singapore 229540; tel: 6737 0811; fax: 6737 9075; email: negara.mns@ meritus-hotels.com.sg. Set back from the western end of Orchard Rd, so quieter while remaining well placed for the shopping area, MRT and buses. Good, personalised service, and large, well-appointed rooms. Pool with limited shade, and jacuzzi, fitness centre and business facilities. 200 rooms. Single S$300–400, double S$320–460, suite S$560–3,200. Recommended. *Nearest MRT* Orchard (NS line)

Hilton Singapore 581 Orchard Rd, Singapore 238883; tel: 6737 2233; fax: 6732 2917; email: hitels@pacific.net.sg. Well located at western end of Orchard Rd, within a short walk of the MRT. Imposing entrance with sculptures and a lobby area containing expensive boutiques and top, designer labels. Well-fitted rooms. Small roof-top pool, good fitness facilities and business centre. Restaurants include the Harbour Grill and Oyster Bar (continental), Inn of Happiness (Chinese), Checkers Brasserie (international and well known for its Philadelphia cheesecake), Tradewinds (poolside, local and North Indian) and Kaspia bar. 423 rooms. Single S$360–90, double S$360–400, suites S$520–820. *Nearest MRT* Orchard (NS line)

Royal Plaza 25 Scotts Rd, Singapore 228220; tel: 6737 7966; fax: 6737 6646; email: royal@royalplaza.com.sg. Undergoing renovation and rebuilding in 2002, although still open. Well placed in Scotts Rd for the shopping areas of Orchard Rd and near MRT and bus routes. Well-decorated rooms. Pool, fitness centre and business centre.

2 restaurants: Café Vienna (international) and Bella Donna (small Italian, at lobby level). 497 rooms. Single S$350–460, double S$370–480, suite S$540–3,600. Recommended once refurbishment complete. *Nearest MRT* Orchard (NS line)

Grand Hyatt Hotel Singapore 10–12 Scotts Rd, Singapore 228211; tel: 6738 1234; fax: 6732 1696; email: reservations.sg@hyattintl.com. Impressive, sweeping entrance on Scotts Rd, and near shopping area, MRT and main bus routes. Relaxing retreat from bustle outside. Tree-lined pool, garden and sundeck area on 5th floor, tennis and squash courts, jacuzzi and sauna, good fitness centre and business facilities. Restaurants: Mezza9 (9 open kitchens, Asian), Paris Café (international, buffet lunch and dinner), Pete's Place (basement, cosy, Italian pizzas and pasta), Oasis Bar (poolside), Brannigans Bar (basement). 693 rooms. Single S$500–600, double S$500–600, suite S$1,000–4,000. Recommended. *Nearest MRT* Orchard (NS line)

Singapore Marriott Hotel 320 Orchard Rd, Singapore 2338865; tel: 6735 5800; fax: 6735 9800; email: smhsales@singnet.com.sg. Impressive site at corner of Orchard and Scotts roads, surmounted by green-tiled pagoda-style roof. Spacious marble lobby area. Roof-top pool, good fitness centre and business facilities. Restaurants include the Marriott Café on the ground floor (excellent buffets), Wan Hao (Cantonese fine dining), Crossroads Café (open-air bar and coffee house beside pavement, where you can sit and watch the world go by), and Garden Terrace Café (poolside Western grill bar). 373 rooms. Single S$380–420, double S$380–420, suite S$650–1,880. Recommended. *Nearest MRT* Orchard (NS line)

Goodwood Park Hotel 22 Scotts Rd, Singapore 228221; tel: 6737 7411; fax: 6732 8558; email: enquiries@goodwoodparkhotel.com.sg. Set high on a small hill past the shopping area on Scotts Rd. Well-known, historic building offering colonial or modern-style rooms. Lovely pool area in garden set away from the bustle. Fitness and business centres. Several good restaurants. 235 rooms. Single S$385–3,000, double S$425–3,000, suite S$525–3,000. Recommended. *Nearest MRT* Orchard (NS line)

Le Meridien Singapore 100 Orchard Rd, Singapore 238840; tel: 6733 8855; fax: 6732 7886; email: meridien_sales@pacific.net.sg. Open lobby with rooms arranged on terraces and lots of orchids. Some rooms with balconies overlook the pool area. Good pool, but bare surrounding area. Fitness and business centres. Restaurants, but also positioned above Kopitiam (open-air food court in basement), and near eating places in Cuppage Place. 407 rooms. Single S$300–60, double S$330–90, suite S$400–1,800. *Nearest MRT* Somerset (NS line)

Holiday Inn Park View 11 Cavenagh Rd, Singapore 229616; tel: 6733 8333; fax: 6734 4593; email: info@holidayinn.com.sg. Quiet location just north of central part of busy Orchard Rd. Impressive entrance into triangular-shaped atrium. Good pool, fitness and business centres. In-house restaurants, but also near selection of restaurants at Cuppage Place and bars at Peranakan Place. 312 rooms. Single S$300, double S$320–40, suite S$600–60. *Nearest MRT* Somerset (NS line)

Mandarin Singapore 333 Orchard Rd, Singapore 238867; tel: 6737 2200; fax: 6738 2382; email: resvn.tms@meritus-hotels.com. One of first high-rise hotels in Singapore. Disappointing lobby area but large, well-appointed rooms. Sizable pool in uninspiring surroundings, and fitness and business centres. Well-known revolving restaurant, Top of the M, on 39th floor. 1200 rooms. Single S$360–420, double S$360–420, suite S$580–2,800. *Nearest MRT* Somerset (NS line)

Sheraton Towers Singapore Hotel 39 Scotts Rd, Singapore 228230; tel: 6737 6888; fax: 6737 1072; email: sheraton.towers.singapore@sheraton.com. Near Newton MRT, but long walk from Orchard Rd. Lots of flowers and waterfalls in lobby area. Good, well-designed rooms. Roof-top pool with bar. Fitness and business centres. Restaurants serving Italian and Chinese food. 413 rooms. Single S$400, double S$400, suite S$1,000. Recommended. *Nearest MRT* Newton (NS line)

Luxury

Traders Hotel Singapore 161A Cuscaden Rd, Singapore 249716; tel: 6738 2222; fax: 6831 4314; email: ths@shangri-la.com. At western end of Orchard Rd, near Botanic Gardens, with spacious lobby area but smallish check-in desk. Good-sized rooms – choose those overlooking the excellent free-formed pool, with trees and shrubs and sundecks, located at the 4th level on top of the adjacent Tanglin Mall. Linked to the shopping mall by 2 walkways, and bills at several restaurants and bars can be charged to your hotel account. A Shangri-la hotel, also with cross-signing at these hotels. Fitness and business centres, and many business customers. Restaurants: Traders Café at lobby level (overlooking waterfall from pool level during main meal hours), Ah Hoi's Kitchen (at pool level, open-air and fan-cooled, well known for local food; speciality is chilli crab), Rumpoles Bar (for drinks and quick snacks). Shuttle bus to Orchard Rd. 547 rooms. Single S$210, double S$230, suite S$330. Recommended. *Nearest MRT* Orchard (NS line)

Orchard Parade Hotel 1 Tanglin Rd, Singapore 247905; tel: 6737 1133; fax: 6733 0242; email: ophrsv@singnet.com.sg. Recently refurbished, with entrance set back from road and well placed for shopping end of Orchard Rd (adjacent to store selling Manchester United goods and memorabilia!). Near open-air bars and restaurants. Pool, fitness area and business centre. 387 rooms. Single S$280–380, double S$320–420, suite S$400–80. *Nearest MRT* Orchard (NS line)

Orchard Hotel Singapore 442 Orchard Rd, Singapore 238879; tel: 6734 7766; fax: 6733 5482; email: orcharde@singnet.com.sg. At western end of Orchard Rd, with adjacent shopping area. Good rooms containing bathrooms with separate showers. Large and impressive ballroom. Fairly sparse pool area, fitness and business centres. 672 rooms. Single S$290–400, double S$320–430, suite S$650–1,800. *Nearest MRT* Orchard (NS line)

York Hotel 21 Mount Elizabeth, Singapore 228516; tel: 6737 0511; fax: 6735 1217; email: enquiry@yorkhotel.com.sg. In quiet area to the north of, and short walk from, Orchard Rd. Pool, fitness and business centres. Restaurants. 406 rooms. Single S$270–90, double S$290–310, suite S$460–910. *Nearest MRT* Orchard (NS line)

Crown Prince Hotel 270 Orchard Rd, Singapore 238857; tel: 6732 1111; fax: 6732 7018; email: cphs@cmihotels.com. 332 rooms. Single S$290–320, double S$310–40, suite S$600. *Nearest MRT* Somerset (NS line)

Hotel Phoenix Singapore 277 Orchard Rd, Singapore 238858; tel: 6737 8666; fax: 6732 2024; email: rsvp@phoenix.com.sg. Well positioned on busy Somerset Rd (just behind Orchard Rd) and beside Somerset MRT. Guests are primarily tourists. Fitness centre but no pool. Restaurants adjacent. 392 rooms. Single S$260–310, double S$280–330, suite S$380–680. *Nearest MRT* Somerset (NS line)

Copthorne Orchid Singapore 214 Dunearn Rd, Singapore 299526; tel: 6250 3322; fax: 6250 9292; email: roomres@orchidsing.com.sg. Some distance from Orchard Rd so shuttle bus is essential (or taxis or buses to nearest MRT stations). Spacious lobby area and helpful staff. Smallish pool at ground level in garden setting, but next to busy road. Small fitness area and business centre. Shuttle bus (hourly until early evening) to west end and centre of Orchard Rd and SunTec City. Restaurants: Palm Court (lobby level, Asian and international buffet or à la carte), Charming Garden (well-known Chinese). 457 rooms. Single S\$300–60, double S\$300–60, suite S\$400–2,000. *Nearest MRT* Newton (NS line)

Mid-range

Hotel Grand Central 22 Cavenagh Rd/Orchard Rd, Singapore 229617; tel: 6737 9944; fax: 6733 3175; email: accommodations@grandcentral.com.sg. Just off Orchard Rd, behind Le Meridien Hotel and Shopping Centre with its Kopitiam food centre in basement. Business facilities but no pool or fitness centre. 390 rooms. Single S\$190–210, double S\$210–30, suite S\$300. *Nearest MRT* Somerset (NS line)

Sloane Court 17 Balmoral Rd, Singapore 259803; tel: 6235 3311; fax: 6733 9041; email: sloane@singnet.com.sg. Small and inexpensive, with clean but basic facilities. Thirty-minute walk from Orchard Rd. 35 rooms. Single/double S\$80–100, triple S\$110. *Nearest MRT* Newton (NS line)

Garden Hotel 14 Balmoral Rd, Singapore 259800; tel: 6235 3344; fax: 6235 9730; email: garden@pacific.net.sg. Uninspiring hotel some distance from Orchard Rd and offering no shuttle bus service (so half-hour walk or taxi necessary). Small roof-top pool. Restaurant. 216 rooms. Single S\$190, double S\$210. *Nearest MRT* Newton (NS line)

Budget

South East Asia Hotel 190 Waterloo St, Singapore 187965; tel: 6338 2394; fax: 6338 3480; email: seahotel@singnet.com.sg. In middle of shopping area near Bugis Village. Clean rooms. No pool, fitness or business facilities. Restaurant. 51 rooms. Single S\$75–85, double S\$75–85, suite S\$95–110. Cash only. *Nearest MRT* Bugis (EW line)

YMCA International House 1 Orchard Rd, Singapore 238824; tel: 6336 6000; fax: 6337 3140; email: hostel@ymca.org.sg. Dull exterior, but clean and surpasses the standards of most youth hostels. The old YMCA building was used by the Japanese as an interrogation centre during World War II. Roof-top pool, sports courts, and fitness centre. Restaurant and McDonalds on ground floor. 111 rooms. Single S\$60. Recommended at this price. Popular, and thus frequently full. *Nearest MRT* Dhoby Ghaut (NS/NE interchange)

YWCA Fort Canning Lodge 6 Fort Canning Rd, Singapore 179494; tel: 6338 4222; fax: 6337 4222; email: ywca@mbox3.singnet.com.sg. At foot of Fort Canning Pk, this large, new building, with tennis courts and pool, is no ordinary youth hostel. Cheap and well located for exploring colonial and Orchard Rd shopping areas. 212 rooms. Single S\$80. Recommended at this price. *Nearest MRT* Dhoby Ghaut (NE line)

Lloyd's Inn 2 Lloyd Road, Singapore 239091; tel: 6737 7309; fax: 6737 7847; email:mail'lloydinn.com. Quiet position between Orchard Rd and River Valley Rd. Small, but very clean, rooms. Restaurant. 34 rooms. Single S\$60. *Nearest MRT* Somerset (NS line)

Metropolitan Y Lodge 60 Stevens Rd, Singapore 257854; tel: 6737 7755; fax: 6235 5528; email: marketing@mymca.org.sg. Newly renovated, with large pool. Clean, efficient, good-value accommodation. Bus ride to Scotts Rd and Orchard Rd MRT or long walk. 92 rooms. Single S$60. Recommended for this price level. *Nearest MRT* Orchard (NS line)

Where to eat

Chatterbox (Mandarin Hotel, 333 Orchard Road; tel: 6737 4411) is a coffee shop which opens 24 hours, and offers primarily local food. It is a little on the pricey side considering its rather humble setting, but the portions are healthy and the Hainanese chicken rice well worth a try.

Outside meal times, the food at the **Coffee Garden** (Shangri-la Hotel, 22 Orange Grove Road; tel: 6737 3644) consists of the usual 'coffee shop' items and, as a consequence, is not especially exciting. However, it is set amidst the hotel's well-known gardens by the swimming pool, and is a wonderful place to visit for a snack and a drink during the early hours of the morning. Open 24 hours.

Blu (Shangri-la Hotel, 24/F, 22 Orange Grove Road; tel: 6730 2598) is an innovative restaurant which combines European, American and Asian influences, and, from our experience, can arouse very different reactions in diners (ranging from 'excellent' to 'awful'). A particular speciality is the prawn and pistachio bisque. Even if the food is not to your taste, however, the vivid blue décor (complete with fabulous contemporary art), the live jazz performances and the stunning view from the top floor of the hotel (particularly after dark) should prove ample compensation. Be aware that both the food and wine are very expensive. Open Mon–Sat 19.00–22.00. The bar is open 17.00–01.00 Mon–Thu, 17.00–02.00 Fri–Sat. Both closed Sun.

The **Chang Jiang Shanghai Restaurant** (Goodwood Park Hotel, 22 Scotts Road; tel: 6730 1752) won 'Best Dining Experience' at Singapore's Tourism Awards in 1998. The *Wu Xi* spare ribs are highly recommended, and taste all the better for being eaten with the golden chopsticks that are this restaurant's trademark. Expect to pay about S$60 per head. Open daily 12.00–14.30 for lunch, 19.00–22.30 for dinner.

Displayed on the walls of the elegant **Li Bai** (Sheraton Towers, 39 Scotts Road; tel: 6737 6888) are paintings of the renowned poet after which the restaurant is named. The Cantonese food is good, with a varied and interesting specials menu and tasty *dim sum* served on opulent jade, fine bone china and silver. You should not find yourself spending any more than S$50 per person. Booking necessary. Open daily 12.00–14.30, 18.30–22.30.

Great *dim sum* – and considerably more besides, including imaginative dishes like baked snail and fried eel – can be found at **Jiang Nan Chun** (Four Seasons Hotel, 190 Orchard Boulevard; tel: 6734 1110). The art nouveau interior is surprisingly subtle and oozes class, while the service is of the very highest quality. A meal here will be correspondingly expensive, but you get what you pay for. Lunch served daily 11.30–14.30, dinner 18.00–22.00.

Au Jardin (EJH Corner House, Singapore Botanic Gardens, Cluny Road; tel: 6466 8812) is a pretty and deeply romantic French restaurant housed in a black and white bungalow in the Botanic Gardens. You will dine finely here, choosing from several fixed menus which range from a 'light' three-course lunch for under S$100 to an extravagant eight-course dinner costing the best part of S$200. Unusually for Singapore, there are only a small number of tables and booking is essential. Open for lunch Mon–Fri 12.00–14.00; for dinner Mon–Sat 19.00–21.00. Closed Sun.

Les Amis (Shaw Centre, #02-16, 1 Scotts Road; tel: 6733 2225) is lauded well beyond the shores of Singapore, and it certainly ranks among the best of the island's restaurants. The French cuisine is exquisite in taste and presentation, the pan-fried foie gras a particular favourite. Very expensive. Open Mon–Sat 12.00–14.00, 19.15–22.00. Closed Sun.

Go underground at **Pete's Place** (Grand Hyatt Hotel, 10–12 Scotts Road Basement; tel: 6738 1234), a relaxed restaurant whose brickwork and checked tablecloths (in red and blue) make it feel like a cross between a continental café and a wine cellar. Its fare is traditional Italian, and the portions are of a good size and not overly expensive in price. Open every day 11.30–14.30, 18.00–23.00.

Top Of The M (39/F Mandarin Hotel, 333 Orchard Road; tel: 6737 4411) is Singapore's tallest revolving restaurant, and the 39th-floor position affords spectacular views of the island. The location, as well as the French and Italian haute cuisine, makes it popular with businessmen, but it is also ideally suited for romantic special occasions. The exclusive dining experience is an expensive one, and you are likely to pay upwards of S$100 per person. Open daily 12.00–14.30, 18.30–22.30.

Lingzhi (Liat Towers, #05-01, 541 Orchard Road; tel: 6734 3788) is an enduringly popular Chinese vegetarian restaurant (an unusual combination) which has recently changed premises. The food is mid-range in price (likely to cost less than S$40), although wine is not served and there is no 'bring-your-own' option. Open 11.30–14.30, 18.00–21.30 every day.

If you're feeling seriously hungry, drop in to **Nadaman** (Shangri-la Hotel, 22 Orange Grove Road; tel: 6737 3644) for a *kaiseki* (traditional and decadent ten-course Japanese meal). A set dinner such as this will cost well over S$100, but, if this is a little steep, you can try a good-value mini-*kaiseki* for under S$40. Open daily 12.00–14.30, 18.30–22.30.

Food centres in the area worth trying are Scotts Picnic Place on Scotts Road (indoor), Kopitiam in the Meridien Hotel's basement, Cuppage Road (outdoor restaurants in the evening, indoor food stalls during the day), Tanglin Mall, Takashimaya Mall (food courts in the basement), and Orchard Point Mall (basement). The Newton Circus **hawker centre** is found next to the MRT station, at the point where Scotts and Bukit Timah roads meet.

Nightlife

Bar None (Singapore Marriott Hotel, 320 Orchard Road; tel: 6831 4656/4657) claims to 'bar nobody and bar nothing'. There is good live music. Happy hour 19.00–21.00.

Brix (Grand Hyatt Hotel, 10–12 Scotts Road; tel: 6738 3108) is frequented by trendy 20- and 30-somethings. It has a wine-and-whisky bar and a piano bar. Happy hour Mon–Sat 18.00–21.00.

The **Elephant Public House** (Winsland House, 165 Penang Road; tel: 6835 1110) is located in a mansion built in the middle of the Victorian reign, and is furnished with antiques. It serves good bar food, and has a very creditable selection of 30 beers, eight of which are draught. Happy hour Tue–Sun 11.00–21.00, Mon all night.

There is a cluster of bars and pubs in the pedestrianised stretch of Emerald Hill Road. **No 5 Emerald Hill Cocktail Bar** (5 Emerald Hill Road/Peranakan Place; tel: 6732 0818) is a bar and restaurant in a restored shop-house. A guitarist plays live blues and jazz in the upstairs bar, and you can also sit outside. Happy hour Tue–Sun 12.00–21.00, Sun 17.00–21.00. **Que Pasa** (7 Emerald Hill Road/Peranakan Place; tel: 6235 6626) is a quiet wine bar which serves Spanish tapas. **Ice-Cold Beer** (9 Emerald Hill Road/Peranakan Place; tel: 6735 9929), is a considerably livelier venue, with loud music and a wide choice of beers kept in ice under the bar. Happy hour is 17.00–21.00.

Muddy Murphy's (Orchard Hotel Shopping Arcade, #B1-01-06, 442 Orchard Road; tel: 6735 0400) is an Irish pub with bands playing between 20.30 and 24.30. The Guinness is on the pricey side. Happy hour 11.00–19.00.

Venom (12/F Pacific Plaza Penthouse, 9 Scotts Road; tel: 6734 7677) is a relatively new – and fairly exclusive – nightclub, on the top floor. There are regular theme nights.

What to see and do
Parks and gardens
Towards Orchard Road's western end, on the corner of Cluny and Holland roads, are the **Singapore Botanic Gardens** (Cluny Road, Singapore 259569; tel: 6471 9955). These used to be overrun with monkeys, picnickers and even snake charmers, but today they make a glorious oasis of (relative) calm, and are alone worth the trip to the island. The gardens date back almost 150 years, and have had important roles to play, both recreationally and economically, during that time. In the late 19th century, for instance, the seeds of the Brazilian rubber tree were first successfully planted here and helped give rise to the great Malayan rubber plantations. The island's more recent campaign to cultivate a 'greener' face – by planting along highways and around buildings – has been put into practice using flora from the Botanic Gardens. This is also an important centre for botanical research.

Within the 52 hectares are landscaped gardens along with an area of wilder, virgin forest unlike anything to be found in other city centres around the world. There are lakes, and lawns where outdoor orchestral concerts are sometimes held. A newer, and beautifully laid out, attraction is the **Ginger Garden**, with an informative exhibition covering the ginger family – its members include arrowroot, turmeric, chekur, edible canna, cardamon, galangal, and even bananas. Here also is the **National Orchid Garden**, where the products of the gardens' breeding programme are held. It boasts the largest collection of orchids in the world, including the national flower of Singapore, the Vanda Miss Joaquim, and a display of varieties named after famous visiting dignitaries. You can buy orchid jewellery, made by dipping real flowers into gold, at the Entrance Pavilion.

The gardens are enjoyed as much by locals as tourists and horticulturists, and they are popular with families. In the early mornings and evenings you will see joggers working out, and at weekends newly weds use the gardens as a backdrop for their bridal photos. Botanic Gardens open daily 05.00–24.00; admission free. Orchid Garden open 08.30–19.00 (latest entry 18.00); admission S$2 adult, S$1 concession.

Getting there Orchard MRT (NS line), then 20-minute walk, or bus (Nos 7, 105, 106, 123, 174) from Orchard MRT along either Orchard Boulevard (on the way) or Orchard Road (return).

Places of worship

Sri Thandayuthapani Temple (15 Tank Road), also known as **Chettiar Temple**, has a magnificent ceiling comprising 48 engraved glass panels, positioned to catch the rays of the sun at sunrise and sunset. One of the most splendid temples in Singapore (and beyond), its interior houses shrines to a range of Hindu gods. It plays a prominent role in the festivals of Thaipusam and Navarathiri (see *Chapter 3, Holidays, Celebrations and Events*, pages 90 and 96). During the former, devotees pierce their bodies with hooks and skewers in a particularly impressive (and gruesome) display of devotion.

Getting there MRT to Dhoby Ghaut (NS line), then walk south towards Penang Road and left into Clemenceau Avenue. Tank Road runs parallel to Clemenceau Avenue on the side away from Fort Canning Park.

Other places of interest

About midway down Orchard Road, just before Centrepoint, are **Peranakan Place** and **Emerald Hill**. This area was once a nutmeg plantation owned by William Cuppage, but the Seah brothers bought the land in 1901 and built houses where the Peranakans (the original Singaporean mix of Malay and Chinese people) were gathered. The five shop-houses facing Orchard Road are now shops and bars, and are collectively known as Peranakan Place.

If you turn north, up past the bars, into Emerald Hill, you will leave behind the noise and bustle of Orchard Road and see beautifully restored three-storey terraced houses that have amazing architectural details. There are lovely old Chinese blue-and-green roof tiles, wall tiles with flower designs which are typically Peranakan, intricately carved wooden doors and first-storey wooden shutters in Malay tradition, and Chinese-style gates at the entrances. Most of these houses are privately owned – and some still by Peranakan families.

Getting there MRT to Somerset (NS line) and cross Orchard Road to Peranakan Place, or take any bus down Orchard Road to the stop for Somerset.

The brown-coloured **Cathay Building** (2 Handy Road), constructed in 1939, was Singapore's first skyscraper. Its 16 storeys contained a cinema – the first to be fully air-conditioned – a luxury restaurant, 32 fashionable apartments and a hotel. It was ideally positioned to attract people from the two busiest sections of the town – Shenton Way and Orchard Road. During World War II, the building was frequently used as an air-raid shelter, with people sleeping in the cinema corridors even while shows were going on. The British Malaya Broadcasting Corporation operated from the Cathay Building until the Japanese invasion, and crowds of people often waited anxiously outside for the latest news about the war.

General Percival flew the Japanese flag from the top of the building for ten minutes on February 15 1942 as a sign that he had accepted the surrender conditions. The Japanese Broadcasting Commission then used the premises until the end of the war, after which it was the site of Admiral Lord Louis Mountbatten's headquarters before it was returned to Cathay in 1946.

Although the restaurant and hotel were closed for periods during and after the war, the cinema continued to show films throughout all these changes and only closed finally in 2000. However, the building is still there, looking rather sorry for itself, and there are plans to reopen it as a national monument.

Getting there MRT to Dhoby Ghaut (NS line), or any bus down Orchard Road to Dhoby Ghaut and walk a short way further east. The Cathay building is set back on the left.

Just beyond Le Meridien Hotel and shopping centre on Orchard Road, a large open space forms the impressive entrance to the **Istana** (*istana* means 'palace' in Malay). The gates, which are manned by guards, open on to a long avenue leading up to what is now the residence of the president of Singapore. Opposite the entrance is the small, attractive **Istana Park**, sandwiched between Orchard and Penang roads. It was designed by the Japanese landscape architect Ren Matsui, with gardens, a reflecting pool and the 16m concrete-and-steel Festival Arch.

The Istana was constructed between 1867 and 1869 by convict labour for Sir Harry St George Ord, the first governor of Singapore. In 106 acres of a former nutmeg plantation, it was built as the Government House, and was subsequently the home for successive governors. During the Japanese invasion it was badly damaged, but the governor of the time, Sir Shenton Thomas, along with his wife and servants, remained until the very last moments. On leaving, they removed the Union Jack that was kept hidden during the occupation.

In 1959, Singapore attained self-rule and when Yusof Ishak became the first local head of state he moved into Government House and renamed it the Istana. The grounds are open only five days a year – for New Year's Day, Chinese New Year, Raya Puasa, Labour Day and Deepavali. You can watch the changing of the guards on the first Sunday of every month from 17.45 to 18.15.

Getting there MRT to Dhoby Ghaut on NS line and walk back up Orchard Road, or any bus down Orchard Road.

The **Goodwood Park Hotel** (22 Scotts Road) stands in an imposing position on a hill at the northern end of Scotts Road, approached by a steep drive or flight of steps, and was listed as one of Singapore's national monuments in1989. It started life as the clubhouse for the 'Teutonia Club', a society for German or German-speaking people who met to sing national songs. When the club was first formed at the end of the 19th century, it was sited on North Bridge Road; a few months afterwards it moved to Blanche House on Mount Elizabeth. Thirty years later the membership had outgrown the building, and the castle-like clubhouse on Scotts Road was constructed.

During World War I, the Germans were considered enemy forces by the British, so the club was seized and most of the Germans sent to Australia. In 1918 the building was bought by the Manassah brothers and opened in 1922 as Club Goodwood Hall, an entertainment centre. By 1929 they had decided to turn it into a sumptuous hotel, adding rooms to the tower wing, turning houses into suites and laying out 14 tennis courts. It was named Goodwood Park Hotel and became renowned as one of Asia's finest. Senior Japanese officers were housed here during World War II, while after the war a war crimes court was established under canvas in the grounds.

Since then, the hotel has been extensively renovated and restored: in the 1950s it was the first to have a swimming pool (which is now a car park), and it even has its own hall of fame recording the names of distinguished guests who have graced its rooms over the years.

Getting there MRT to Orchard Road (NS line) and walk up Scotts Road. The hotel is on the right, after the Far East Plaza shopping centre.

LITTLE INDIA TO ARAB STREET
Little India

When he first arrived in Singapore, Raffles was accompanied by 120 Indian assistants and soldiers who settled in the Chulia, south of the river. However, by the late 19th century, there was a great influx of Indians seeking work as road builders, swamp clearers or in positions in the civil service. With the introduction of cattle farming in the fertile land around the Rochor River by rich Indians, such as a Mr Belilos from Calcutta, the Indians then began to settle in that area and the banana plantations gave way to a flourishing commercial centre surrounding Serangoon Road. Little India had arrived.

Today it is still the centre for Indian culture, commerce and leisure and is a fascinating area to explore. The five-foot covered ways fronting the shop-houses are lined with small shops whose wares spill out into the passageways (see *Shopping*, page 70). There are shops packed with colourful rolls of vivid silks and saris, jewellery shops brimming with Indian gold head-dresses, bracelets, necklaces and rings, shops selling spices whose scents fill the air, shops displaying a huge variety of Indian cakes and sweets (see box, page 119), and shops housing garland makers and fortune tellers (see box, page 116), not to mention fish-head curry restaurants serving food on palm leaves. All go

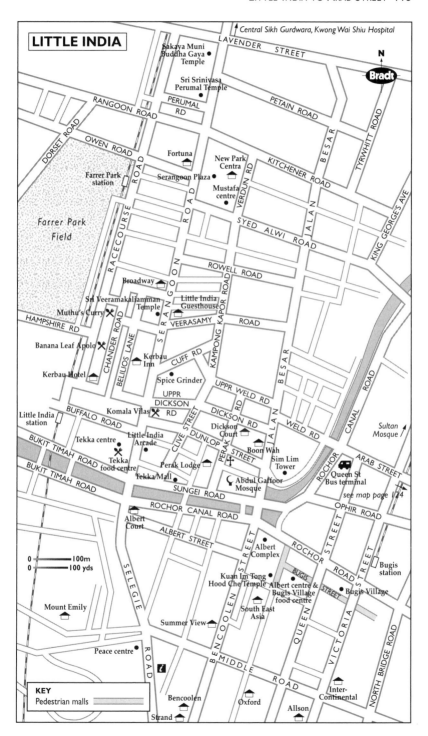

LITTLE INDIA

↑ Central Sikh Gurdwara, Kwong Wai Shiu Hospital

LAVENDER STREET

Sakaya Muni Buddha Gaya Temple ●

Sri Srinivasa Perumal Temple ●

PETAIN ROAD

N

Bradt

RANGOON ROAD

PERUMAL RD

DORSET ROAD

OWEN ROAD

Fortuna

New Park Centra

KITCHENER ROAD

BESAR

TYRWHITT ROAD

Farrer Park station

Serangoon Plaza

RACECOURSE ROAD

Mustafa centre

VERDUN RD

ALAN

KING GEORGE'S AVE

Farrer Park Field

SYED ALWI ROAD

ROWELL ROAD

Broadway ●

SERANGOON ROAD

Sri Veeramakaliamman Temple

Little India Guesthouse

KAPOR ROAD

Muthu's Curry ✕

VEERASAMY ROAD

HAMPSHIRE RD

CHANDER ROAD

Banana Leaf Apolo ✕

BELILIOS LANE

Kerbau Inn

CUFF RD

KAMPONG KAPOR

BESAR

Kerbau Hotel

Spice Grinder ●

UPPR WELD RD

CANAL ROAD

Little India station

BUFFALO ROAD

Komala Vilas ✕

UPPR DICKSON RD

DICKSON RD

WELD RD

JALAN

Sultan Mosque

BUKIT TIMAH ROAD

Tekka centre

Little India Arcade

CLIVE STREET

DUNLOP STREET

Dickson Court

Boon Wah

Sim Lim Tower

ROCHOR

ARAB STREET

BUKIT TIMAH ROAD

Tekka food centre

Perak Lodge

PERAK ROAD

Queen St Bus terminal

Tekka Mall ●

SUNGEI ROAD

Abdul Gaffoor Mosque

see map page 124

ROCHOR CANAL ROAD

Albert Court

OPHIR ROAD

ALBERT STREET

STREET

Albert Complex

ROCHOR ROAD

STREET

Bugis station

0 —— 100m
0 —— 100 yds

SELEGIE ROAD

Kuan Im Tong Hood Che Temple

BUGIS STREET

Albert centre & Bugis Village food centre

● Bugis Village

Mount Emily

BENCOOLEN STREET

South East Asia

VICTORIA STREET

Summer View ●

QUEEN STREET

Peace centre ●

ROAD

MIDDLE ROAD

NORTH BRIDGE ROAD

i

KEY
Pedestrian malls

Bencoolen

Oxford

Allson

Inter-Continental

Strand

FORTUNE-TELLERS

Interested in finding out what the future holds? Visit a fortune-teller in Little India. Usually these soothsayers will use a bird – a ring-necked parakeet, a tree sparrow, or a common or pied mynah – to help them with their craft. As the fortune-teller lays out a pack of cards, the bird is released from its tiny cage. It picks up a card with its beak before hopping back across the table and into its cage. In its choice lies your destiny. It's up to you whether you treat it as a bit of fun or subsequently live your life in a state of fevered expectation; either way, however, it makes an intriguing spectacle.

about their business accompanied by the sound of Indian music blaring from the numerous CD stores.

During the festival of Deepavali (see *Chapter 3, Holidays, Celebrations and Events*, page 97) the streets are hung with lights. Dance displays, plays and entertainment are provided at temporary theatres, market stalls abound and all head for the temples in their finest clothes. The Thaipusum festival (see page 90) sees Hindu devotees pierce their bodies with skewers, and walk from the temple of Sri Srinivasa Perumal in Serangoon Road to the Sri Thandayuthapani Temple on Tank Road.

It is worth noting that on Sundays the local Indian population throngs into the area and the streets and shops are very crowded.

Getting there

The nearest MRT station (opening at the end of 2002) is Little India on the NE line. Alternatively, take a bus (64, 65, 111, 97 or 85) from Orchard Road.

Where to stay
Luxury

New Park Hotel 181 Kitchener Rd, Singapore 208533; tel: 6291 5533; fax: 6297 2827; email: newpark@plazapacifichotels.com. On the northeast edge of Little India, this hotel is large and fairly ordinary. Free shuttle buses to Orchard Rd leave at 10.00, 13.45 and 17.45. Small pool with a few sunbeds and some shade on level 6. 3 restaurants: pool terrace (Chinese/Asian steamboat); Hai Xiang (Chinese); coffee lounge (Japanese, Chinese and Western). 531 rooms. Single S$200–20, double S$350, suite S$400–700. *Nearest MRT* Farrer Park on NE line (from end 2002)

Mid-range

Albert Court Hotel 180 Albert St, Singapore 189971; tel: 6339 3939; fax: 6339 3252; email: sales.mktg@albertcourt.com.sg; web: www.albertcourt.com.sg. A unique boutique hotel converted from Peranakan shop-houses, situated just over the canal at the south end of Serangoon Rd. It is airy and full of character, and furnished in Peranakan style (note some rooms have bigger windows than others). Currently housing 136 rooms, there is an extension planned (for late 2002 until the end of 2003)

Above left Merlion (JW)

Above right Raffles Hotel (VG)

Below Arab Street (VG)

Above left A pierced devotee during the Hindu festival of Thaipusam (STB)

Above right Lion dance (VG)

Below Dragon-boat race (STB)

to the 2-storey shop-houses on the opposite side of the courtyard (quieter) and linked with the existing hotel. No pool, but guests may use pools at Golden Landmark or Orchard Parade hotels. 2 restaurants: Shish Mahal (North Indian vegetarian); Good Chance (local and Western). 136 rooms. Single S$190–210, double S$210–30, suite S$280. Recommended – but check the state of the building works! *Nearest MRT* Little India on NE line (from end 2002)

Fortuna Hotel 2 Owen Rd, Singapore 218842; tel: 6295 3577; fax: 6294 7738; email: fortuna@singnet.co.sg. Small hotel catering mainly for Indian independent travellers. Unexciting concrete block at the northern end of Serangoon Rd, on the corner of Owen Rd. Helpful staff. No pool. 1 restaurant (Indian). 85 rooms. Single/double S$128–48, suite S$148–68. *Nearest MRT* Farrer Park on NE line (from end 2002)

Budget

Broadway Hotel 195 Serangoon Rd, Singapore 218067; tel: 6292 4661; fax: 6291 6414; email: bw030303@asianconnect.com. Ugly block on the busy Serangoon Rd, near the Sri Veeramakaliamman Temple. It is immersed in the buzz of Little India and has friendly staff. Many restaurants and food courts near by. No pool. 1 good restaurant: New Delhi (North Indian, Western and Chinese). 63 rooms. Single S$80, double S$90. FIT/group rates: single S$55++, double S$60++. *Nearest MRT* Farrer Park on NE line (from end 2002)

Dickson Court Hotel 3 Dickson Rd, Singapore 209530; tel: 6297 7811; fax: 6297 7833; email: dicksonl@magix.com.sg. A small, bright, airy and very good budget find in the middle of the conservation area. It is located near Sim Lim Tower, one of Singapore's huge electronic shopping centres. Coffee shops and restaurants very near by serving local and North and South Indian food. Recommended. No pool or restaurant. 51 rooms. Single S$60–100, double S$80–135, suite S$110–60. *Nearest MRT* Bugis (EW line)

Grandmax 51 Desker Rd, Singapore 209588; tel: 6299 3688; fax: 6292 2188; email: grandmax51@hotmail.com. This is the newest hotel in Little India, and at the time of writing had not yet even produced its own brochure. It is fairly uninspiring and could be called bleak. Opposite Serangoon Plaza and Mustafa shopping centres. 1 restaurant. 54 rooms. Single S$50, double S$55–60, suite S$80–120. Accepts cash only at present. *Nearest MRT* Farrer Park (NE line, from end 2002).

Kerbau Inn 22 Belilos Lane, Singapore 219962; tel: 6291 2291; fax: 6291 9291; email: kerbauinn@pacific.net.sg. This offers very basic accommodation, but it is cheap and clean, and every room has its own fridge. It is located very near the Sri Veeramakaliamman Temple, and the restaurants in Race Course Rd and hawker food stalls at Tekka Centre are all within easy reach. Same management as Kerbau Hotel. 49 rooms. Single/double S$60. *Nearest MRT* Little India on NE line (from end 2002)

Kerbau Hotel 54/64 Kerbau Rd, Singapore 219178; tel: 6297 6668; fax: 7297 6669. Cheap and cheerful, with no lift or in-room fridges. Near new Little India MRT, and the temples and restaurants of Little India. 31 rooms. Single/double S$50. *Nearest MRT* Little India (NE line)

Perak Lodge Guesthouse 12 Perak Rd, Singapore 208133; tel: 6299 7733; fax: 6392 0919; email: reservations@peraklodge.net. This hotel, a restored shop-house building with lots of character, is worth trying. It is a surprising find tucked away in a back street near Little India Arcade. Close to restaurants and food courts. No pool. Small restaurant/coffee shop for breakfast. 34 rooms. Single/double S$80–100, triple S$110. Recommended. *Nearest MRT* Little India (NE line)

Boon Wah 43A Jalan Basar, Singapore 2008804; tel: 6299 1466; fax: 6294 2176. This is very cheap accommodation, but adequate and clean. There are en-suite facilities, but the plumbing is a little dubious in some rooms. It stands in the back streets of Little India, behind the Little India Arcade. There are coffee shops and food outlets near by. No pool or restaurant. 37 rooms. Double S$55. *Nearest MRT* Little India (NE line)

Little India Guesthouse 3 Veerasamy Rd, Singapore 207309; tel: 6294 2866; fax: 6298 4866. Small, clean and cheap, although only 5 air-conditioned rooms. Situated near temples. Mainly Indian devotees and backpackers. 26 rooms. Single S$35, double S$40 or less. *Nearest MRT* Little India (NE line)

Where to eat

Little India has a multitude of small restaurants. The following are the best known.

For spicy, South Indian food served, of course, on banana leaves, try **Banana Leaf Apolo** (56–58 Race Course Road; tel: 6293 8682). Located in the heart of Little India, at a point midway between Rotan Lane and Hampshire Road, this restaurant is informal and unpretentious. The fish-head curry is reputed to be among the best in the country, and is mid-range in price. Note that wine is not served, although beer is. The construction of the MRT is currently affecting business. However, the owners have bought up the adjacent properties, and should be well placed for more custom when the station at Farrer Park opens at the end of 2002. Open daily 10.30–22.00.

Up the road, on the corner where Race Course Road meets Rotan Lane, stands **Muthu's Curry** (76–78 Race Course Road; tel: 6293 2389). The north Indian food is great, but the service is a bit hurried. Like Banana Leaf Apolo, it overlooks the new MRT line, so is fairly empty, but is optimistic that customers will return when work on the MRT is complete. Mid-range in price; open daily 10.00–22.00.

Komala Vilas (12–14 Buffalo Road; tel: 6293 3664) serves good vegetarian food in a café-style atmosphere. Expect to pay around S$20 per head, and note the unusually early opening time. Open daily 07.00–22.30.

The Bugis Village **hawker centre** can be found next to the MRT station at Bugis, to the east of Little India.

What to see and do
Walking tour

The best place to start is at the left-hand side of the southern end of Serangoon Road, with a visit to the **Tekka Centre**. The original market which stood here was called the K K Market, from the Malay '*kandang kerbau*', meaning 'cattle pen'. In the basement you will find a **wet-market** (so called because the floors are washed daily and are wet, as distinct from the dry floors of supermarkets) where stalls are packed with fruit, vegetables, fish, spices, crabs, prawns, chickens and other kinds of meat. This is where the locals do their daily shopping and it is a pleasure to wander through the narrow aisles looking at

SWEET SENSATIONS

There are many sweet shops in Little India, carrying large selections of gaudy Indian confectionery. The very sight sends children running to their money boxes and adults to their dentists. *Laddoos* are bright yellow sweets about the size of table-tennis balls, made from millet or gram flour and heaving with calories. Wrap yourself around some *jelabies*, which are sticky tangles of orange worms, or *pista barfi*, bright green and made from pistachio nuts. Best of all (infinitely better than the more recognised *gulab jamin*) are *rasgoolah*, heavenly white spheres that come awash with rose-flavoured syrup. If you really fancy pigging out, you can even sit at one of the tables that these shops frequently provide for customers – just don't tell the kids!

everything on display. See if you can find the black chickens, which are sold for medicinal purposes. Ensure you go in the morning, as stall holders start to pack up at lunchtime.

The floors above the wet-market are crammed with stalls selling food, clothes, electrical goods – in fact, everything you can think of – and you can bargain here. There's a hawker centre too, next to the wet-market, and you can walk up and down past stalls selling a variety of food and drink. The sweet, hot tea sold in glass mugs, with or without evaporated or condensed milk, is surprisingly refreshing in the heat of Singapore – and only costs about 70 cents!

After this, walk north up Serangoon Road to Belilos Road and the **Sri Veeramakaliamman Temple** (see page 120). This is a typical Hindu temple with its shrine for the gods, a hall for worship and a *kopuram* – tower – covered in statues of the deities and built so that it can be seen from afar. It closes between 12.30 and 16.00 daily. Remember to remove your shoes before entering (rest assured that they will still be there when you come out). Walk around the outside walls of the temple compound to see the statues of animals on top of the walls.

If you cross the road here and wander back down Serangoon Road, opposite the temple you will pass garland makers preparing the brightly coloured and beautifully scented garlands which are offered as gifts for the gods. Turn left into Cuff Road and look for one of the last spice-grinding shops, then back to Serangoon Road and left into Dunlop Street. Here you will find the **Abdul Gaffoor Mosque** (see page 121).

Returning to Serangoon Road, turn left once more and you will come to the **Little India Arcade**, which is an area of restored shop-houses. Walk inside and explore the stalls selling Indian crafts, jewellery, gifts, traditional Indian sweets and snacks, and medicines, and taste some of the wares at the food stalls. In the food court area, try the *wada* (pronounced 'waday'), which are made of flour and fried – rather like doughnuts – and eaten with curry and coconut gravies. Alternatively, try *putumayam*, (white, string-like pancakes, eaten with grated coconut and orange sugar), or *thosai* (chewy rice flour and lentil pancakes, eaten with pastes and curries), and drink hot tea made with condensed milk. Remember to eat with your right hand only; there are sinks where you can wash afterwards. Also visit the small cultural corner where you can see old pictures of the area and read about the meaning of many Indian traditions.

If you have time, continue further north along Serangoon Road to another Hindu temple, **Sri Srinivasa Perumal** (see below), and then round the next corner into Race Course Road, which runs parallel to Serangoon Road, where there is the Buddhist **Temple of a Thousand Lights** (see opposite). Be warned, however, that this is a long, hot walk!

Places of worship
Sri Veeramakaliamman Temple (Belilos Road/Serangoon Road) is a small Hindu temple built by the Bengali community in 1881, and is dedicated to Kali, the wife of Siva. It is decorated with many brightly coloured statues of gods and animals and contains the usual three main elements – a shrine, a worship hall, and a tower or *kopuram*. The *kopuram* is covered with sculptures of gods, goddesses and beasts, and is tall and thus visible from a distance to enable devotees to say their prayers without even entering the temple. The main shrine contains a jet-black statue of Kali, with many pairs of arms and hands, each carrying weaponry, and her two sons Ganesha (the elephant god) and Murugan. Tuesdays and Thursdays are holy days. As you enter, look out for the bright murals on the wall adjacent to the temple. Note that women undergoing the monthly cycle are considered unclean and forbidden from entering the temple grounds. Closed daily 12.30–16.00.

Getting there Walk north from Little India Arcade along Serangoon Road, and the temple is on the left.

Sri Srinivasa Perumal Temple (Serangoon Road) is the only Hindu temple in Singapore which is dedicated to Vishnu. Followers of Vishnu believe the god becomes incarnate in animal or human form. The temple was founded in 1855 by Narasimhaloo Naidu, a wealthy Indian businessman who donated the land on which it was built. Later the government took over its administration; in the 1960s it was renovated, and a new statue brought from India and the *kopuram* added. It has a large prayer court, and on the left is the chariot in which the deities are ceremoniously carried. On the right is a thulasi plant, a symbol of faith and womanhood. The perimeter of the temple is lined with life-size statues.

During the festival of Thaipusam (see page 90), this temple is the starting point for the procession of devotees, each of whom has his tongue pierced with skewers and his body with spikes or hooks as an act of thanksgiving or penance. Those in the procession walk the 3km carrying elaborate *kavadis*, or frames, on their shoulders as far as the Sri Thandayuthapani Temple in Tank Road. Incredibly, there is no blood lost during these acts of self-mutilation, and participants walk in a trance-like state, surrounded and supported by their families, and apparently feeling no pain. Open daily 06.30–12.00 and 18.00–21.00.

Getting there A longish walk north up Serangoon Road from the Little India Arcade. Alternatively (by the end of 2002), take the MRT to Farrer Park on the NE line, walk right to Owen Road, left into Serangoon Road. Continue as far as Perumal Road and you will find the temple on the left.

Sakaya Muni Buddha Gaya Temple (Race Course Road) is known as the Temple of a Thousand Lights because a huge, 15m statue of the seated Buddha is surrounded by 1,000 light bulbs which are switched on every time a donation is made. There is also a small statue of the reclining Buddha. The temple has a pair of enormous and very impressive lions at the door. Despite all this, it is not particularly inspiring. Open daily 08.00–16.45.

Getting there Follow the directions to Sri Srinivasa Perumal Temple (see above), walk left along Perumal Road, and right into Race Course Road. The temple will be on your left. If you want to take the bus, catch Nos 64, 65, 106 or 111 from Orchard Road which go up Serangoon Road (one way) past Little India. You will need to join these from Jalan Besar for the return journey.

The original **Abdul Gaffoor Mosque** (41 Dunlop Street) was built of wood in 1884 and was called the Shaik Abdul Gapore Mosque. By 1884 it had become one of Singapore's landmarks and Abdul Gaffoor was given permission to build a new mosque on the same site in 1887. The small, brick-built mosque was completed in 1910 and contains the family tree of Muslim prophets. The beautiful, stained-glass cupola is supported by pillars in a Roman/Saracen style, and the whole cream-coloured building, with its dark green ornamentation, is a blend of Arabic and Renaissance architecture. The central part was closed for renovation during 2002, but it is due to reopen by the end of the year. When visiting, remember to observe temple etiquette by covering your legs and taking off your shoes.

Getting there Walk north up Serangoon Road past Little India Arcade to Dunlop Street, and turn right to the end of the street.

The **Central Sikh Gurdwara** (Towner Road) is to the north of Little India, and was built to celebrate the 518th anniversary of the founder of Sikhism, Guru Nanak. There are around 15,000 Sikhs in Singapore, and this is their main centre of worship. The gurdwara received an architectural design award in 1986.

Getting there Either take a taxi to the junction of Towner Road and Serangoon Road, or take an SBS bus (Nos 64, 65, 106 or 111) from Orchard Road up Serangoon Road, and alight outside the Kwong Wai Shiu Hospital. It is a short walk from here.

MY FAVOURITE PART OF SINGAPORE
Andrew Rudd

Little India: possibly the most colourful and exciting quarter in Singapore, and without doubt my favourite. The Indian society resulted from the landing of Sir Stamford Raffles in 1819, arriving with a number of Indian aides who first settled in the area around Chulia Street. As cattle rearing expanded near the Rochor River, Little India shifted to its present location, centred by Serangoon Road.

My travelling companion and myself were lucky enough to be in Singapore during the run up to Deepavali, the Hindu 'Festival of Lights', which celebrates the triumph of good over evil and normally falls between October and November. The festival only lasts two days, but the preparations begin weeks in advance.

As we neared Serangoon Road for the first time, it was instantly obvious that we'd arrived. The road was strikingly colourful, with buildings so much more interesting than those to be found elsewhere in Singapore. Such sights encouraged us to look further and discover more. Streamers and banners littered the thoroughfare; lights were strung between street posts and people were busily cleaning and decorating. We fought our way along the narrow footpath, peeking into different shops along the road, many apparently dedicated to gold jewellery while others sold more general goods. Every few footsteps a strong aroma would strike us, begging to be investigated, and usually leading to small restaurants where locals and tourists alike feasted on delicious Indian meals.

One of the best things about Little India is that it is almost impossible to

Shopping centres
The following shopping centres are located in this area: Tekka Centre, Serangoon Plaza, Mustafa Centre, Tekkamal (opposite the Tekka Centre and opening at the end of 2002) and Sim Lim Tower.

Arab Street and the Kampong Glam
In the 1823 plan for Singapore, Raffles assigned areas to the north of the Singapore River to the Arabs and to the Malayan Sultan of Singapore and his followers. Arab seamen had traded in the Indian Ocean for hundreds of years before the founding of Singapore, but when the free port was established they left their bases in Indonesia and the British Protectorate of Arabia and Hadramut and moved to the island.

Temenggong Abdul Rahman, the island's chief, and Sultan Hussain, Shah of Jahore, were granted the use of the Kampong Glam for their residence. *Kampong* means 'village' in Malay, and the area was named after the glam tree which grew there, and whose bark and oil the Buginese and Malays would use to caulk their ships and make medicine. Hussain built a palace (*istana* in Malay) and next to it the original Sultan Mosque between 1824 and 1826.

explore it all. A walk down Serangoon Road gives an indication of what lies hidden in small alleys, but the main road is just a front, the location of the intricately carved and extravagantly decorated temples. The real charm lies off the beaten track between and behind the shabby buildings, brimming with character, and inspiring curiosity. To experience the area properly it is essential to investigate the side streets and not to be put off by a lifeless-looking road. If you open your eyes, it is a window to a fantastically interesting way of life.

By abandoning Serangoon Road we stumbled into the haggling world of a bustling market. The smells of various spices and food stalls wafted around as we walked, fighting our way around the tables and squeezing past people busy arranging prices for bizarre vegetables or bags of seemingly deadly spices. The paths were dirty, boxes were strewn everywhere and random pieces of bright material hung from all available railings. But there was something strangely reassuring in the fact that, in such a modern city, with skyscrapers dominating the landscape, there is still a place that remains so culturally rich. It's a stark contrast to the supremely clean, and at times characterless, CBD; this small enclave attempts to encapsulate the essence of the population's homeland, recreating it and keeping tradition alive.

Staying in Little India is another great experience. It is both fascinating and rewarding to fully immerse yourself in the place, and absorb the culture it has to offer. We stayed on Veerasamy Road in a perfectly decent guesthouse, learning more from that brief stop than from any other visit. My only regret is that we couldn't spend more time there. An absolute must see.

The Islamic influence in Singapore – which began in the 15th century when Malays first occupied the island, and continued in the 19th century with the settling of wealthy Arab traders on land in the area surrounding Arab Street – meant that this whole region became a centre for the Muslim community. Surrounding roads have names like Baghdad Street, Bussorah Street, Kandahar Street, Haji Lane and Shaik Madrash Lane, stemming from the time when Singapore was the primary departure point for pilgrims from east Asia bound for Mecca. Many shops still trade in *haj* supplies such as prayer rugs and skullcaps.

Today the shops on Arab Street display the cultural items of the island's Muslim community, and sell batik, lace, silk, rugs, brassware and jewellery, while cane, straw, palm-leaf ware and baskets spill out on to the walkways. In the streets around you can find all types of Muslim or *halal* food, from crispy *roti prata* (a tossed and lightly fried flaky bread) to delicious, piping hot *murtabak* (a *prata* filled with meat and vegetable, or vegetable alone). Both are served with curry sauce.

It is best to visit the area early as most shops close after 17.00.

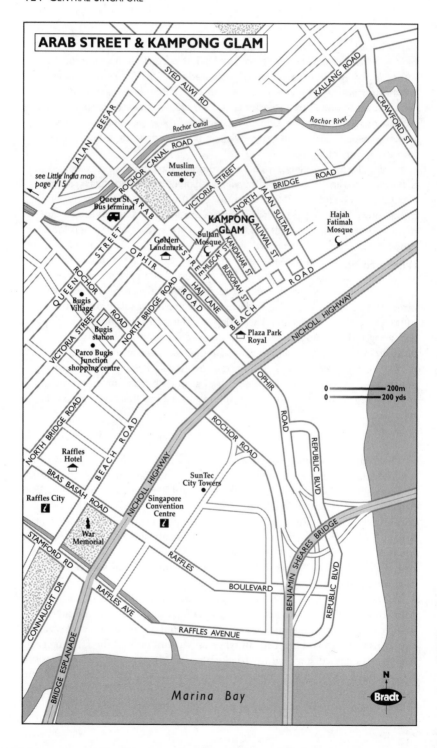

ARAB STREET & KAMPONG GLAM

Where to stay
Luxury
Golden Landmark Hotel 390 Victoria St, Singapore 188061; tel: 6297 2828; fax: 6298 2038; email: landmark@mbox3.singnet.com.sg; web: www.goldenlandmark.com.sg. This is a large hotel, whose Arabic-style architecture is reflected in its Moorish arched windows. It is located very near the Sultan Mosque. Swimming pool. 1 restaurant: Landmark Café (local and Western food). 393 rooms. Single S$220–80, double S$240–300, suite S$500. *Nearest MRT* Bugis (EW line)
Plaza Hotel 7500A Beach Rd, The Plaza, Singapore 199591; tel: 6298 0011; fax: 6296 3600; email: plazahtl@mbox2.singnet.com.sg. At the eastern end of Arab St, this is a large hotel with a pool area landscaped in Balinese style. 3 restaurants: Sichuan Dou Hua Seafood (Chinese), Café Plaza (international) and a coffee lounge. 350 rooms. Single S$270–360, double S$270–370, suite S$390–570. *Nearest MRT* Bugis (EW line)

Where to eat
There are various small Muslim and *halal* restaurants in the streets near the Sultan Mosque (see below), selling *murtabak* and other local food.

What to see and do
Places of worship
The original **Sultan Mosque** (North Bridge Road) was built in 1824, thanks to a grant of S$3000 from Sir Stamford Raffles. When North Bridge Road was extended in 1925, it had to be diverted around the mosque, which accounts for the road's kink!

By its centenary year in 1924, the original mosque had become too small for the expanding Muslim community and, as it had also fallen into a state of disrepair, the trustees approved a plan to build a new mosque. The present building took four years to complete and was designed by Denis Santry, who combined a mix of Persian, Moorish, Turkish and classical themes to create its Islamic-Saracenic style, including domes, minarets and balustrades. With its large golden dome, and a prayer hall that can accommodate 5,000 people, it is an imposing place and the principal mosque in Singapore. Sultan Ali, the Sultan of the Faithful, is buried here. He was the grandson of Sultan Hussain, the signatory of the original treaty signed with Raffles in 1819 (see *History*, page 14).

During the holy month of Ramadan (see *Chapter 3, Holidays, Celebrations and Events*, page 97), *tarawih* prayers are performed, and in the evenings food stalls in Bussorah Street sell traditional Malay foods to the local Muslims who are breaking their daily fast. During the festival of Hari Raya Haji (see page 92), sheep and goats are ritually slaughtered as sacrifices and the meat is given to the poor and deserving. The main entrance is in Muscat Street, and the old shop-houses in the area have been restored.

Getting there Take the MRT to Bugis (EW line). Walk east along Rochor Road, left into North Bridge Road, and cross over Arab Street.

Hajjah Fatimah Mosque (4001 Beach Road) is the only mosque in Singapore named after a female. Hajjah Fatimah was a wealthy Malayan woman from Malacca who married a Bugis sultan from the Celebes. It was built in 1845 and, while its minaret is in Malaccan style, the spire resembles the tower and spire on the second Church of St Andrew. The building has Doric pilasters, Chinese glazed parapet grills and Malayan house features – an amazing mix of styles. Interestingly, the building has an undeniably British-Victorian look.

Getting there Take the MRT to Lavender (EW line), walk south down Victoria Street, left into Jalan Sultan and left again into Beach Road. Because they are close to each other, you could combine a visit here with one to the Sultan Mosque. After paying a visit to the latter, walk along Arab Street to Beach Road and turn left towards the Hajjah Fatimah Mosque.

Bugis Street

Between Arab Street (to the northeast) and the city centre lies Bugis Street. The first Bugis settlers arrived in Singapore in 1820 from the Riau islands. Originally allocated land in the Kampong Glam by Raffles, they later established themselves in an area then known as Kampong Bugis, which stood on the edge of the Rochor River, near where Kallang Bridge is today.

Over the years, this became notorious as the colourful haunt of transvestites and prostitutes (and the soldiers and sailors who sought their services). Hawker stalls here did a roaring trade, providing food long into the night for characters who kept unusual hours. During the early 1960s, the scene started to change. By the 1990s, the old shop-houses had been demolished, and Bugis Junction was built in 1995. The area is now made up of offices, restaurants and a shopping centre – very different from the Bugis Street of the past, before the arrival of the MRT. The old streets are covered by a glass roof.

Bugis Village, across Victoria Road, teems with market stalls displaying gifts, souvenirs, clothes, watches and jewellery. Bargains can be sought here. There's also a good food centre – the Albert Centre. It is best visited in the evenings, when the whole place comes alive.

In the pedestrian mall at the northern end of Waterloo Street, on the far side of the food centre, is the **Kuan Im Tong Hood Che Temple**. This was first built in 1884 and is a very good example of Chinese temple architecture. Its flower sellers now offer lotus flowers to the thousands of temple devotees who arrive daily to pray to the Goddess of Mercy. It is busiest on the eve of Chinese New Year, when the temple stays open all night and the street is packed.

Getting there MRT to Bugis Street.

CITY CENTRE, COLONIAL AREA AND MARINA AREA

In Raffles' plan for Singapore, Fort Canning Hill was set aside for military use, the Padang area for the colonial government and Beach Road for the European settlers. These days, the buildings around the Padang are the only remaining

Singaporean examples of the colonial appetite during the 1920s for grand and imposing structures, while land reclamation has had the effect of moving the area further and further from the sea.

For newcomers to the island, it is difficult to imagine that Raffles Hotel once overlooked the sea and that Beach Road really did run alongside the beach. The modern structures of SunTec City and the towering grand new hotels in the Marina area now block the sea and its ships from view – except from the elevated heights of some hotel windows.

In 1825, Beach Road held 20 large seaside houses – in fact its Chinese name was 'Twenty House Street'. By the 1880s, however, these houses were being transformed into hotels or eating places to cater for the increasing numbers of people coming to the island, and when the process of land reclamation distanced the road from the sea it also became a less fashionable place to live.

The rapid land reclamation programme has continued to alter the landscape of this area. As recently as the late 1990s, for instance, one could look out from the Padang and Esplanade Park over a flat area of reclaimed land towards the sea. Now the new Esplanade – Theatres on the Bay Arts Centre (see *Arts and entertainment*, pages 73–4), due to open towards the end of 2002, stands in this position.

Getting there
Take the MRT to City Hall (NS/EW interchange). Alternatively, any bus that goes down Orchard and Bras Basah roads towards Chinatown will pass through this area.

City centre
Where to stay
Super-luxury
Carlton Hotel Singapore 76 Bras Basah Rd, Singapore 189558; tel: 6338 8333; fax: 6339 6866; email: RoomReservations@Carlton.com.sg. Recently refurbished and good position near Singapore Art Museum, CHIJMES and colonial area. Main pool and children's pool, fitness centre and jacuzzi, business centre. Good *dim sum* Chinese restaurant. 623 rooms. Single S$330–80, double S$350–400, suite S$480–1,500. *Nearest MRT* City Hall (NS/EW interchange)

Hotel Inter-Continental Singapore 80 Middle Rd, Singapore 188966; tel: 6338 7600; fax: 6338 7366; email: singapore@interconti.com. Attractively renovated art deco shop-houses backed by high block. Good rooms and bathrooms (shop-house rooms are more expensive). Roof-top pool with jacuzzi, fitness centre and business centre. Near Bugis Village and Parco shopping centre. 406 rooms. Single S$440, double S$440, suite S$600–4,000. *Nearest MRT* Bugis (EW line)

Hotel Rendezvous Singapore 9 Bras Basah Rd, Singapore 189559; tel: 6336 0220; fax: 6337 3773; email: reservations@rendezvous.com.sg. Good position (at corner of Bras Basah Rd) for Fort Canning Pk and within walking distance of CHIJMES and colonial area. Pool and business centre. Restaurant, and near local coffee houses. 300 rooms. Single S$300–80, double S$330–410, suite S$480–800. *Nearest MRT* Dhoby Ghaut (NS line)

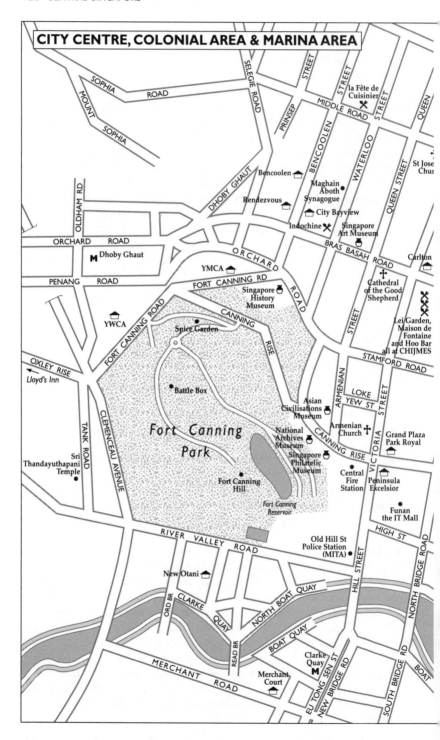

CITY CENTRE, COLONIAL AREA & MARINA AREA

SOPHIA ROAD

MOUNT SOPHIA

SELEGIE ROAD

PRINSEP STREET

MIDDLE ROAD

STREET

STREET

QUEEN

la Fête de Cuisinier

BENCOOLEN STREET

WATERLOO STREET

QUEEN STREET

St Jose Chu

DHOBY GHAUT

OLDHAM RD

Bencoolen

Maghain Aboth Synagogue

Rendezvous

City Bayview

Indochine

Singapore Art Museum

BRAS BASAH ROAD

Carlton

ORCHARD ROAD

M Dhoby Ghaut

ORCHARD ROAD

Cathedral of the Good Shepherd

PENANG ROAD

YMCA

FORT CANNING RD

STREET

Lei Garden, Maison de Fontaine and Hoo Bar all at CHIJMES

Singapore History Museum

FORT CANNING ROAD

YWCA

CANNING RISE

Spice Garden

STAMFORD ROAD

OXLEY RISE

Lloyd's Inn

Battle Box

ARMENIAN STREET

LOKE YEW ST

Asian Civilisations Museum

Armenian Church

Grand Plaza Park Royal

TANK ROAD

CLEMENCEAU AVENUE

Fort Canning Park

National Archives Museum

Singapore Philatelic Museum

CANNING RISE

VICTORIA STREET

Sri Thandayuthapani Temple

Fort Canning Hill

Fort Canning Reservoir

Central Fire Station

Peninsula Excelsior

Funan the IT Mall

RIVER VALLEY ROAD

HIGH ST

Old Hill St Police Station (MITA)

NORTH BRIDGE ROAD

New Otani

ORD BR

CLARKE QUAY

NORTH BOAT QUAY

HILL STREET

READ BR

BOAT QUAY

Clarke Quay M

Merchant Court

MERCHANT ROAD

EU TONG SEN ST

NEW BRIDGE RD

SOUTH BRIDGE RD

BOAT

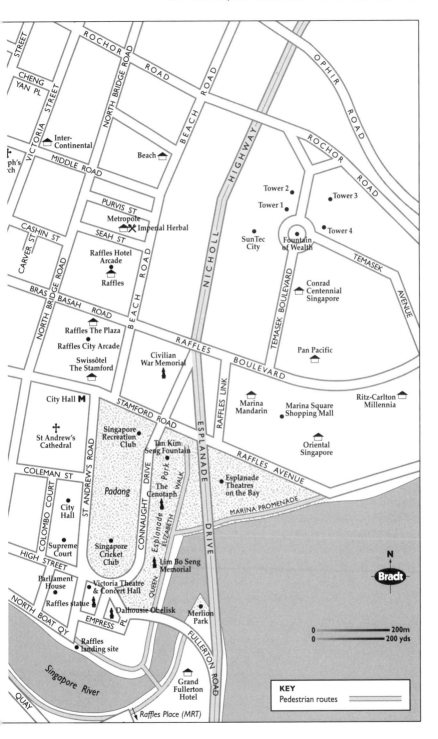

KEY
Pedestrian routes

0 _____ 200m
0 _____ 200 yds

Raffles Hotel 1 Beach Rd, Singapore 189673; tel: 6337 1886; fax: 6339 7650; email: raffles@raffles.com; web: www.raffleshotel.com. The most famous hotel in Singapore, with superb suites and facilities – but at a price. Impressive approach lined with frangipani trees, doorman in magnificent costume and spacious entrance lobby with beautiful central floral displays. In-room computer ports, and pool and business centre. Excellent restaurants within the hotel and Raffles Arcade: Raffles Grill (French), Tiffin Room (curry buffet and high tea), Bar and Billiard Room (buffet lunch, high tea and Sunday brunch), Raffles Courtyard (alfresco Mediterranean, with open grill and live music and dancing in the evening), Ah Tengh's Bakery (snacks), Seah Street Deli (American), a Tapas Bar, Doc Cheng's (trans-ethnic), Empress Room (Cantonese). Bars: Long Bar and Bar Indochine. 103 rooms. Suite S$650+. Recommended if you can afford it. *Nearest MRT* City Hall (NS/EW interchange)

Raffles The Plaza, Singapore 2 Stamford Rd, Singapore 178882; tel: 6338 8585; fax: 6338 2862; email: emailus.plaza@raffles.com. Previously the Westin Plaza, this newly upgraded hotel has a central position at City Hall. Large and impersonal entrance lobby, but impressive rooms, all with views of the harbour, city skyscrapers or colonial area. Amazing modern bathroom fittings. Pool, business centre and computer ports in rooms. Restaurant: Prego (Italian). 769 rooms. Single S$340–400, Suite S$600–1,700. Recommended, but expensive. *Nearest MRT* City Hall (NS/EW interchange)

Swissôtel, The Stamford, Singapore 2 Stamford Rd, Singapore 178882; tel: 6338 8585; fax: 6338 2682; email: emailus.singapor@swissotel.com. Previously The Westin Stamford. The tallest hotel in Singapore, upgraded and re-decorated at the end of 2001 under the Raffles group. Spacious – although bare – entrance lobby with coffee area, but superb views of the harbour area, city business area or colonial area from the luxurious and well-fitted rooms. Good pool, business centre and in-room computer ports. Restaurants: on 71st and 72nd floors (with fantastic views on a clear day of Singapore, Malaysia and Indonesia), Equinox (Asian buffet lunch, high tea and à-la-carte French in the evening, with views of Boat Quay and the skyscrapers), Jaan (French and expensive), New Asia (bar and grill, local foods), Jazz 70, and City Space. Introbar (drinks and *dim sum*), on ground floor beside the lift to the top floors (which takes a full 20 seconds), is a good meeting place. 1,263 rooms. Single S$340–400, double S$340–400, suite S$600–1,700. *Nearest MRT* City Hall (NS/EW interchange)

Grand Plaza Park Royal 10 Coleman St, Singapore 179809; tel: 6336 3456; fax: 6339 9311; email: grandplaza@plazapacifichotels.com. Stark, marble-clad building with more friendly interior. Pool and jacuzzi, fitness centre and business centre. Two restaurants. 330 rooms. Single S$330–50, double S$330–50, suite S$600–1,200. *Nearest MRT* City Hall (NS/EW interchange).

Mid-range

Beach Hotel 95 Beach Rd, Singapore 189699; tel: 6336 7712; fax: 6336 7713; email: bhotel@singnet.com.sg. Ugly building but inexpensive, clean rooms. Not far from SunTec City and short walk from colonial area. 33 rooms. Single S$90. *Nearest MRT* Bugis (EW line)

The City Bayview Hotel Singapore 30 Bencoolen St, Singapore 189621; tel: 6337 2882; fax: 6338 2880; email: bayviews@mbox4.singnet.com.sg. Friendly staff, small rooms. Reasonably priced and well placed for attractions in city and colonial area. Roof-top pool. Restaurant. 131 rooms. Single S$115–25, double S$125–35, suite S$170–80. *Nearest MRT* Dhoby Ghaut (NS/NE interchange)

Peninsula Excelsior Hotel 5 Coleman St, Singapore 179804; tel: 6337 2200; fax: 6339 3847; email: pehbizcentre@ytchotels.com.sg. Originally two separate hotels, recently refurbished and combined. Well placed for colonial sites and near Funan, the IT shopping centre. Pool, fitness centre, business centre. Restaurant. 578 rooms. Single S$220–40, double S$240–60, suite S$400–1,400. *Nearest MRT* City Hall (NS/EW interchange)

Metropole Hotel 41 Seah St, Singapore 188396; tel: 6336 3611; fax: 6339 3610; email: metropole@metrohotel.com. Small, inexpensive and basic. Near Beach Rd, Raffles and SunTec City. 54 rooms. Single S$92–124, double S$98–136. *Nearest MRT* City Hall (NS/EW interchange).

Budget
Hotel Bencoolen 47 Bencoolen St, Singapore 189626; tel: 6336 0822; fax: 6336 2250; email: bencoolen@pacific.net.sg. Small, basic, clean and cheap hotel near to Bras Basah Rd. Small pool on 2nd floor. Complementary breakfast at coffee shop outside. 74 rooms. Single S$65, double S$85. *Nearest MRT* Dhoby Ghaut (NS/NE interchange)

Where to eat
La Fête du Cuisinier (161 Middle Road; tel: 6333 0917), on the corner of Middle Road and Waterloo Street, was originally a chapel with a courtyard and retains the latter to create a charming and intimate setting. The furnishings are sumptuous, with gold leaf on the ceiling, crystal chandeliers, Victorian mirrors, oriental carpets and an extravagant landscape mural. The French Creole cooking is nicely presented, and includes dishes of crayfish, large oysters, duck, chicken and steak imported from America. Allow for about S$100 per person for three courses. Open Mon–Sat 12.00–14.00, 19.00–22.30. Closed Sun.

Indochine (42 Waterloo Street; tel: 6333 5003) is located at the Action Theatre, an informal dinner performance venue. There is a comfortable and romantic outdoor eating area, candle-lit at night, and set with Buddhas and tapestries that conjure a Vietnamese/Laotian atmosphere. As the name suggests, the fare is Indochinese, and there is an impressive range of main courses. Budget for S$40–50. Open daily 12.00–15.00, 18.00–23.00. Chinatown's Club Street holds a sister branch, and there is a cheaper café, **Siem Reap**, in Holland Village.

The **Imperial Herbal Restaurant** (3/F Metropole Hotel, 41 Seah Street; tel: 6337 0491), to the north of Raffles, employs a resident herbalist who, if you wish, will give you a brief medical check and suggest the dishes best suited to enhance your mental and physical health. Among the restorative tonics available is deer penis wine, and scorpion is also on the menu. Expect to pay around S$40 a head; it is advisable to book. Open daily 11.30–14.30 for lunch, 18.30–22.30 for dinner.

Enjoy succulent Cantonese cuisine at **Lei Garden** (30 Victoria Street, #01-24, CHIJMES; tel: 6339 3822) in a modern, sophisticated setting complete with large tanks of fish. There is a healthy selection of dishes, including legendary *dim sum* and good vegetarian options. The Peking duck is to die for. Expect to pay around S$50. Open 11.30–15.00, 18.00–23.00.

Maison de Fontaine (30 Victoria Street, #01-26/27, Caldwell House, CHIJMES; tel: 6336 0286) has cultivated a French rustic feel, and also has an outdoor area. Generous portions of French cuisine. Expect to pay about S$60 per person for three courses from the à-la-carte menu; set menus start at the S$40 mark. Open 12.00–14.30, 18.30–24.00.

The famous **Raffles Grill** (Raffles Hotel, 1 Beach Road; tel: 6331 1611) captures the colonial feel of a bygone era, with vast window drapes and rows of chandeliers. Smoked salmon and suckling pig are two specialities, and underline the restaurant's reputation for fine dining at its very finest. The range of wines on offer is extraordinary. Unsurprisingly, such quality comes at a price, and a meal here is likely to set you back considerably more than S$100; if you can afford to splash out, however, the experience is worth the expense. You will need to book. Open Mon–Fri 12.00–14.00, and daily 19.00–22.00.

Also found at Raffles, on the ground floor, is the **Tiffin Room** (Raffles Hotel, 1 Beach Road; tel: 6331 1612), where you can eat amid classic Victorian splendour. There is an à-la-carte menu, but the place is most noted for its tiffin curry buffet. It is good but, unsurprisingly given its renown, you pay a lot for what you get – S$35 for lunch or S$45 for dinner. T-shirts and shorts are prohibited, and you will need to book. Open daily 12.00–14.00, 19.00–22.00.

Enjoy breathtaking views over the river as it passes Boat Quay and the skyscrapers of the CBD at **Equinox** (70/F Swissôtel The Stamford, 2 Stamford Road; tel: 6431 6156) on the 70th floor. Buffet lunch, high tea and à-la-carte dinner available. Open daily 12.00–14.30, 18.30–22.30.

Prego (Raffles The Plaza, 2 Stamford Road; tel: 6431 5156) is very popular, and has a bustling yet relaxed atmosphere. The Italian fare is good, the thin-crust pizzas especially so, and moderately priced. Open 11.30–14.30 for lunch, 18.30–22.30 for dinner. Booking recommended. There is also a drinks and snack bar, serving during the afternoon and in the evening until after midnight.

Inagiku (Raffles The Plaza, 2 Stamford Road; tel: 6338 8585) is divided between several sections serving different types of Japanese food. It is best to choose one of the speciality rooms, where the ambience and service are better than in the main dining room. The food is excellent – *sashimi* at its best – and the presentation impeccable. It is also very expensive. Open daily 12.00–14.30, 18.30–22.30.

Patara (Raffles The Plaza, 2 Stamford Road; tel: 6339 1488) offers good-quality and reasonably priced Thai food in a comfortable setting whose centrepiece is a groaning dessert buffet table. Open 12.00–14.30, 18.00–22.00. There is a sister restaurant in Tanglin Mall, on Tanglin Road.

SINGAPORE SLING

If you fancy making your own Singapore Sling – as originally conceived in 1915 by Ngiam Tong Boon in the Long Bar at Raffles – the recipe consists of:

2 measures gin
1 measure cherry brandy
1 measure fresh orange, lemon and pineapple juices
drop of angostura bitters
drop of Cointreau

Shake well with ice, and serve the drink in a tall glass garnished with pineapple and a cherry.

There is a Kopitiam **food centre** on Bras Basah Road, near the Singapore Art Museum.

Nightlife

The **Bar and Billiard Room** (Raffles Hotel, 1 Beach Road; tel: 6337 1886) is a place to have a drink before moving on elsewhere. Its atmosphere is relaxed, and you can play billiards on one of the two original tables or play a tune on the piano. Jazz is played in the evening. A tiger was found – and duly shot – hiding under the Billiard Room in 1902. Open 11.30–24.00 daily. The famous **Long Bar**, where the Singapore Sling was first invented (see box above), is also in Raffles Hotel. One quirky feature is that customers are provided with peanuts and are encouraged to discard the shells on the floor. There is no dress code.

Hu'u Bar (Singapore Art Museum, 71 Bras Basah Road; tel: 6338 6828) is located in the art museum, and is popular during the afternoon. In the evenings it attracts the younger, trendier set.

Paulaner Brauhaus (9 Raffles Avenue; tel: 6883 2572) specialises in good beer, and serves German cuisine. Happy hour 11.30–19.00.

Somerset's Bar (3/F Raffles The Plaza, 2 Stamford Road; tel: 6338 8585) is named after Somerset Maugham, the English novelist and playwright, and features live jazz by established overseas musicians. Happy hour 17.00–20.00.

China Jump Bar and Grill (Fountain Court, #B1-07/08, 30 Victoria Street, CHIJMES; tel: 6338 9388) has won the Singapore Tourism Board's award for Nightspot of the Year in the past, and, as a consequence, there are frequently queues for admission. It serves unexciting American food, but after 22.00 the dining area is cleared and becomes a dance floor. There is a 'dentist chair' where patrons have spirits poured into their mouths directly from the bottle. Smart dress code.

What to see and do: a walking tour

The city centre, as with the colonial and marina areas, is best visited on foot. The following sites of interest are arranged as part of a walking tour that takes about 2½ hours (excluding time spent visiting the museums). It starts at City Hall MRT (NS and EW interchange); exit through City Hall shopping mall towards Bras Basah Road and Raffles. It concludes by the old Hill Street Police Station near Clarke Quay, where you could have a bite to eat before heading for Clarke Quay MRT (new NE line).

Raffles Hotel
The world-famous hotel at 1 Beach Road began life in a small house facing the sea and belonging to a Captain and Mrs George Julius Dare. In 1870 they started to use their home as a 'tiffin room' for the many travellers coming to the area. Tiffin was the name for the midday meal, consisting of several small dishes – the packed lunches of the day – that Indian and Sri Lankan workers took with them to work.

The Sarkies brothers built a small hotel next door in 1887, eventually taking over the Dares' establishment. After adding wings, the French-Renaissance-style building opened as Raffles Hotel on November 18 1896, with a tiffin room on the site of the Dares' house.

The hotel became increasingly popular. The last tiger in Singapore was shot in the bar in 1902 (see page 133), and in 1903 Ngiam Tong Boon created a gin-based cocktail which he called the 'Singapore Sling' (see page 133). During the depression of the 1930s, however, the Sarkies lost ownership and the hotel passed into new hands.

The hotel was used as accommodation for top Japanese officers during the occupation. After the war, it reverted back to a hotel, and then struggled to survive as competing establishments sprang up in Singapore. The threat of demolition hung over it for a while, but in 1987 it was listed as a national monument. It closed in 1989 for restoration and refurbishment, before reopening in 1991 and cementing its reputation as one of the island's most prestigious places to stay.

CHIJMES
CHIJMES (pronounced 'chimes'), or the Convent of Holy Infant Jesus, is opposite the Cathedral of the Good Shepherd (see opposite), on the corner of Victoria Street and Bras Basah Road. During the 19th century it was a convent, before being redeveloped into the site of shops, art galleries, bars and restaurants which it is now. As a result, the building features a curious blend of modern restorative and classical architecture. Inside, a neo-Gothic chapel (added in the early 20th century) displays some stunning stained glass and frescos. The complex also contains Caldwell House, the oldest free-standing building in Singapore, which was designed by George Coleman, the architect responsible for other prominent structures like the Coleman Bridge (see page 157) and Parliament House (see page 143). There is an attractive sunken forecourt and pleasing waterfalls and fountains. Shops open 11.00–22.00, restaurants 11.00–late.

Getting there MRT to City Hall (NS/EW interchange), or bus (Nos 7, 14 or 16) from Orchard Road.

GRAND FOOTSTEPS
Hannah Postgate

It seems fitting that Sir Stamford Raffles be immortalised in Singapore's history past and present, and in what better way than arguably the world's most famous hotel? Gone are the days of sitting in the Long Bar of Raffles Hotel and enjoying the sunset over the harbour with a gin and tonic. Nowadays the hotel has only skyscrapers for a view, as the city wades further and further into the sea. However, Raffles – the man and the hotel – continue to be enduring symbols of Singapore.

It was the man's vision for this small backwater in the Straits of Johore that allowed Singapore to become the giant it is today. Acting on behalf of the British East India Company, Raffles saw its potential as a trading base for operations in the region. The company annexed the land in 1819 and bought the entire island from the Sultan of Sumatra in 1824. Raffles realised his vision for the city in a few short years and the population grew to a staggering 81,000 by 1860.

The Raffles Hotel bears the name of the city's founding father and was opened in 1887 by the Armenian Sarkies brothers. It quickly became the celebrated sanctuary of the chattering classes and hastened the rise of the swinging scene for which Singapore became famous. This playground for wealthy Europeans lasted until World War II, with imported pastimes from home such as tennis, cricket and horse racing.

Originally little more than a sprawling bungalow, Raffles Hotel has grown into its colonial stature over the years. It has become, not only architecturally but also culturally, a building of great importance. With few 19th-century hotels of this kind still in use today, Raffles was declared a national monument in 1987 and was fully restored in 1991. The Sarkies brothers built a smaller hotel, also renowned for its inimitable style, called The Strand in Rangoon, Burma, or Myanmar, as the country is known now. The properties have lost some of their colonial charm and faded grandeur through their rather over-zealous refurbishment.

I still like to imagine myself sitting in the same chair my grandfather sat in at Raffles while he took afternoon tea in 1941. For a glimpse of its grandiose past, go to the museum on the third floor which has a collection of photographs taken over the last hundred years. It conjures up sounds of gently whirring ceiling fans and the baby grand wafting up from the bar below.

Cathedral of the Good Shepherd
The oldest Roman Catholic church in the country, the Cathedral of the Good Shepherd (4 Queen Street) was completed in 1847 and is listed as a national monument. It is also home to the Archbishop of Singapore. Its conception was a fraught one. A dispute arose between two architects, J T

Thomson and D L Sweeney, each of whom wanted to design the cathedral. Thomson eventually prevailed, although his plans were considerably more expensive than those of his rival. A year later, a third architect, Charles Dyce, added a tower and a spire.

Getting there MRT to City Hall (NS and EW interchange), walk past CHIJMES and cross Victoria Street

Singapore Art Museum
The art museum (71 Bras Basah Road; tel: 6332 3222) is housed in a magnificent colonial building, formerly a Roman Catholic boys' school called St Joseph's Institution. The collection here comprises a mixture of contemporary and traditional works by artists throughout Southeast Asia. There is also a display of 20th-century art on large television monitors: it is interesting to note the differences between the works of local artists and those from further afield. There are free guided tours in English at 11.00 and 14.00 Tue–Fri, 11.00, 14.00 and 15.30 at weekends. Open Tue–Sun 09.00–17.30 (Wed 09.00–21.00). Closed Mon. Admission S$3 adult, S$1.50 child.

Getting there MRT to Dhoby Ghaut (NS/NE interchange), and walk to Bras Basah Road. Alternatively, take MRT to City Hall (NS/EW interchange) and walk along Bras Basah Road towards CHIJMES. Museum is on the north side of the road.

Singapore History Museum
Across the square, this museum (Stamford Road; tel: 6837 9940) contains informative exhibits relying on the latest technology to chart the island's history, including a 3-D film. The idea for a national museum was originally proposed by Raffles himself. Frustratingly, only a small amount of the museum's collection is ever on show at one time, and, because only a few of the displays are permanent, it is impossible to know what you are going to see beforehand. However, there is a fascinating section covering Peranakan culture and tradition, including a re-creation of the interior of a Peranakan house complete with furnishings and dress, and an extensive collection of jade. There are free daily guided tours in English at 11.00 and 14.00 (and additionally at 15.00 Sat and Sun). Open Sat–Thu 09.00–18.00, Fri 09.00–21.00. Closed Mon. Admission S$3 adult, S$1.50 child (S$4/S$2 to include 3-D show). Free Fri after 18.00.

Getting there Dhoby Ghaut MRT station (NS/NE interchange), and short walk past YMCA to Stamford Road.

Fort Canning Park and the Battle Box
In 1819, what is now Fort Canning Park (51 Canning Rise, Singapore 179872; tel: 6332 1200; fax: 6339 9715; web: www.nparks.gov.sg) was known as Bukit Larangan, meaning 'forbidden hill'. It was thought to be the site of an ancient palace and commoners were forbidden from setting foot in the

area. It subsequently went through several changes of name, including Government Hill, Singapore Hill and simply The Hill. Raffles built a small house here in 1822 that was also used by the resident councillor and later, until 1858, by the governor.

A Christian cemetery replaced an older graveyard on the hill, and this was extended in 1846 and bounded by a brick wall with lovely Gothic gates that are still standing. It is intriguing to peruse the inscriptions on the gravestones and slabs lining the walls.

The top of the hill was flattened in 1859 and a military fort established with a barracks, a hospital, and seven 68-pounder guns facing the Straits. The area was called Fort Canning Hill, after Lord George Canning, the first Viceroy of India. In 1920 it became the headquarters of the British army and the old fort was replaced with a massive underground operations centre called the Battle Box (tel: 6333 0510). It was here that General Percival finally decided to surrender to the Japanese during World War II. Visitors can watch a short film describing the history of Singapore's fall before touring the various sections of the bunker itself, including the command and radio rooms containing wax figures of the military staff. There is a recorded commentary. Open Tue–Sun 10.00–18.00. Admission S$8 adult, S$5 child.

Today, you can climb fairly steep paths and steps and visit the tomb of an old Malay prince. There is also a spice garden (on the site of the old Botanic Gardens) containing examples of the spices grown in this part of the world such as nutmeg, lime and clove trees, curry bushes, cinnamon, ginger and lemon grass. It was originally established by Raffles in 1822 but has since been improved and restocked.

Getting there MRT to Doby Ghaut station (NS/NE interchange) and walk towards Park Mall on Penang Road. It is not far, but quite an ascent into the park. Alternatively, any bus travelling up or down Orchard Road or up Penang Road towards Orchard Boulevard will stop near by.

National Archives of Singapore (or the Oral History Department)

Formerly the Anglo-Chinese Primary School, this building on Coleman Street became the home of the National Archives of Singapore (1 Canning Rise; tel: 6337 4464) in 1997. There are some fascinating photographs depicting the Singapore of the past, together with old maps and other documents. A major project was undertaken about ten years ago to encourage older citizens to record and share their experiences in the forms of oral anecdotes and stories for the benefit of future generations. Some of these contributors could not write and most of the recordings are in a variety of Chinese dialects, though written translations are available. Open Mon–Fri 09.00–17.30, Sat 09.00–13.00. Closed Sun. Admission free.

Getting there MRT to City Hall (NS/EW interchange), walk down North Bridge Road, and past St Andrew's Cathedral to Coleman Street. Turn right and pass the Armenian church. The archives stand opposite the end of Armenian Street, on the left.

Singapore Philatelic Museum

To the south of the National Archives is the Singapore Philatelic Museum (23B Coleman Street; tel: 6337 3888), housed in a grand colonial building. Here you can trace the history of stamps from Singapore and the rest of the world, learn about the stamp-making process and even design your own. There is also a collection of postcards. Guided tours are available, and can be arranged either through reception on arrival or in advance by telephone. Open Tue–Sun 09.00–18.00. Admission S$2 adult, S$1 child.

Getting there MRT to City Hall (NS and EW interchange), walk down North Bridge Road and right into Coleman Street.

Asian Civilisations Museum

Located in a former Chinese school called Tao Nan, the Asian Civilisations Museum (39 Armenian Street; tel: 6332 3015) charts the development, over thousands of years, of Asian culture (primarily Chinese). The displays – featuring traditional exhibits and others relying on the latest computer technology – include furniture, silk, jade, ceramics, jewellery and calligraphy. Particularly interesting is information detailing the intricacies of Chinese belief systems and symbolism. Free guided tours in English are available each day at 11.00 and 14.00 (extra tour at 15.30 at the weekend). Open Tue–Sun 09.00–18.00 (Wed 09.00–21.00). Closed Mon. Admission S$3 adult, S$1.50 child. Free admission Wed 18.00–21.00. A second wing to the museum has recently opened at Empress Place (see page 144).

Getting there MRT to City Hall (NS and EW interchange) and walk along Stamford Road.

Armenian Church

This church (60 Hill Street), the oldest in Singapore, is still used by the Armenian community. It was built in 1835 and dedicated to the monk St Gregory the Illuminator, the first patriarch of the Church in Armenia. The building was listed as a national monument in 1973.

Designed by George Coleman, the original plans were based upon St Gregory's Church in Echmiadzin in north Armenia. However, the blueprint was adapted to suit Singapore's climate, with wooden louvre windows to filter the sun yet let in the breeze, and pews made from woven ratten as a cooler alternative to the traditional solid wood. The structure is British neo-classical, and its interior circular (resembling the Round Church in Cambridge, England) on a square plan with porticoes on all four sides. Those on the north, south and west sides were designed to allow horse-drawn carriages to pull right up to the doors so that the occupants could step straight into the church without muddying their clothes on the ground outside. The original bell turret was replaced with a square tower spire in 1847, followed by the present spire in 1853.

Outside the church are the Memorial Gardens. The tombstones here, which all came from the Chinese cemetery in Bukit Timah in 1988, commemorate many of Singapore's famous Armenians. They include the

Sarkies brothers, who owned Raffles Hotel, Catchik Moses, who established the *Straits Times* in 1845, and Miss Agnes Joaquim, who discovered Singapore's first hybrid orchid in 1893. It was named Vanda Miss Joaquim after her and declared the national flower of the island in 1981. (There is also a small park in Tan Yin Road in Chinatown that celebrates Miss Joaquim's find.)

Getting there MRT to City Hall (NS and EW interchange), walk west along Stamford Road away from St Andrews Cathedral and left down Hill Street. The church is on the opposite side of the road. Alternatively, take bus No 190 from Orchard Road.

Central Fire Station
This fire station building (62 Hill Street) was completed in 1908, with a watchtower and living areas for the firemen. Initially there were only four portable water pumps, but gradually the fire brigade improved to such an extent that during the Japanese occupation the British fire-fighters were retained in their posts rather than being imprisoned. There is a Civil Defence Force Gallery here depicting the history of fire-fighting on the island.

Getting there As for the Armenian Church, above.

Old Hill Street Police Station (now the Ministry of Information and the Arts)
The old police station at 140 Hill Street is another neo-classical building that opened in 1934 to help control the Chinese secret societies. During the war, it was used by the Japanese to hold (and possibly torture) prisoners, before reverting to a police station once more at the war's conclusion. The police eventually moved out, and in 1983 the place was renamed the Hill Street Building and subsequently used to house the National Archives.

It has been refurbished, its shutters painted in a variety of bright colours, and is now home to the Ministry of Information and the Arts. It contains art galleries and a central atrium where exhibitions are held.

Getting there As for the Armenian Church, above.

Leaving the Hill Street Building, you find yourself on the north bank of the river. You have reached the end of the walking tour, so cross the road to Clarke Quay and find a bar or restaurant for a relaxing drink or meal. You can return to Orchard Road by taking the MRT from Clarke Quay (NE line) to Dhoby Ghaut.

Other places of interest
In addition to the sights covered by the walking tour, the following places of worship are also worth visiting if you have the time and the energy.

Maghain Aboth Synagogue
The synagogue (24/26 Waterloo Street; tel: 6337 2189) was built during the Victorian era and serves Singapore's small Jewish community.

Getting there MRT to Dhoby Ghaut (NS line), walk southeast along Orchard Road into Bras Basah Road, and left into Waterloo Street (beside the Plaza by the Park). Or take any bus down Orchard Road towards Raffles.

St Joseph's Church
The Roman Catholic church (143 Victoria Street; tel: 6338 3167) was built a century ago on the site of an earlier Portuguese church. Every Good Friday the congregation forms a procession around the grounds.

Getting there MRT to Bugis (EW line), then turn south down Victoria Street, past Middle Road and towards Bras Basah Road.

Colonial area
Packed with historic buildings of interest to tourists, the colonial area has few hotels and restaurants. If you wish to stay or eat in the vicinity, it is best to find somewhere in the city centre or marina area.

What to see and do: a walking tour
The following sites of interest have been arranged as a circular walking tour taking about 2½ hours, which should probably allow time to wander into St Andrew's Cathedral but not to visit the second wing of the Asian Civilisations Museum at Empress Place. The start (and end) point is City Hall MRT (NS and EW interchange). Exit towards St Andrew's Road for St Andrew's Cathedral.

St Andrew's Cathedral
The cathedral on St Andrew's Street stands directly above City Hall station. There used to be another cathedral on this site, fashioned in the early Gothic style and consecrated in 1838. However, following considerable lightning damage, it was demolished in 1852 and replaced with the present building in 1856. Its glossy-white-icing look is the result of a mixture of shell-lime, egg-white and sugar which was used to coat the exterior of the building. The ceiling inside is wooden-beamed and painted dark blue, and the structure cooled by substantial fans suspended from the roof. Guided tours are available, and there is an interesting visitor centre. Services are held on Sundays in Chinese or English. There is a board outside on which the times are displayed, or your hotel concierge should be able to tell you.

Getting there City Hall MRT (NS and EW interchange) and follow exit signs to St Andrew's Cathedral.

The Padang
Just across St Andrew's Road is a wide and open grassy space called the Padang – which means 'flat field' in Malay – with its two pavilions, one at either end. Originally known as Raffles Plain, Raffles had planned that it should be used for government buildings. However, after some early houses were built on the site, he decreed that the area should remain the centre around which the town of Singapore would be constructed, and stopped all further construction.

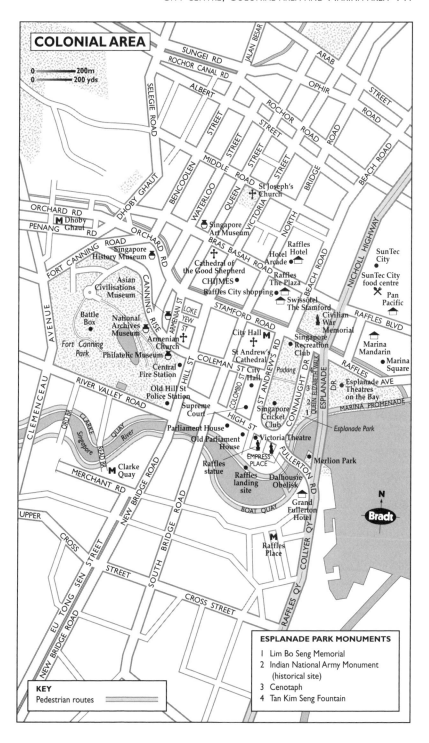

COLONIAL AREA

0 — 200m
0 — 200 yds

SUNGEI RD
ROCHOR CANAL RD
JALAN BESAR
ARAB STREET
OPHIR ROAD
ALBERT STREET
SELEGIE ROAD
DHOBY GHAUT
ORCHARD RD
PENANG RD
BENCOOLEN STREET
WATERLOO STREET
MIDDLE ROAD
QUEEN STREET
VICTORIA STREET
ROCHOR ROAD
ROAD
BRIDGE ROAD
NORTH BRIDGE
BEACH ROAD

M Dhoby
Ghaut

St Joseph's
✝ Church

ORCHARD RD
FORT CANNING ROAD
CANNING RISE

🏛 Singapore
Art Museum

Singapore
History Museum 🏛

✝ Cathedral of
the Good Shepherd
CHIJMES ●
Raffles City shopping ●

Raffles
Hotel
Hotel
Arcade ●
Raffles
The Plaza
BRAS BASAH ROAD
BEACH ROAD

SunTec
City
SunTec City
food centre
✗ Pan
Pacific
NICHOLL HIGHWAY

Asian
Civilisations
Museum

Battle
Box ●
Fort Canning
Park

National
Archives
Museum 🏛
Armenian ✝
Church
Philatelic Museum ●
Central ●
Fire Station
Old Hill St
Police Station
Supreme
Court ●
Parliament House ●
Old Parliament
House

ARMENIAN ST
LOKE YEW ST
STAMFORD ROAD

City Hall M

St Andrew's
Cathedral ✝
COLEMAN ST
HILL ST
COLOMBO ST
CITY
Hall
Padang
HIGH ST

Swissotel
The Stamford

🚩 Civilian
War
Memorial
RAFFLES BLVD

Singapore
Recreation
Club

Singapore
Cricket
Club

CONNAUGHT DR
QUEEN ELIZABETH WLK
ESPLANADE DR
MARINA PROMENADE

Marina
Mandarin
● Marina
Square

● Esplanade AVE
Theatres
on the Bay
RAFFLES

Esplanade Park

AVENUE
CLEMENCEAU
RIVER VALLEY ROAD
OLD BR
CLARKE BR
READER BR
QUAY

Singapore River

MERCHANT RD
M Clarke
Quay

UPPER
CROSS STREET
EU TONG SEN STREET
NEW BRIDGE ROAD
SOUTH BRIDGE ROAD
CROSS STREET

Raffles
statue ●
Raffles
landing
site ●
Victoria Theatre
EMPRESS
PLACE
Dalhousie
Obelisk
BOAT QUAY
Grand
Fullerton
Hotel

FULLERTON RD
COLLYER QY
RAFFLES QY

● Merlion Park

N
Bradt

M
Raffles
Place

KEY
Pedestrian routes ▭▭▭

ESPLANADE PARK MONUMENTS
1 Lim Bo Seng Memorial
2 Indian National Army Monument
  (historical site)
3 Cenotaph
4 Tan Kim Seng Fountain

During the 1820s, horses were exercised here, and it was the venue for the New Year's Sports. At that time the area was still fronted by the sea (the policy of land reclamation was yet to begin), and aquatic events took place as well as those on land. Soon afterwards it was renamed the Esplanade and, although it was still only about half its present size, cricket was played here in the 1830s; in 1852 the southern end became the home of the newly founded Singapore Cricket Club. In 1885, the northern end was given over to the Singapore Recreation Club, catering specifically to the Eurasian community (whose members were prohibited from joining the cricket club).

The present cricket club building was erected in 1907, and contains wrought-iron pillars and verandas from an earlier pavilion. The recreation club, despite several renovations since first appearing at its present location in 1904, still looks much the same. Other sports played during the mid- to late 19th century included fives, followed by lawn tennis and bowls in the 1870s, football and rugby in the 1880s, and hockey in the 1890s.

It was at the Padang where, in 1942, the Japanese gathered the surrendered British soldiers before marching them to Changi and Selarang prisoner-of-war camps. It is also where the British paraded in victory in 1945. Today it is the site of speeches and other major events that take place annually in August to celebrate National Day (see page 94).

City Hall

Across Coleman Street from St Andrew's Cathedral is City Hall (3 St Andrew's Road). Originally the Municipal Building, it was constructed between 1926 and 1929. During their occupation of Singapore, the Japanese ran the island from here, and it was also where they surrendered to the British on September 12 1945.

In recognition of Singapore's elevation to city status, the building's name was changed to City Hall in 1951. Lee Kuan Yew proclaimed self-rule for Singapore from its steps in 1959 and, four years later, declared the country's independence by reading the Malaysian Proclamation from the same spot. A year after Singapore finally separated from Malaysia on August 9 1965, becoming a sovereign and independent state, the first National Day Parade was held on the Padang, in front of City Hall.

Supreme Court

Next to City Hall, overlooking the Padang, is the Supreme Court (1 St Andrew's Road). Before the building was constructed, this site had held not only colonial houses but also the Grand Hôtel de l'Europe – a rival establishment to Raffles Hotel. Rudyard Kipling advised, 'Travellers take note – stay at the Raffles but eat at the Hôtel de l'Europe'. The area was handed over to the Chief Justice in 1939.

The Supreme Court is noted for the work of the Italian sculptor, Calvalieri Rudolfo Nolli, who came to the island in 1921. He also created the lamps depicting the Singapore lion that can be seen on Elgin Bridge (see page 157) near Parliament House. The structure is composed of four blocks positioned around a circular library, with an imposing dome and classic Corinthian columns. Nolli, who specialised in pre-cast iron, imitation stone and decorative plasterwork, created these columns as well as the sculpture of justice in the pediment. Every hour there is a free tour of the place, including its 11 courtrooms and judges' chambers. There is also a multimedia gallery where you can watch presentations focusing on the judiciary.

Old Parliament House
High Street, North Bridge Road and Hill Street were the first thoroughfares laid in Singapore by Lieutenant Henry Ralfe, who was a gunnery officer on one of the ships that arrived with Raffles. He was ordered to cut back the jungle around the river and clear a spot for the signing of the treaty between Sultan Temenggong and Raffles (see page 14). There is also archaeological evidence of a settlement on the banks of the river here in the 13th or 14th centuries.

Old Parliament House (Parliament Place, formerly 1 High Street) is the oldest government building in Singapore. It was designed by George Coleman in 1827, commissioned as a grand private residence for a Scottish merchant, John Maxwell. However, Maxwell was never to enjoy living in the two-storey, neo-Palladian structure. Instead, it was immediately leased to the government. The front portion was used to house courtrooms, the side rooms were inhabited by the resident councillor, and the Land Office filled the ground floor. The walls and piers of the central tower of the original house can still be seen.

The building has been extended and renovated several times over the years; there have also been variations in the type of official – whether judicial or governmental – who worked within it. Between 1839 and 1875 it was occupied solely by government figures, after which it was re-occupied by the judiciary until the opening of the new Supreme Court in 1939. Reverting to government space, in 1954 it became the location for the Legislative Assembly and the office of David Marshall, Singapore's first chief minister. It was finally renamed Parliament House in 1965, when Singapore became an independent republic.

In the grounds you can see a bronze **statue of an elephant**, presented to Singapore by King Chulalongkorn of Siam (now Thailand) to commemorate his first state visit in 1871. If you are interested in listening to a parliamentary debate, you can enter the new Parliament House next door. Opened in 1999, it has colonnades that face on to North Bridge Road, and a café open to the public.

Victoria Theatre and Concert Hall
Walking back towards the Padang, you come to the Victoria Theatre. This was originally the town hall, designed by John Bennett, and completed in 1862. The decorative building contained large halls on each of its two floors for concert performances, and side rooms used as offices.

When Queen Victoria died in 1901, a commemorative hall and clock tower were added to one side in the same architectural style. The Victoria Memorial Hall, featuring a grand sweeping staircase up to the first floor, was completed in 1905, and the clock tower, with faces on all four sides and a bell turret, in

1906. In 1909, the Victoria Theatre and Memorial Hall opened with a performance of *The Pirates of Penzance*, and Noel Coward acted there in 1930.

During the Japanese occupation, it was used as a hospital and later as a war crimes court. The ballots for the first elections in Singapore in the mid-1950s were counted under the clock tower, and Lee Kuan Yew was declared leader of the new People's Action Party. Finally, between 1978 and 1980, the Memorial Hall was converted into the impressive Victoria Concert Hall, now home to the Singapore Symphony Orchestra.

Stamford Raffles statue
In front of the Victoria Concert Hall is an eight-foot bronze statue of Sir Stamford Raffles. Mounted on a granite pedestal bearing his coat of arms, it depicts Raffles with folded arms and a map at his feet which has fallen from his grasp. The sculpture was commissioned to mark Queen Victoria's Diamond Jubilee, and was designed by T Woolner. It initially stood on the Padang but was moved here in Singapore's centenary year of 1919.

Empress Place and the Asian Civilisation Museum
Turning towards the river, you now reach Empress Place (1 Empress Place). During the colonial era, this building housed government offices and – appropriately enough – was known as Government Offices. It was renamed Empress Place in honour of Queen Victoria in 1907.

Up until the 1980s, the Immigration Department was based here. After that, however, it was replaced by the Empress Place Museum, and had an amazing exhibition of artefacts from the Qing Dynasty, some of which had never been seen outside China. Unfortunately, the building began to suffer severe structural problems and was closed in 1995 for extensive renovations. It reopened in 2002 as the second wing of the Asian Civilisations Museum (see page 138).

Dalhousie Obelisk
As you turn back towards the Padang, you will come across the Dalhousie Obelisk. When the Marquis of Dalhousie, Governor-General of India, visited Singapore in 1850, it was decided to name the new harbour entrance Dalhousie Ghaut and to erect this obelisk as a harbour mark in his honour.

The obelisk was designed by John Turnbull Thomson, and resembles Cleopatra's Needle on the Thames embankment in London. The obelisk's position became inconvenient when the construction of Connaught Drive was planned in the 1880s – it would have stood in the middle of the projected route. It was therefore carefully dismantled and re-erected in its present location – ironically nearer where Dalhousie actually landed than its previous site.

Now use the underpass to cross to Esplanade Park.

Esplanade Park
This is a peaceful area from which you can see the sea and get a good view of the Merlion statue on the point at the river's mouth. It is possible that you might find a snake charmer practising his art here, and you can buy local ice-

cream. It is also the site of the Esplanade – Theatres on the Bay Arts Centre, due to open at the end of 2002 (see *Arts and entertainment*, pages 73–4).

Walking north through the park along the Queen Elizabeth Walk you come to a series of memorial monuments. The first of these is the **Lim Bo Seng Memorial**, a marble pagoda in memory of the man who led the anti-resistance movement against the Japanese during World War II. He died in his mid-30s, after being captured in Malaya in 1944. He was also one of the founders in 1939 of the Chung Cheng High School, established with the aim of preserving Chinese culture and tradition through education.

Near by is the **Indian National Army Monument**, a plaque erected in 1995 to mark the site of the original Memorial to the Unknown Soldier of the Indian National Army. The army was formed in 1942 to co-opt Indians in Singapore into joining the fight for India's independence. The Japanese hoped that they could persuade the Indians to sabotage the British Army. This plan failed, and the army was disbanded in 1943 (although it was revived briefly under Subhas Chandra Bose, a well-known Indian revolutionary). The memorial was built in the final months of the Japanese occupation but was demolished shortly afterwards by the British.

Midway up the park, on Connaught Drive, is the **Cenotaph**, unveiled in 1922 by the then Prince of Wales (who later abdicated from Britain, after briefly serving as King Edward VIII, because of his love for an American divorcee). It was built to commemorate the lives of the 124 Singapore soldiers who died during World War I. After World War II, a further dedication was added to the reverse of the monument to include those sacrificed during the subsequent conflict. The words engraved on the base of the monument read, 'They died so that we might live.'

Next you will come to the **Tan Kim Seng Fountain**, a beautiful Victorian fountain erected in 1882. This recognised the generous contribution made by Tan Kim Seng, an immigrant from Malacca in 1840 who became an important businessman and prominent Chinese community leader. It was he who arranged a supply line bringing free fresh water from Bukit Timah to the town. Originally placed in front of the Fullerton Building, the fountain was moved to Queen Elizabeth Walk in 1952.

Civilian War Memorial

Cross over Stamford Road to the memorial that is known to all the locals as 'the chopsticks'. It recalls those civilians massacred by the Japanese during their occupation of the island, and was erected after Chinese mass graves were found at various sites on the island in 1962. The four pillars, each 67m high, are joined at the base and symbolise unity between the four major ethnic groups in Singapore – the Chinese, Eurasians, Indians and Malays. A memorial service is held here annually, on February 15, to commemorate the fall of Singapore to the Japanese in 1942.

Cross back over Beach Road to Raffles City and City Hall MRT at the end of the walk.

Marina area

The Marina area around Marina Square primarily features hotels and shopping malls (SunTec City, among others), although it is also pleasant to walk along Marina Promenade, which hugs the water's edge.

Marina South comprises an area which has only fairly recently been reclaimed from the sea. Such land has to be given time to settle before it is considered stable enough for concentrated building, and, as such, it is relatively undeveloped at present. While it has its own MRT station (Marina Bay on the NS line), holds the Superbowl Golf and Country Club, and will doubtless welcome shops and hotel complexes in time, the only current site of any interest to the visitor is **Marina City Park**. Open daily, the park contains an array of statues, including one of Confucius, and a brass-and-steel sculpture called the Spirit of Youth and Sculpture Fountain reaching 40 feet in height.

Getting there MRT to Marina Bay station and then bus No 400.

Where to stay
Super-luxury

Marina Mandarin Singapore 6 Raffles Blvd, 01-00 Marina Sq, Singapore 039594; tel: 6338 3388; fax: 6845 1001; email: marina.mms@meritus-hotels.com. Three blocks built in a triangle around a large, full-height atrium. Jungle atmosphere, with plants and birds. Pool, fitness centre, business centre and restaurants. 575 rooms. Single S$380–470, double S$380–470, suite S$600–3,000. *Nearest MRT* City Hall (NS/EW interchange)

The Oriental Singapore 5 Raffles Ave, Marina Sq, Singapore 039797; tel: 6338 0066; fax: 6339 9537; email: orsin@mohg.com. Triangular atrium with lifts on the outside. Outward-facing rooms have good harbour views. Main pool and children's pool, fitness centre and business centre. Restaurants: Chinese Cherry Garden, Liana's (Californian), Pronto (poolside, Italian). 524 rooms. Single S$390–480, double S$390–480, suite S$520–1,080. *Nearest MRT* City Hall (NS/EW interchange)

The Pan Pacific Hotel Singapore 7 Raffles Blvd, Marina Sq, Singapore 039595; tel: 6336 8111; fax: 6339 1861; email: panpac@pacific.net.sg. Open, triangular atrium, reaching 36 storeys. All rooms have views over the city, the harbour or the town. Pool, fitness centre, 2 tennis courts and business centre. Mainly business customers. Its restaurant is the well-known Keyaki (Japanese), overlooking a Japanese garden on 4th floor. 784 rooms. Single S$390–650, double S$410–700, suite S$645–1,495. *Nearest MRT* City Hall (NS/EW interchange)

Conrad Centennial Singapore 2 Temasek Blvd, Singapore 038982; tel: 6334 8888; fax: 6333 9166; email: conradsg@mbox4.singnet.com.sg. Large contemporary rooms with good views. Pool, fitness centre and business centre. Amazing collection of art on display. Near SunTec City, so good for business travellers. 509 rooms. Single S$380–600, double S$380–600, suite S$550–3,300. Recommended. *Nearest MRT* City Hall (NS/EW interchange)

The Ritz-Carlton Millennia Singapore 7 Raffles Ave, Singapore 039779; tel: 6337 8888; fax: 6338 0001; email: reservation@ritz-carlton.com.sg. Modern furnishings in appealing rooms with great views of the harbour and the river. Large pool and jacuzzi in lovely garden setting, fitness centre and business centre. 608 rooms. Single

S$465–545, double S$515–95, suite S$698–5,288. Recommended. *Nearest MRT* City Hall (NS/EW interchange)

Where to eat

In the Marina area to the top of Marina Bay, **Keyaki** (4/F Pan Pacific Hotel, 7 Raffles Boulevard, Marina Square; tel: 6434 8335) is a classy – and consequently expensive – Japanese restaurant, with an elegant interior and roof-top garden containing waterfalls and pools. Dinner will cost at least S$100 a head. Open daily 12.00–14.30, 18.30–22.30.

Summer Pavilion (The Ritz-Carlton Millennia, 7 Raffles Avenue; tel: 6337 8888) is a beautiful, glass-enclosed Cantonese restaurant set in a garden. Its menu – decorated, incidentally, with gold silk – is extensive, and it is a good idea to let the helpful staff offer advice when making your choices. The food is high quality and beautifully presented – the bird's nest soup with seafood, for example, is served in a coconut shell. A meal is expensive (expect to pay about S$80–90 per person) but well worth splashing out on. Open Mon–Sat 11.30–14.30 and 18.30–22.30; Sun 10.00–14.30 and 18.30–22.30.

Oscar's (Conrad Centennial Singapore, 2 Temasek Boulevard; tel: 6432 7481) has some splendidly extravagant puddings, including red-chilli-and-chocolate ice-cream, which makes it a great place to take the children. You can eat here at any time, as it stays open throughout the night.

Golden Peony (3/F Conrad International Centennial Hotel, 2 Temasek Boulevard; tel: 6334 8888) offers top-quality Cantonese food in a sophisticated dining area, decorated in gold and displaying gorgeous vases and paintings. Expensive. Open every day 11.30–14.30, 18.30–22.30.

There is a large **food centre**, together with a number of restaurants, at SunTec City Mall, on the ground floor overlooking the Fountain of Wealth.

SINGAPORE RIVER AND THE CBD

It is easy to overlook the delights of the Singapore River, but there is much to see and do here. The area includes Boat and Clarke quays, the Melaka Mosque and the Tan Si Chong Su Temple, bars and nightclubs along Mohamed Sultan Road, good eating places along the banks, and even a large Merlion (the island's national symbol) squirting water from its mouth. Furthermore, Singapore, like most great cities, traces its early beginnings to the mouth of its river.

In 1819, Raffles landed on the north bank. Today the site is marked with a gleaming, white poly-marble statue (see below, page 157), erected in 1972; this was moulded from plaster casts of a bronze statue originally placed on the Padang to mark Queen Victoria's golden jubilee in 1887. The bronze sculpture, designed by T Woolner, was moved to its present site outside the Victoria Memorial Hall in 1919, Singapore's centenary year.

During the first two decades of the 19th century, the headland was lined with mangrove and the riverbanks covered with rhododendron, myrtle and eugenis trees. It was here on the firm ground of the north bank that the Temenggong of Singapore lived (see *History*, page 14). However, when the

Temenggong signed the agreement with Raffles allowing the British to establish a free port and use the island as a trading base, the river area changed. The north bank was allocated to the government, the Temenggong was moved to Telok Blangah, and the swamps on the south bank were filled with earth (obtained by levelling the hill where Raffles Place now stands) so that merchants could construct warehouses on the land. These warehouses became known as 'godowns', an Anglo-Indian word that probably derived from the Malay *gudang* (meaning 'a place to keep goods or tools').

As Singapore's importance as a port grew, the river became increasingly busy, and pollution from sewage, rubbish and the by-products of local industry became unbearable. In 1977, Prime Minister Lee Kwan Yew decided to act, declaring, 'in ten years time, let us have fishing in the Singapore River – it can be done'. Such statements of intent are usually acted upon in Singapore. Polluting industries were quickly re-located, hawkers were licensed and moved to areas with proper sewage facilities, barges (with large eyes painted on their bows to ward off evil spirits) were shifted to the west coast, and proper systems were put in place for the collection and burning of refuse. The river was also dredged, and gradually marine life returned to the cleaner waters. Indeed, on April 16 1984 a group of 400 people swam across the river, and in December of the same year the first Singapore River Regatta was held to celebrate the end of the river's use for commerce.

Today, the banks have been shored up, re-paved and redeveloped, and most of the old godowns have been demolished or upgraded. Some still stand upstream at Robertson Quay, but they are in a fairly dilapidated state, and it is to be hoped that they will be rescued and restored.

It is now possible to walk from the Anderson Bridge (near the mouth of the river), down well-laid-out paths on both sides. You can go along Boat Quay or the other bank by Empress Place and North Boat Quay, past Clarke Quay or the Riverwalk on the opposite side, upstream as far as Robertson Quay, passing new hotels and private condominiums, and on to the Kim Seng Bridge beyond the Grand Copthorne Waterfront Hotel. Bumboats or river taxis travel from the pier at Clarke Quay (and also from UOB Plaza, at the eastern end of Boat Quay, when the tide is high enough). A trip on one of these is a very pleasant and relaxing way of learning the history of the river.

Getting there and around

MRT to Clarke Quay on the new NE line (due to open end of 2002) or Raffles Place (NS line), and walk north towards the river. Bus No 190 from Orchard Road drops passengers between Boat and Clarke quays. This area of the Singapore River is readily explored on foot. However, bumboats or river taxis also ply their trade here, and you can travel from Clarke Quay to UOB Plaza for S$1 in peak hours (11.00–14.30) and S$2 in non-peak hours. Alternatively, river taxis leave from Raffles Landing Site going to Boat Quay or UOB Plaza (for S$2), or to Clarke Quay, Riverside Point or Clifford Pier (the old landing site for cruise ships, just outside the mouth of the river towards the docks) for S$3. Traffic is currently only permitted as far as the Clemenceau Bridge at

Above Skyline at night (JM)

Below Singapore Harbour (JM)

Next page Boat in Singapore Harbour (DL)

Clarke Quay; however, there are plans to allow river taxis to go to Robertson Quay by the end of 2002. Certainly landing points have been constructed, ready for the trade, at various places along the newly concreted riverbanks.

Where to stay
Super-luxury
Grand Copthorne Waterfront 392 Havelock Rd, Singapore 169663; tel: 6733 0880; fax: 6737 8880; email: rsvnsgrandcopthorne@copthorne.com.sg. Opened in 1998, this 5-star hotel is located in a lovely setting at the quiet end of the Singapore River area. River taxi due to open at end 2002. Shuttle bus to Great World Shopping Centre, Orchard Rd and Chinatown. Small pool, 2 tennis courts. Restaurants: Café Brio (terrace café with some tables on riverside; cosmopolitan and Asian), Pontin (Italian). 537 rooms. Single S$300–450, double S$330–500, suite S$550–800. Recommended. *Nearest MRT* Outram Park (NE/EW interchange)

The Fullerton Singapore 1 Fullerton Sq, Singapore 049178; tel: 6733 8388; fax: 6735 8388; email: info@fullertonhotel.com. Opened in 2001 by the prime minister, this 5/6-star hotel in the converted 1928 building has a commanding position at the entrance to Singapore River and overlooking Boat Quay and the old colonial area. At night, its floodlit Doric columns and Palladian architecture make a spectacular sight. Immensely luxurious, with ambitions to be the world's best hotel, it competes with Raffles as the most prestigious place to stay in Singapore. It has an amazing lobby area, and all rooms have magnificent views either inwards over the atrium or outwards to the city skyscrapers, the river or Marina Bay. Superb pool (looking over the river), spa, business centre. Restaurants: Town (Mediterranean, Continental and Japanese), Courtyard (coffee, afternoon tea, curry or chocolate buffet), Jade (Cantonese), Lighthouse (on the top floor – fine dining – an 8-course set dinner with wine for 2 could set you back S$800!), Post Bar (cocktails and jazz). 400 rooms. Single S$450–530, double S$450–530, suite S$650–4,800. Recommended – if you have cash to burn. *Nearest MRT* Raffles Place (NE/EW interchange)

Luxury
Concorde Hotel 317 Outram Rd, Singapore 169075; tel: 6733 0188; fax: 6734 3968; email: singapore@concorde.net. Circular building of 27 floors on busy intersection. All rooms look outwards, with views towards the harbour and city skyscrapers at the western end of the river area. Magnificent atrium to full height of building, with glass roof and decorated with Chinese kites. Shuttle to Orchard Rd. Pool, business centre and tennis court. Restaurants: Melting Pot (Western, continental), Xin Cuisine (East/West fusion, Cantonese). 515 rooms. Single S$240–320, double S$260–340, suite S$650–1,600. Straddles the divide between luxury and super-luxury. *Nearest MRT* Outram Park (NE/EW interchange)

Novotel Apollo Singapore 405 Havelock Rd, Singapore 169633; tel: 6733 2081; fax: 6733 1588; email: novotel@novotelapollo.com. Large, open lobby area with café overlooking small waterfall. Resort-like terrace with sundeck, jacuzzi, and 7 tennis courts in tropical setting. Shuttle bus to Orchard Rd and Chinatown. Access from hotel to adjacent night-club, so busy in evening until late. Restaurants: The Square (international and Nonya), Kintammani (Indonesian), Hae Bok (Korean). 480 rooms.

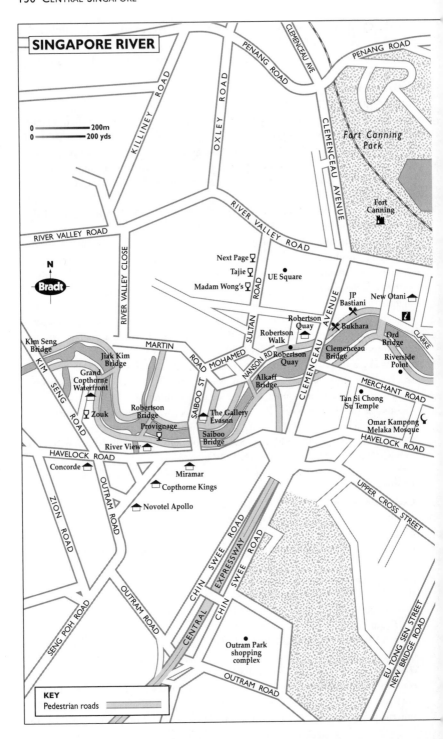

SINGAPORE RIVER

CLEMENCEAU AVE

PENANG ROAD

KILLINEY ROAD

OXLEY ROAD

PENANG ROAD

CLEMENCEAU AVENUE

Fort Canning Park

Fort Canning

0   200m
0   200 yds

RIVER VALLEY ROAD

RIVER VALLEY CLOSE

RIVER VALLEY ROAD

N

Bradt

Next Page

Tajie

Madam Wong's

UE Square

SULTAN ROAD

JP Bastiani

New Otani

Robertson Quay

Robertson Walk

Robertson Quay

Bukhara

Ord Bridge

Riverside Point

CLARKE

Kim Seng Bridge

Jiak Kim Bridge

MARTIN ROAD

MOHAMED

NANSON RD

Clemenceau Bridge

CLEMENCEAU AVENUE

MERCHANT ROAD

Grand Copthorne Waterfront

Zouk

Robertson Bridge

Provignage

River View

SAIBOO ST

Alkaff Bridge

The Gallery Evason

Saiboo Bridge

Tan Si Chong Su Temple

Omar Kampong Melaka Mosque

HAVELOCK ROAD

KIM SENG ROAD

HAVELOCK ROAD

Concorde

Miramar

Copthorne Kings

Novotel Apollo

OUTRAM ROAD

ZION ROAD

UPPER CROSS STREET

CHIN SWEE ROAD

CENTRAL EXPRESSWAY

CHIN SWEE ROAD

SENG POH ROAD

OUTRAM ROAD

Outram Park shopping complex

EU TONG SEN STREET

NEW BRIDGE ROAD

OUTRAM ROAD

KEY
Pedestrian roads

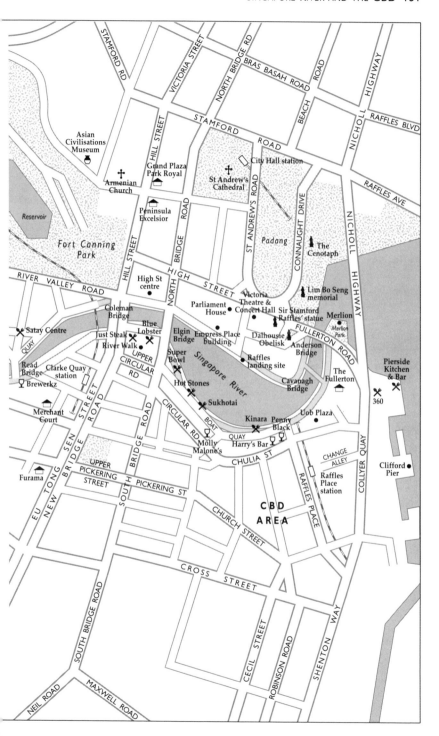

Single S$240–80, double S$260–300, suite S$450. *Nearest MRT* Outram Park (NE/EW interchange)

Copthorne Kings Hotel Singapore 403 Havelock Rd, Singapore 169632; tel: 6733 0011; fax: 6235 1462; email: rooms@copthornekings.com.sg. All rooms have balconies with flowers and shrubs hanging over edges. Pool, gym and business centre. Restaurants: Tien Court (Chinese), Princess Terrace (local and Western), Mino-Q (Japanese). 314 rooms. Single S$220–90, double S$220–90, suite S$500–650. *Nearest MRT* Outram Park (NE/EW interchange)

Hotel Miramar 401 Havelock Rd, Singapore 169631; tel: 6733 0222; fax: 6733 4027; email: miramar@pacific.net.sg. Busy, friendly and newly refurbished. Situated near Chinatown, and just across the road from the river. Large pool in tropical garden. Restaurants: Fern Tree Café (with bright, checked cloths at lobby level; local and Continental buffets), Ikoi (Japanese), Orient Ocean (Cantonese). 346 rooms. Single S$220–60, double S$240–80, suite S$400–1,000. *Nearest MRT* Outram Park (NE/EW interchange)

Hotel New Otani Singapore 177A River Valley Rd, Singapore 179031; tel: 6338 3333; fax: 6339 2854; email: newotani@singnet.com.sg. Four-star hotel on top of Liang Court Shopping Complex (70 shops, boutiques and supermarket). Breezy pool on 7th floor, with a few small trees set between the 2 towers of rooms overlooking river, fitness centre and business centre. No shuttle, but very near Singapore Trolley stop at Clarke Quay. Next to restaurants and bars at Clarke Quay. 408 rooms. Single S$260–300, double S$280–320, suite S$600–800. *Nearest MRT* Clarke Quay (NE line)

Merchant Court Hotel 20 Merchant Rd, Singapore 058281; tel: 6337 2288; fax: 6334 0606; email: info@merchantcourt.com.sg. Became part of Raffles/Swissôtel group in 2002. Excellent position in centre of river area, immediately opposite Clarke Quay and next to new Clarke Quay MRT (opening end 2002). Beautiful lobby with embroidered panels on walls. Free-form pool and sundeck on 2nd floor, with trees and shrubs, jacuzzi, pool terrace and bar. Ellenborough Café on lobby level (Straits Chinese and local) is very busy and popular – speciality is *durian* pudding. 476 rooms. Single S$285–375, double S$315–405, suite S$810–1,200. *Nearest MRT* Clarke Quay (NE line)

The Gallery Evason 76 Robertson Quay, Singapore 238254; tel: 6846 8686; fax: 6836 6666; email: general@galleryhotel.com.sg. On river overlooking old *godowns* at Robertson Quay. Change of ownership spring 2002. Very minimalist décor, with security lifts above lobby level (4th floor). Pool on 5th floor surrounded by glass walls. Restaurants: lobby level (East/West fusion; 3 computers available for guests to use free of charge), Kei (Japanese), 2nd floor (Middle East and Asian). Every room currently contains a computer, which can be used without extra payment. New river taxi service (by end June 2002) will provide better access to city area. 222 rooms. Single S$295–345, double S$345–75, suite S$375–570. *Nearest MRT* Clarke Quay (NE line)

Mid-range

River View Hotel 382 Havelock Rd, Singapore 169629; tel: 6732 9922; fax: 6731 0890; email: river382@singnet.com.sg. First hotel to open on river (in 1985). Shuttle bus to Orchard Rd. Pool and business centre. Restaurants: River Café (sit outside under trees), Ginga Restaurant (Japanese), River Palace (Chinese). 470 rooms. Single S$180–200, double S$200–20. *Nearest MRT* Outram Park (NE/EW interchange)

Robertson Quay Hotel 15 Merbau Rd, Singapore 239032; tel: 6735 3333; fax: 6738 1515; email: sales@robertsonquayhotel.com.sg. Built in 1998, this 3-star hotel has small rooms at a medium price, and claims that 80–90% of guests return. Near restaurants at Clarke Quay and beside Singapore Arts Theatre. Small pool, spa and gym. No restaurant, but in-house breakfast in small lobby lounge, and beach bar on riverside just outside. 150 rooms. Single S$120–50, double S$150, suite S$200. *Nearest MRT* Clarke Quay (NE line)

Where to eat

Top Aussie tucker is served at **The Moomba** (52 Circular Road; tel: 6438 0141), where you can sample kangaroo and crayfish, and wash it all down with ice-cold Australian lager. There are also good wines from New Zealand and Australia. The furnishing is refreshingly understated, broken by energetic Aboriginal artwork. The menu is mid-range in price (approximately S$50 a head). Open Mon–Fri 12.00–14.30, 18.30–22.00; Sat 18.30–22.00. Closed Sun and Sat lunch.

For no-nonsense, immensely filling steaks and ribs, head for **Just Steak** (20 Upper Circular Road; tel: 6438 5522). Enjoy the prime beef at a prime location overlooking the river. Three courses will cost around S$80. Open Mon–Sat 11.00–14.30, 18.00–22.00. Closed Sun.

Dine outside, overlooking the ships in the harbour, at the **Pierside Kitchen and Bar** (Unit 01-01, One Fullerton, 1 Fullerton Road; tel: 6438 0400). Excellent and imaginative seafood. Expect to pay about S$60. Open Mon–Sat 11.30–14.30, 19.00–22.30. Closed Sun.

If you don't mind sitting fairly close to other diners on bench-style seats, eat inside at **Super Bowl** (81 Boat Quay; tel: 6538 6066). More sensible is to ask for a table outside by the river. The Chinese food is inexpensive. Open daily 11.00–15.00, 18.00–23.00.

Sukhothai (47 Boat Quay; tel: 6538 2422) offers unpretentious Thai food, including good fresh seafood. You're unlikely to spend much more than S$50 per person. Open Mon–Fri 11.30–14.30, 18.30–23.00, Sat and Sun 18.30–23.00. Closed Sat and Sun lunch.

Also at Boat Quay is **Kinara** (57 Boat Quay; tel: 6533 0412), which serves Mogul food and features a decent choice of tandoori meat dishes (although there are also vegetarian options). It has a sister restaurant (on Lorong Mambong, Holland Village) in the west of the island. Open 11.30–14.30, 18.00–23.00.

One of four outlets in Singapore, the **House of Sundanese** (55/55A Boat Quay; tel: 6534 3775) offers typical, flavoursome and cheaply priced Indonesian cuisine. The interior is disappointing – and is not air-conditioned – but the location by the river is some compensation. Open Mon–Sat 11.00–14.00, 18.00–22.00. Closed Sun.

Lucerne-by-the-River (The Riverwalk, #B1-46/47, 20 Upper Circular Road; tel: 6535 8700) serves Swiss food, including good fondues. Open 12.00–15.00, 18.00–22.30.

The Lighthouse (The Fullerton Hotel, 1 Fullerton Square; tel: 6877 8932) is as exclusive as anybody could wish; it offers set menus of classic French cuisine. As you would expect, the décor is unfailingly tasteful and the prices reassuringly heart-stopping. An evening meal will cost at least S$200, and more probably nearer S$300. It goes without saying that booking is essential. Open Mon–Fri 12.00–14.00, 19.00–21.30, Sat 19.00–21.30. Closed Sat lunch and Sun.

The **Blue Lobster** (20 Upper Circular Road, #B1-49/50, The Riverwalk; tel: 6538 0766) has a fish market above the restaurant, and is therefore able to guarantee the freshness of its ingredients. The fare revolves primarily around seafood dishes from Australia, although there is meat (including kangaroo) on the menu, and options inspired by the cuisine of other countries. The riverfront location makes for a great atmosphere. Prices are at the lower end of the expensive bracket. Open Mon–Sat 12.00–14.30, 19.00–22.30, Sun 11.30–14.30, 19.00–22.30.

Bukhara (3C River Valley Road, #01-40/44, Clarke Quay; tel: 6338 1411) is housed in a former godown. It specialises in Indian kebabs. Budget for around S$50. Open daily 12.00–14.30, 18.30–22.30. **J P Bastiani** (3A River Valley Road, #01-12, Clarke Quay; tel: 6433 0156) offers good Mediterranean cuisine for a similar price. Prime location, overlooking the river. There is a wine bar on the first floor.

Pontini (Grand Copthorne Waterfront Hotel, 392 Havelock Road; tel: 6233 1133) is a spacious and modern restaurant which nevertheless retains a familiar and comfortable atmosphere. The Italian pasta dishes are very good, and seafood lovers will be well served here. Expensive. Open Mon–Fri 12.00–14.30, 18.30–22.30, Sat 18.00–22.00. Closed Sat lunch and Sun.

Hot Stones (53 Boat Quay; tel: 6534 5188) is an informal restaurant which, with its giant sculpture of a dinosaur skeleton, bears more than a passing resemblance to a museum of natural history. The favourite dish – 'hot stones' – comprises seafood and chicken cooked at the table on hot plates. A meal should not exceed S$45. Open Mon–Sat 12.00–15.00, 18.00–22.30, Sun 18.00–22.30. Closed Sun lunch.

360 (One Fullerton, 1 Fullerton Road, #02-02; tel: 6220 0055) serves a range of modern dishes in a relaxed setting facing the river. The service is helpful and efficient, and there is an extensive selection of drinks. Not enormously expensive – budget for around S$60 each (less for lunch). Note that there is a subway link to the Grand Fullerton Hotel. Open Mon–Sat 12.00–14.30, 18.30–22.30. Closed Sun.

In the evenings, pay a visit to the **Satay Centre** at Clarke Quay. Stalls and tables are set out in the road where you can order satay and rice dishes, and buy drinks. The chicken, pork, beef and lamb satays are very reasonably priced. Stallholders may strongly recommend the king prawns – these are (as you'd expect) more expensive. There are also several open-air restaurants in this area.

Nightlife
The décor at **Amoeba** (207 River Valley Road, #01-59, UE Square; tel: 6735 6193) appears curiously dated. From Monday to Thursday you can listen to acid jazz, garage and house music.

Bar (11 Unity Street, #01-23/24, Robertson Walk; tel: 6738 1108) has a minimalist style to its interior which gives it a strangely outmoded, 1970s appearance. Happy hour Mon–Sat 18.00–21.00.

Situated by the river, **Crazy Elephant** (3E River Valley Road, #01-07, Trader's Market, Clarke Quay; tel: 6337 1990) has seating outside near the water's edge. The bar currently has four resident bands – Elephant Jam, Don Victor Band, Graham Neill Band and Heritage – who play rock music every day except Mon. Happy hour Tue–Sun 17.00–21.00, and all night Mon.

East Side (207 River Valley Road, #01-51/52, UE Square; tel: 6235 6418) claims to be where the East meets the West. It is decorated with Buddhas, and has a pool table. Happy hour Mon–Sat 17.00–21.00.

At the eastern end of the busy Boat Quay is **Harry's Bar** (28 Boat Quay; tel: 6538 3029), a large venue patronised by city workers. One of its dubious claims to fame is that it was a favourite haunt of the rogue trader Nick Leeson, whose financial gambles ultimately brought down Barings Investment Bank in the mid-1990s. There are live jazz bands in the evening (except Mon), food is available, and it is invariably very busy. Happy hour Tue–Sun 11.00–21.00, all night Mon.

Go to **Lush** (207 River Valley Road, #01-75, UE Square (off Unity Street); tel: 6733 6388) for acid, funk and trip-hop music, played within a sparse setting.

If you're yearning for a little piece of England, try **Penny Black** (26–27 Boat Quay; tel: 6538 2300), which is a two-storey building styled to look like a typical English pub. It serves ales from the UK, and traditional pub grub. Happy hour 11.00–20.00. If it's Ireland you're after, head for **Molly Malone's** (42 Circular Road) just to the west of Boat Quay. Here you can order a glass of the black stuff on tap, listen to Irish bands, and choose from a selection of Irish dishes.

Provignage (30 Robertson Quay, #01-12/13, Riverside View; tel: 6834 1490) is a rather upmarket wine bar designed to look like a concrete cave. It is beside the river, and only a short walk from Clarke Quay, but can be a little difficult to find. There are frequent wine-tasting sessions.

To the west of Clarke Quay is Mohamed Sultan Road, where there is an increasing number of bars and clubs to be found. **Club Eden** (25 Mohamed Sultan Road; tel: 6738 0720) is not for the faint of heart; the décor would not look out of place in a Turkish brothel, and the club music from America's west coast is turned up loud. **Next Page** (17 Mohamed Sultan Road; tel: 6235 6967) has a slightly more relaxed atmosphere, with soft lighting and a pleasing, wood-panelled interior. There is a pool table, and the place is popular among expats. Happy hour 15.00–21.00 daily. There is frequently a queue to enter nearby **Tajie** (27 Mohamed Sultan Road; tel: 6887 0007), which is bedecked in red and orange, with prominent Chinese calligraphy. Happy hour Sun–Thu 18.00–21.00. Go one door down for '80s music, and a distinctly Chinese flavour, at **Madam Wong's** (28–29 Mohamed Sultan Road). **Sugar** (13 Mohamed Sultan Road; tel: 6836 0010) is a trendy bar where the décor is altered every three months. There is '70s disco and house music.

Just across the river from Clarke Quay is **Brewerkz** (Riverside Point, #01-05, 30 Merchant Road; tel: 6438 7438), a microbrewery which serves several locally made beers. It also offers food such as pizza, steak and chicken for reasonable prices. It is a good place to have a drink by the river. Happy hour 12.00–20.00.

If you walk down Eu Tong Sen Street towards the river, near the junction with Merchant Road, you will find **Lan Kwai Fong** (50 Eu Tong Sen Street; tel: 6534 3233). This atmospheric night spot has a main bar downstairs, with an enormous dance floor, and a wine bar upstairs. Situated in a grand old building, with various colonial artefacts inside, it is highly recommended. Happy hour 18.00–21.00 Sun–Thu, 18.00–20.00 Fri.

Zouk (17 Jiak Kim Street; tel: 6738 2988) is a popular nightclub housed in an old warehouse. Happy hour Wed–Sat 19.00–21.00.

What to see: a walking tour

The river area is best visited on foot. The sites which follow have been arranged as a walking tour, starting on the north bank by Anderson Bridge near the southern end of the Padang, walking up the river towards Robertson Quay, crossing the river by Kim Seng Bridge and walking back along the south bank. If you don't have time to conduct the whole of this relatively lengthy route, which takes about two hours (excluding stops), then simply pick and choose the sites that most appeal. It is possible to miss out parts by moving to and fro across the river using the many pedestrian or road bridges. Ideally, do the quieter, historical parts during the cooler parts of the day and the livelier restaurant and bar areas of Clarke Quay and Boat Quay in the evening. Do remember to take a bottle of water with you, as well as an umbrella to shield you from the sun or protect you from sudden tropical rainstorms.

North Bank

Named after Sir John Anderson, governor of the Straits Settlement from 1904 to 1911, **Anderson Bridge** was built in 1910 when Cavenagh Bridge was no longer able to cope with Singapore's increasing volume of traffic. Cavenagh Bridge was then closed and all heavy traffic diverted to Anderson Bridge.

Cavenagh Bridge is the oldest bridge across the river. It was constructed in 1868 to commemorate Singapore becoming part of the Straits Settlement and was the first road link between the north and south banks. Before this the only way of crossing the river was by ferry – a great nuisance when visiting the post office (where the courthouse now stands) or the Master Attendant's Office on the north bank from the commercial district on the south.

It is the only suspension bridge in Singapore, designed by John Turnbull Thomson, and made from steel shipped from Glasgow. The original intention was to call it the Edinburgh Bridge, after the Duke of Edinburgh, who was the first to use it while on a visit to the island; ultimately, however, it was named after the popular Colonel Sir William Orfeur Cavenagh, who had served between 1859 and 1867 as the last governor appointed by the East India Company. Unfortunately it was not tall enough for boats to pass underneath at high tide, and, up until 1983 (when they were banished from the river), queues of bumboats were forced to wait on either side of the bridge until the water level had fallen.

When Anderson Bridge was built, Cavenagh Bridge was closed to 'oxcarts, horses and vehicles over 3cwt'. A sign stating this can still be seen on the Empress Place (north) side of the bridge. It is now only a pedestrian crossing. Look over the railings and see if you can spot a family of Singapore river cats – *kucinta* cats – which are recognised as being one of the smallest breeds in the world. Cats in Singapore often have twisted or stunted tails. This is the result not of cruelty or accidents, but of a common genetic flaw.

On passing this bridge, the river curves and widens out. Its shape here, between the north bank and Boat Quay, is thought to resemble the belly of a carp and so is considered auspicious by the Chinese. The walking route takes you past Empress Place (which now houses the Asian Civilisations Museum, in the colonial area – see page 144) and a new Indochine Bar with its magnificent view over the river to Boat Quay and the skyscrapers of the Central Business District to Raffles Landing Site.

The **site of Raffles' first landing** in Singapore on the north bank is marked by the white poly-marble version of the original bronze statue (which now stands outside the Victoria Memorial Hall). The statue stands with Raffles facing north into the island, with his back to the river, and with a map at his feet.

Continue on towards the **Elgin Bridge**, which carries North Bridge Road/ South Bridge Road over the river – the name changing at the bridge. The first crossing over the river was at this point; it was a wooden drawbridge, built in 1822, and known as the Monkey Bridge. This was the solitary permanent means of moving from one side of the river to the other until the Cavenagh Bridge was erected in 1840. It was replaced in 1843 with a footbridge designed by Thomson (and renamed the Thomson Bridge), until it in turn made way for a new iron bridge, constructed in 1863 and named after Lord Elgin.

Lord Elgin was the governor general of India from 1862 to 1863 and then the British commissioner and plenipotentiary in China. He was in Singapore when the Indian mutiny broke out in 1847 and helped to bring it to a conclusion by diverting ships destined for China to Bengal.

The iron version lasted until 1927, when it was demolished and substituted with the concrete double-bridge, and its graceful arches, which stands here today. The old cast-iron lamps on either side, with a Singapore lion in the pedestals, were designed and signed by Cavalieri Rodolfo Nolli, a master craftsman from India. It is probable that this touch is a reference to the legend in which Prince Sang Nila Utana is supposed to have witnessed what he thought was a lion on the island, and accordingly gave Singapore its name (see pages 13–14).

The **Coleman Bridge**, the next one upstream, has thick white pillars and was completed in 1886. It was named after its architect, an Irishman called George Drumgold Coleman, who also designed Parliament House and St Andrew's Cathedral (see pages 143 and 140). Although this is the fourth bridge to span the river here, the eight lampposts survive from the original structure of 1886.

The original crossing on the site of **Read Bridge** was called Merchant Bridge, and was designed by Captain Faber of the Madras Engineers. Like

Cavenagh Bridge, however, it suffered from the distinct disadvantage of being too low to allow boats to pass under at high tide. In 1887 it was demolished and replaced with the present bridge, named after William Henry Read. Read was one of the most famous figures in Singapore. An outstanding legislator and businessman, whose achievements included organising the first regatta and building the first public library, he was well known for his unorthodox methods of controlling contemporary riots sparked by feuding Chinese clans. These included using clan leaders as special constables to patrol the streets (with police escorts) and quell the violence.

In the past, street hawkers and coolies would meet here in the evenings to listen to storytellers, and today, at certain times of the year, you can see evening performances of Chinese street opera at nearby Clarke Quay. The bridge now links Clarke Quay on the north bank with Merchant Court Hotel, Riverside Point and Riverside Village on the south.

Clarke Quay

This quay derives its name from Sir Andrew Clarke, the second governor of Singapore, and was once a busy commercial area. Its warehouses stored goods brought by boats sailing upriver from ships moored in the docks. These warehouses have now been restored and converted into over 50 shops and 30 restaurants. As a result, Clarke Quay is still a lively, bustling place, and the atmosphere is terrific at night.

During the day, you can visit a traditional barber, a small antiques shop and other arts and crafts stores; after dark, the eating places – including floating restaurants on barges – and the bars come into their own, while the Satay Centre (see page 154) takes over one of the side streets. There are also numerous stalls and carts selling all kinds of gifts, souvenirs and foods in the evenings, and there are various street performances that take place during Singapore's many festivals. You can take bumboat rides from the pier (run 09.00–23.00; cost S$10 adult, S$5 child) and there is a flea market on Sunday mornings.

Ord Bridge dates from 1886 and is named after Sir Henry St George Ord, who was the first governor of the Straits Settlement, appointed by the Colonial Office in London. It is now a pedestrian crossing, and street artists and buskers often perform here.

Passing under the wide **Clemenceau Bridge**, which also carries the expressway, you may see men sleeping perched precariously on the walls of the river's edge. This was the furthest navigable point after the reclamation of the river, but river taxis are expected to be able to travel upstream to Robertson Quay and on to the riverside hotels by the end of 2002.

Robertson Quay

This area and beyond was used mainly for storage warehouses and godowns, and, although some have been restored as bars and restaurants, it is nevertheless very quiet during the day. Several new pedestrian bridges have been built on this stretch of the river and the old Rodyk Street godowns, built in 1877, and Jiak Kim Street godowns (three art deco ones) can be seen between the Robertson and Jiak Kim bridges.

South Bank

Cross the river either at the Jiak Kim pedestrian bridge or, a little further on, the Kim Seng road bridge and walk back along the south bank. Pause for a refreshing drink under the trees at the Riverside Café of the Grand Copthorne Waterfront Hotel (see page 149), and then continue past the new and luxurious private condominium blocks with their swimming pools and gated entrances.

Pass under the Clemenceau Bridge, turn right and leave the river for a short diversion to visit the **Tan Si Chong Su Temple** (Magazine Road, Singapore 059567), which you will find by walking to Merchant Road, turning left and then first right into Magazine Road. This is an ancestral Hokkien temple, doubling as a community centre for the Tan clan. It was financed by Tan Lim Cheng and Tan Beng Swee, two Fujian merchants, and built in 1878 from stones brought out to Singapore in ships as ballast.

Wonderfully ornate, it has a blazing pearl on the roof, ceramic flowers and dancing dragons for celestial power and potency, and intricate carvings of lotuses and phoenix at the entrance. A pair of red-and-gold dragons greets you as you enter the courtyard and there are door-gods that guard the side entrances from evil spirits. Above the altar is a sign in Chinese characters which means 'Help the world and the people'. During Chinese New Year, celebrations here involve the use of sugarcane plants. This looks back to an ancient story that describes the Hokkien hiding in a sugarcane field to escape marauding Mongols. On leaving the temple, turn right to Riverside Village.

Getting there If you are not doing the rest of the walking tour, the best way to reach the temple is by taking the MRT to Clarke Quay (new NE line, opening end 2002). Walk away from the river past the Merchant Court Hotel towards Merchant Road, and turn right and then left into Magazine Road.

Riverside Village and Riverside Point

These new developments are situated opposite Clarke Quay. **Riverside Village** consists of Central Mall, Central Square and Merchant Square, and stands where once a community of squatters lived – along with cockroaches and rats! Nowadays it is a great night-spot, with restaurants, bars and discos. Walking back towards the river, you reach **Riverside Point**, with more restaurants and a micro-brewery where you can drink freshly brewed beer. In the past, this area held opium dens, secret societies and prostitutes.

Walk back to the riverside itself and continue past the new Clarke Quay MRT station. Go under Coleman Bridge, past the Riverwalk and its restaurants, to Elgin Bridge and Boat Quay.

Boat Quay

In 1822 Raffles allocated the area south of the river to the Chinese. Boat Quay was completed in 1842. Although the conditions were extremely squalid, trade flourished and hundreds of bumboats would struggle for the limited berths available. It continued to be an important trading area, even after the new harbour at Tanjong Pagar was opened in 1852, until the 1960s. However, trade on the river gradually declined and, in the late 1980s, the whole area was designated for conservation and restoration.

Boat Quay has always been a popular eating-place. Hawkers used to sell their wares from stalls, and, with no supply of clean water, each was forced to wash his or her bowls in a single bucket that was subsequently emptied into the river! In the days before the river was cleaned up, the smell must have been dreadful. The old shop-houses have since been converted into restaurants and bars, and this is a great – though fairly expensive – place to eat, to watch people and river boats, and to admire the view of the old colonial buildings on the north bank.

Each restaurant has its own group of tables on the riverside. In the evenings the area throngs with tourist and local diners, while the bars are busy during the lunch hours and early evenings as workers from the nearby skyscraper banks and financial offices unwind after busy days.

A river taxi service runs from Boat Quay to Clarke Quay when the tide is high enough.

Walk on along the promenade past **United Overseas Bank (UOB) Plaza**, with its modern statues by Fernando Botero and Salvador Dalí, and the city skyscraper banks. Behind and to the south of UOB Plaza is the **Central Business District** (or **CBD**). This is the heart of the financial sector, full of hi-tech, glistening skyscrapers, and the primary source of the country's wealth. Many of the buildings are aligned according to the principles of *feng shui* – indeed, *feng shui* experts are invariably consulted before new buildings are constructed. This is also where the trader Nick Leeson famously brought about the downfall of Barings Bank in the 1980s. His favourite haunt was Harry's Bar (see page 155), and it (along with other bars in Boat Quay) is still frequented by city types. The CBD is made up of four main roads – Shenton Way, Raffles Place, Cecil Street and Robinson Road – and their buildings contribute to Singapore's distinctive, thrusting skyline. However, there is little to occupy the casual visitor.

Lying between Cavenagh Bridge and the pedestrian Anderson Bridge, you will find the **Fullerton Hotel** (see page 149) in the old Fullerton Building. Fullerton Square was the site of Fort Fullerton, which was built in 1829 to defend Singapore from attack, before being demolished in 1873. The Exchange Building then stood on the site, and was used by the Chamber of Commerce and the Singapore Club, until being replaced by the Fullerton Building in 1928.

Named after Robert Fullerton, who was the first governor of the Straits Settlement, it housed the General Post Office and other government departments. There was even a subway from the post office under Fullerton Road to Clifford Pier to make the task of moving the mail to and from the ships easier. When the Fullerton Building was completed it was a landmark for ships sailing into the harbour, and the Fullerton Light, which was installed on the roof in 1958, could be seen from 15 miles away.

The building has since been refurbished as a five-star hotel but the exterior has been carefully preserved. Floodlit in the evenings, it is a very impressive sight in its commanding position at the entrance to the Singapore River.

Getting there For those looking for the hotel, but not doing the rest of the tour, take the MRT to Raffles Place (NS and EW interchange) and walk north towards the river.

To the southeast of the Fullerton Building is **Clifford Pier**. The original reclamation of the swampy ground south of the Singapore River enabled Boat Quay and Commercial Square (now Raffles Place) to be created. This meant that development could take place at the waterfront (which at that time lay back where the buildings on Collyer Quay now stand), comprising the godowns and jetties belonging to the different merchants and businesses.

Further reclamation, and the appearance of a sea wall in the 1860s, led to the construction of Collyer Quay. Two-storey houses lined the quay, complete with hanging verandas from which the merchants could watch the arrival of their ships.

Johnston's Pier was an iron structure, built in 1854, and named after the pioneering merchant, Alexander Laurie Johnston, who arrived at Raffles' invitation in 1819. He was the founder of the Chamber of Commerce and also one of the first magistrates of the town. The pier was often called Lampu Merah (the 'red-lamp pier' in Malay) after the red oil lamp that was strung from the pier to guide the seamen.

Demolished in 1933, it was replaced by Clifford Pier, a little further along Collyer Quay. This was named after Sir Hugh Clifford, who spent most of his working life in the Far East and was governor between 1927 and 1929. The pier then became the landing spot for the many immigrants and sea passengers flocking to Singapore. These days, passenger-bearing ships dock in the harbour area and the pier is used as a departure point for bumboats and water taxis running tourists to the river and the harbour, or for Chinese junks providing short cruises to the islands of Kusu and St John's. (Ferries to Kusu and St John's run from the World Trade Centre. See page 37.)

Getting there MRT to Raffles Place and walk east through Change Alley towards Collyer Quay and the pier. Alternatively, take a bus (Nos 167 or 700) from Orchard Road.

North of here, on the land at the southern entrance to the river, is the small **Merlion Park**, the location for the strange white statue of the Merlion (which is half-fish and half-lion, and the symbol of Singapore). It is the place where Prince Sang Nila Utana supposedly spied a lion (*singla*), giving the island its name (see pages 13–14). The piscine half of the mutated figure represents the island's standing as an old and famous port.

The statue periodically spouts water from its mouth – the postcards certainly show this – although you have to be in the right place at the right time to witness it. The best view is from the north side of the river, or from the river taxis that travel from Clarke Quay or Boat Quay around to Clifford Pier.

CHINATOWN

The first junk full of immigrants arrived from Xiamen in the Chinese province
of Fujian in 1819. There followed an influx of immigrants, and Sir Stamford
Raffles allocated the district southwest of the river for the Chinese inhabitants
to develop a *kampong* (village). The Hokkiens bought property along China
Street, Chulia Street and Telok Ayer Street. The Cantonese, who were tailors,
jewellers and restaurateurs, built their premises on Temple Street, Mosque
Street and Pagoda Street, and around Upper Cross Street, New Bridge Road,
Bukit Pasoh and South Bridge Road. The Teochew were farmers and
fishermen, and settled around Boat Quay, Circular Road and part of South
Bridge Road. Even today, the spoken Chinese dialects vary between these areas.

Raffles decreed that the new structures must conform to a specific design.
Each house had to be built with a uniform frontage and a five-foot-wide
veranda. The latter was to be open at the front and at either end in order to
create a continuous walkway on each side of the street, providing protection
for pedestrians from tropical downpours and the heat of the sun. These
famously became known as the 'five-foot ways'. Most of these shop-houses
were two or three storeys high, the number of floors dependent upon the
wealth of the owners. Sadly, many have been demolished both to
accommodate the expanding financial district and as a result of a government
initiative to sanitise the area. The latter was a policy that the government came
to regret on realising that tourists were attracted, rather than put off, by the
original character of the place. During the 1970s, the Urban Redevelopment
Authority (URA) was hastily formed in an attempt to prevent any further
destruction of historic buildings and to oversee a programme of conservation.
Consequently, some shop-houses remain and are still used as stores selling
paper goods to burn at funerals, plastic lanterns for festivals and hundred-year-
old eggs, or are being restored as boutique hotels.

Much of the area along the parallel dual carriageways of Eu Tong Sen
Street (northbound) and New Bridge Road (southbound) has been subject
to massive disruption caused by the construction of the NE line of the
MRT. There are new stations for Clarke Quay and Chinatown, and an
addition to Outram Park. The line is due to open at the end of 2002, and
will improve access to Chinatown. Some new shopping and office blocks
are also being built.

The most interesting parts of Chinatown, though, are bounded by New
Bridge Road to the west, Telok Ayer Street to the east, Cross Street to the
north, and Keong Siak Road and Craig Road to the south. South Bridge Road
bisects this area roughly in a line from north to south.

On one side of Eu Tong Sen Street is **People's Park Complex**, a shopping
mall that has a good basement food market. Stalls close at 07.30, but if you get
there early enough you will see a variety of animals being sold as food. Among
them are imported terrapins, destined for Chinese restaurants that serve them
as turtle soup. The sight of animals packed into small cages – and their
slaughter – can be disturbing, and is not for the weak of stomach. Across the
road are some of the remaining old shop-houses, and their stock is well worth

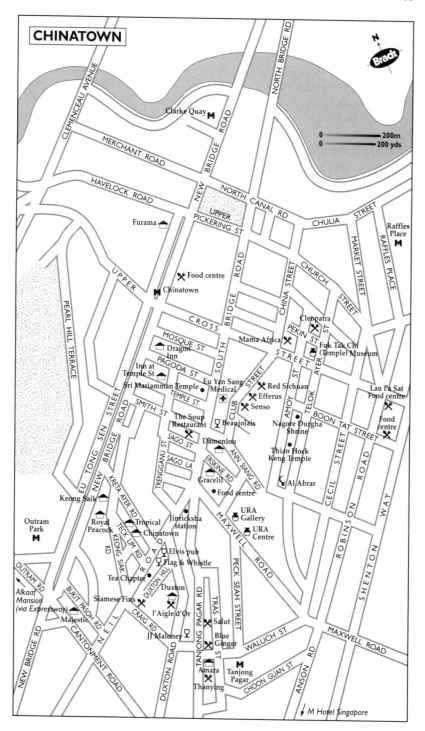

CHINATOWN

N

Bradt

Clarke Quay M

MERCHANT ROAD

NORTH BRIDGE RD

NEW BRIDGE ROAD

HAVELOCK ROAD

NORTH CANAL RD

UPPER PICKERING ST

CHULIA STREET

0   200m
0   200 yds

Furama

Raffles Place M

MARKET STREET

RAFFLES PLACE

Food centre

Chinatown

UPPER

CROSS

BRIDGE ROAD

SOUTH BRIDGE ROAD

CHINA STREET

CHURCH STREET

Cleopatra

PEKIN ST

Mama Africa

Fuk Tak Chi (Temple) Museum

PEARL HILL TERRACE

MOSQUE ST

Dragon Inn

PAGODA ST

Inn at Temple St

Sri Mariamman Temple

Eu Yan Sang Medical

TEMPLE ST

SMITH ST

CLUB STREET

Red Sichuan

Efferus

Senso

AMOY ST

TELOK AYER STREET

BOON TAT STREET

Lau Pa Sat Food centre

Food centre

The Soup Restaurant

Beaujolais

Nagore Durgha Shrine

EU TONG SEN STREET

NEW BRIDGE ROAD

KRETA AYER RD

SAGO ST

Damenlou

SAGO LA

TRENGGANU ST

ERSKINE RD

ANN SIANG RD

Thian Hock Keng Temple

CECIL STREET

ROBINSON ROAD

SHENTON WAY

Gracelit

Food centre

Al Abrar

Keong Saik

Outram Park M

Royal Peacock

Tropical

Chinatown

Jinricksha station

URA Gallery

URA Centre

TECK LIM RD

KEONG SIAK RD

DUXTON HILL

Elvis pub

Flag & Whistle

MAXWELL ROAD

PECK SEAH STREET

Tea Chapter

BUKIT PASOH RD

Siamese Fins

Duxton

l'Aigle d'Or

CRAIG RD

TANJONG PAGAR RD

TRAS ST

Salut

Blue Ginger

WALUCH ST

MAXWELL ROAD

OUTRAM RD

Alkaaf Mansion (via Expressway)

Majestic

NEW BRIDGE RD

CANTONMENT ROAD

JJ Maloney

DUXTON ROAD

Amara

Tanjong Pagar M

Thanying

CHOON GUAN ST

ANSON RD

↓ M Hotel Singapore

a browse. You will discover enamelled mugs from China, toys from Malaysia and India, jewellery from Java, Indonesian batik garments called *kebayas*, and locally produced paper lanterns and painted fans. Most intriguing is 'hell money' – colourful notes which are burnt as offerings to the dead.

If you are interested in the Singaporean passion for **bird singing** (see pages 30–3), Chinatown is a good area to watch. Competitions are held at the corner of Tiong Bahru and Seng Poh roads, between about 07.00 and 10.30 (Sunday mornings are the most popular). You can sit at one of the coffee shops and enjoy the tunes, and have a look at the fascinating range of accessories on sale at a shop across the street.

Getting there
MRT to Chinatown on the new NE line (opening end of 2002). Bus No 190 from Orchard Road will drop passengers by the Sri Mariamman Temple (see page 169).

Where to stay
Super-luxury
Amara Hotel 165 Tanjong Pagar Rd, Singapore 088539; tel: 6224 4488; fax: 6224 3910; email: reserv@amara.com.sg. Another multi-storey, fairly impersonal, international luxury hotel. Has its own shopping centre next door. Recently renovated, with business centre, large pool, gym, and tennis court. Restaurants: Element (Japanese, international and Asian), Wall St Café (char-grill and salad), Silk Rd (Chinese), Thanying (Thai), Café Oriental (style of local coffee shop). 338 rooms. Single S$340–400, double S$360–420, suite S$600–800. *Nearest MRT* Tanjong Pagar (EW line)

M Hotel Singapore 81 Anson Rd, Singapore 079908; tel: 6224 1133; fax: 6222 0749; email: roomres@m-hotel.com.sg. Large, modern, newly renovated and renamed (was Copthorne Harbour View). Minimalist-style lobby and rooms. At southern end of CBD, so very convenient for business travellers. 416 rooms. Single S$380, double S$380, suite S$600–700. *Nearest MRT* Tanjong Pagar (EW line)

Luxury
Furama Hotel Singapore 60 Eu Tong Sen St, Singapore 059804; tel: 6533 3888; fax: 6534 1489; email: sales.fhsg@ furama-hotels.com. Modern, 4-star hotel with well-furnished, upgraded rooms completed in 2002. Situated in ugly block on main street through centre of Chinatown, and near new Chinatown MRT station (opening autumn 2002). Pool, small gym and business centre. Restaurants: Tiffany (Western buffet), Furama Palace (Cantonese), Serabel (Korean). 360 rooms. Single S$240–300, double S$260–330, suite S$380–1,100. *Nearest MRT* Clarke Quay (NE line)

Mid-range
Chinatown Hotel 12–16 Teck Lim Rd (off Keong Saik Rd), Singapore 088388; tel: 6225 5166; fax: 6225 3912; email: enquiries@chinatownhotel.com. Three shop-houses refurbished as a boutique hotel. Family-run and personalised service – the owner was inspired by a small European hotel, and determined to set up similar

establishments in Singapore. Delightful watercolours of old Singapore by local artist Lim Kim Sing in lobby. Hotel has produced its own guide to history of Chinatown and nearby restaurants. Breakfast corner in lobby. Business facilities provided. No pool. 42 rooms. Single S$130–65, double S$170–80. Recommended. *Nearest MRT* Outram Park (NE/EW interchange)

Duxton 83 Duxton Rd, Singapore 089540; tel: 6227 7678; fax: 6227 1232; email: duxton@singnet.com.sg. The first boutique hotel in Singapore, converted from 5 Straits Chinese trading houses. Spacious lobby with marble-carpeted floors and large plate-glass windows, but 1st and 2nd floors are traditional shop-house design. Many bars, karaoke bars and restaurants in Duxton Rd, so busy and noisy in evening. Restaurant L'Aigle d'Or (French) claims to be best in Asia. 48 rooms. Single S$170–210, double S$205–50, suite S$230–90. Recommended. *Nearest MRT* Tanjong Pagar (EW line)

Damenlou Hotel 12 Ann Siang Rd, Singapore 069692; tel: 6221 1900; fax: 6225 8500. A 2-star hotel opened in 1993 in a building constructed by the Tang family in 1927. Unprepossessing to look at, but run by a very helpful and friendly family with many guests who return. Restaurant serves the famous fish-head noodle soup created by owner's father, Tang Kwong Swee, who started life as a hawker in the 1920s, perfecting his recipe over the years until his death in 1999. Basic and inexpensive, but characterful and in heart of Chinatown. Small roof-top restaurant. No pool. 12 rooms. Single/double from S$100–30. Interesting! *Nearest MRT* Tanjong Pagar (EW line)

Majestic 31 Bukit Pasoh Rd, Singapore 089845; tel: 6222 3377; fax: 6223 0907/5111; email: majestichotel@pacific.net.sg. Restored shop-houses at very southern edge of Chinatown offering modern, Chinese-style rooms with bathrooms and air conditioning. Breakfast and simple meals in café. Close to busy road (currently with roadworks for new MRT line at Outram). 56 rooms. Single S$88, double S$98. *Nearest MRT* Outram Park (NE/EW interchange)

The Royal Peacock 55 Keong Saik Rd, Singapore 089158; tel: 6223 3522; fax: 6221 1770; email: rpeacock@cyberway.com.sg. Located in the heritage area (old red-light district), this 7-year-old boutique hotel consists of 10 restored shop-houses. All rooms beautifully decorated with simple Chinese furnishings. Management prides itself on offering traditional values and personal service – consequently, very friendly and helpful staff. American breakfast included. 79 rooms. Single S$145–215, double S$160–230, suite S$250. Recommended. *Nearest MRT* Outram Park (NE/EW interchange)

The Inn at Temple Street 36 Temple St, Singapore 058581; tel: 6221 5333; fax: 6225 5391; email: theinn@singnet.com.sg. Peranakan-style hotel with Peranakan furnishings from 5 restored shop-houses. Small rooms containing shower or bath, all with air conditioning. Breakfast included, with café on lobby floor serving Western and local Peranakan and Chinese food. 42 rooms. Single S$125, double S$145. Recommended. *Nearest MRT* Chinatown (NE line)

Budget

Dragon Inn Chinatown 18 Mosque St, Singapore 059498; tel: 6222 7227; fax: 6222 6116. Two newly renovated 3-storey shop-houses in heart of Chinatown.. Pretty basic rooms with air conditioning and bathrooms. Food in nearby Smith St. 40 rooms. Single S$59, double S$69–79. Be warned, however, that there are also hourly rates and a fairly brisk trade. *Nearest MRT* Chinatown (NE line)

The Keong Saik Hotel 69 Keong Saik Rd, Singapore 089165; tel: 6223 0660; fax: 6225 0660; email: keongsaik@pacific.net.sg. A 4-year-old boutique hotel from 3 refurbished shop-houses. At southern end of Chinatown (previously the red-light district), with better hotels near by. Cramped and unappealing lobby, and very small breakfast area (Continental breakfast included). Plain furnishing. No pool. 25 rooms. Single S$70–80, double S$80–100. *Nearest MRT* Outram Park (NE/EW interchange) **Tropical Hotel** 22 Teck Lim Rd (off Keong Saik Rd), Singapore 088392; tel: 6225 6696; fax: 6225 6626; email: trophot@singnet.com.sg. Boutique hotel from 3 refurbished shop-houses catering mainly for business travellers. At southern end of Chinatown. Well-decorated rooms with usual facilities. 44 rooms. Single S$55–60, double S$75–80. *Nearest MRT* Outram Park (NE/EW interchange)

Where to eat

Mama Africa (88 Telok Ayer Street, #01-01, Far East Square; tel: 6532 9339) is run by the same people as African Heartbeat in the west (see page 173) and, like its sister restaurant, offers delicacies including ostrich and crocodile in a lodge-style setting. Prices are reasonable, and the staff efficient. Open Mon–Fri 11.30–14.30; Mon–Sat 18.30–22.30. Closed Sun and Sat lunch.

Feel devilishly hedonistic amidst the deep crimsons and blood reds which colour the surroundings at the appropriately named **Red** (29 Club Street; tel: 6227 7189). The imaginative décor is matched by creative and well-presented Sichuan cuisine, which costs around S$50 per person. Open daily 11.30–14.30, 18.00–22.30.

L'Aigle d'Or (Duxton Hotel, 83 Duxton Road; tel: 6227 7678) is a light and sunny restaurant, dominated by yellows and creams. The French menu is modern and changes regularly to guarantee the freshest seasonal produce. The foie gras is a speciality, there are some fabulous desserts, and an excellent choice of cheeses. Popular for business lunches. The bill can be expensive, although some of the set menus are less so (lunch for S$35, and dinner options starting at S$75). Open daily 12.00–14.00, 19.00–22.00.

There is a similarly warm atmosphere at **Salut** (25–27 Tanjong Pagar Road; tel: 6225 7555) which, like L'Aigle d'Or, is splashed with the colours of a Mediterranean summer. Foie gras is a favourite here, too. The French cuisine is perhaps not quite so fine, although neither is it quite so pricey, and you should be able to eat for under S$70. Open 11.30–14.30, 18.30–22.30. Lunch is not served on Sun.

To the south of Chinatown, off Henderson Road, is **Alkaff Mansion** (10 Telok Blangah Green, Telok Blangah Hill Park; tel: 6278 6979), which has two dining areas and is a restaurant to savour. The dining hall on the lower level offers a variety of international buffets (dinner only). As well as set Western menus, the upper restaurant features a real treat – *rijsttafel*, an Indonesian feast of rice and a range of side dishes served by waitresses in traditional dress. The colonial mansion conjures a romantic sense of the past, and the leafy views are serene. Budget for around S$80 per head. Open daily 12.00–14.30, 19.00–24.00.

For Middle Eastern food, head just off Telok Ayer Street for **Cleopatra** (Capital Square 3, #01-03, Pekin Street, Far East Square; tel: 6438 2975).

Syrian, Moroccan and Lebanese dishes are available for mid-range prices. While, as you would expect, there is no shortage of meat, there are also vegetarian alternatives. Open every day 11.30–14.30, 18.00–22.30.

Ostensibly Middle Eastern, **Efferus** (47 Club Street; tel: 6324 6768) nevertheless offers an eclectic and curious mix of Mediterranean cuisine ranging across foods such as couscous cakes, crispy duck, veal and cassoulet. Try not to be too baffled by the opening hours, and expect to pay S$50–60. Open Mon–Fri 11.30–14.30, Mon–Thu 18.30–22.30, Fri–Sat 18.30–23.00, Sun 18.30–22.00. Closed lunchtime at weekend.

Also on Club Street, **Senso** (21 Club Street; tel: 6224 3534) has good Italian food and a range of regional wines. There is an alfresco dining area. It is expensive, but not extravagantly so. Open Mon–Fri 12.00–14.30, 18.30–22.30, Sat 18.30–22.30. Closed Sun.

One of five outlets (others are at SunTec City Mall, Seah Street, Causeway Point and Jurong Point), the **Soup Restaurant** (25 Smith Street; tel: 6222 9923) has a range of tasty soups along with other Chinese dishes. The food is inexpensive – you should eat well for under S$30. Open daily 12.00–14.30, 17.30–21.30.

Siamese Fins (45 Craig Road, Tanjong Pagar; tel: 6227 9795) serves Thai-Teochew cuisine in a relaxing ambience. Expect to pay around S$40–50 each. Open daily 11.30–14.30, 18.00–22.00.

Blue Ginger (97 Tanjong Pagar Road; tel: 6222 3928) is situated in a restored shop-house, and has a comfortable, homely feel about it. It serves good Peranakan (or Nonya) cuisine, the traditional blend of Malay and Chinese foods developed by the early settlers in Singapore who arrived from these regions. A meal here is inexpensive. Open 11.30–15.00, 18.30–22.00.

Thanying (Amara Hotel, 165 Tanjong Pagar Road; tel: 6227 7856) is an attractive, characterful restaurant, dominated by light wooden panelling and soft illumination. Its Thai cuisine ranks among the best on the island, and, as such, is reasonably priced at about S$40 per person. Open Mon–Sat 11.00–14.30, 18.30–22.00. Closed Sun.

Food centres can be found on the corner of Maxwell and South Bridge roads (outdoors, but covered), at Lau Pa Sat on Robinson Road (indoors, fan-cooled), next door on Boon Tat Street (evenings only), and at Chinatown Point Mall at the junction of New Bridge Road and Upper Cross Street.

Nightlife

Just off South Bridge Road, the **Beaujolais Wine Bar** (1 Ann Siang Hill; tel: 6224 2227) is romantic and intimate, with candles, fairly priced wines, and seating outside.

Carnegie's (44/45 Pekin Street, #001-01, Far East Square; tel: 6534 0850) first opened in Hong Kong in 1994. It evokes the rock-and-roll era, with appropriate paraphernalia decorating its walls. There is a decent menu and an extensive range of shooters to shoot back. Happy hour 11.00–21.00 Mon–Fri, 17.00–21.00 Sat, all night Sun. If rock and roll is your thing, pay tribute to 'The King' at the shrine that is the **Elvis Pub** (1A Duxton Hill; tel: 6220 1268). A short walk away is a British pub, the **Flag and Whistle** (10 Duxton Hill), and not far from there **J J Mahoney's** (55 Duxton Road), a bar spread over three floors, and offering a games room and karaoke.

What to see and do
A walking tour
Chinatown is most easily explored on foot. A fairly long walking tour (taking at least half a day) is briefly detailed below, covering several of the religious monuments, historical sites, and shopping and food outlets. It starts at Chinatown MRT (NE line).

Walk south to **Temple Street** and left to **South Bridge Road** to visit the **Sri Miriamman Temple** and **Eu Yan Sang Chinese Medical Centre**. Next, go right along **Smith Street** (food street), left down **Trengganu Street** and back along **Sago Lane** to South Bridge Road. Turn right to see the former **Jinricksha Station** and into **Neil Road** to visit a tea house. Back to **Maxwell Road**, and the refurbished food centre at the corner – more refreshment – and then right to **Cecil Street** and left into **Telok Ayer Street** to see the **Thian Hock Keng Temple**, the **Nagore Durgha Shrine** and the **Fuk Tak Chi Temple**. Finally, travel right along **Boon Tat Street** to **Lau Pa Sat** (for a cooling drink and a snack) and then take a short walk up **Robinson Road** to **Raffles Place MRT** (NS and EW interchange). For full details of these places, see below.

Places of worship
The **Fuk Tak Chi Temple** (80 Telok Ayer Street), built by Hakka and Cantonese immigrants, was the first Chinese temple in Singapore. It began life as a shrine in 1824, gradually expanding over the years to become the temple it is today. The temple's entrance, modelled in the style of a Chinese magistrates' court, is symbolic of power and authority. The principal god worshipped here is Tua Pek Kong (in Hokkien) or Dai Bak Kong (in Cantonese). It is a good idea to combine a visit to this temple with trips to the Nagore Durgha Shrine and the Thian Hock Keng Temple (see below) as they are all found on Telok Ayer Street.

Getting there MRT to Raffles Place (NS and EW interchange), followed by a 15-minute walk south down Robinson Road to Boon Tat Street, and a right into Telok Ayer Street.

The **Nagore Durgha Shrine** (140 Telok Ayer Street; tel: 6324 0021) was originally constructed of wood and attap by two Muslim brothers from India. In 1815 it was rebuilt with limestone, before being altered once more three years later with materials brought from India. The result is an interesting blend of architectural styles.

Getting there As for the Fuk Tak Chi Temple, above.

The **Thian Hock Keng Temple** (158 Telok Ayer Street), or the Temple of Heavenly Bliss, is the island's oldest Chinese temple and the most significant for its Hokkien community. Early immigrants from southern China landed at the Telok Ayer waterfront and built the original temple between 1821 and 1822. It was initially a simple joss-house where incense was offered to Ma Cho Po, the goddess of the sea, in thanks for a safe journey. This was rebuilt from 1839 to 1842, and its prayer hall was to provide the setting for a statue of the goddess that arrived from China in 1840.

Many of the timbers, stone columns and tiles were once ballast in Chinese junks, and broken pottery and cutlery from such boats were used in the mosaics of birds' feathers, dragons and flowers which decorate the roof. The temple's architecture is southern Chinese in style, with a grand main entrance and high steps patterned with coloured tiles depicting peacocks, roses, and the green-and-brown Buddhist swastika. Tigers, lions and gods guard the doors, while one pagoda contains a shrine to Confucius and another the ancestral tablets of the immigrant founders.

Getting there As for the Fuk Tak Chi Temple (see opposite).

The outside of the **Sri Mariamman Temple** (244 South Bridge Road) is adorned with vivid statues of Hindu deities and mythological figures. Singapore's oldest Hindu temple, dating back to 1827, it was built by Narina Pillary, a government clerk from Penang, who arrived in 1819 with Stamford Raffles. He was the earliest leader of the Indian community and acquired the site in 1823. The original temple was constructed from wood and attap, but the present brick building was fashioned by skilled craftsmen – who were, in fact, ex-convicts from India – in 1843. Of particular interest are the two Chinese windows in the walls below the *gopuram* (tower). It is believed these were built to allow Chinese believers to pray from outside the temple.

The structure, a national monument, is a favoured venue for Hindu weddings because of its lavish (even gaudy) decoration. It is also the location for the annual Thimithi festival (see *Chapter 3, Holidays, Celebrations and Events*, page 96), when devotees walk across hot coals to demonstrate the depth and purity of their faith.

Getting there MRT to City Hall (NS and EW interchange) and a bus (Nos 61, 103, 166 or 197) from nearby North Bridge Road to the temple. Alternatively, take bus No 190 from Orchard Road, which runs every 5–10 minutes.

Museums and galleries

The **URA Gallery** (URA Centre, 45 Maxwell Road; tel: 6321 8321) charts the history of Singapore's urban development and the conservation schemes of the Urban Redevelopment Authority. This body was set up during the 1970s with the aim of ensuring that what remained of the island's architectural heritage – which was rapidly disappearing – was preserved. In practice, this means the restoration and conservation of the façades of the old shop-houses (the interiors are now largely impractical for modern businesses). There are almost 50 displays, many satisfying the Singaporean love for technological wizardry (with interactive touchscreens and computer-generated exhibits). The centrepiece is an impressive scale model of the country. Open Mon–Fri 09.00–16.30, Sat 09.00–12.30. Closed Sun and public holidays.

Getting there MRT to Tanjong Pagar (EW line) and walk left along Maxwell Road.

Other places of interest
Eu Yan Sang Chinese Medical Centre

When Eu Kwong Pui left China for Malaya in 1800, he was shocked to see miners eating opium to relieve their pains. He therefore decided to start treating them with Chinese medicines instead. In 1879 he opened his first shop in Perak in Malaya. The Eu Yan Sang Chinese Medical Centre (269A South Bridge Road) is the oldest such centre in Singapore. *Yan sang* means 'caring for men'.

Buy ginger liqueur (good for travel sickness and wind!), wolf berries (tossed with spinach and added to Chinese chicken soup to improve the eyesight of young children), chrysanthemum tea (supposedly breaks down cholesterol) or a host of other strange and peculiar-looking offerings and medicines. You can also taste ginseng tea. Combine a visit here with one to the Sri Mariamman Temple almost opposite.

Getting there As for the Sri Mariamman Temple (see above, page 169).

Jinricksha Station

The former Jinricksha Station (1 Tanjong Pagar Road), the white building where Neil and Tanjong Pagar roads meet, is more properly an interesting landmark than a place to visit. It represents the last remaining link with the rickshaws that were so common during the early history of Singapore. The building was erected in 1903 to house the Jinricksha Department, which had been established 15 years earlier to ensure that every rickshaw was registered and licensed. At the end of the 19th century, there were at least 1,000 owners of rickshaws; by 1919 the number had grown to 9,000 rickshaws pulled by 20,000 men working in shifts. These workers lived in squalid conditions in Chinatown, and, until two-seaters were banned in 1914, often toiled away pulling vehicles containing whole families or heavy loads of commercial goods.

Rickshaws were eventually replaced first by trishaws and electric trams, and finally by buses and cars. They were phased out entirely by the government after World War II. The trishaws to be found today off Bras Basah Road offering tours around Little India, and the occasional ones seen in Chinatown, are reminders of a quieter and more leisurely form of transport. For details of trishaw tours, see page 58.

Getting there MRT to Chinatown (new NE line, opening end 2002), and walk east along Upper Cross Street and south down South Bridge Road. Pass the Sri Miriamman Temple to Maxwell Market Food Centre, and Jinricksha Station is where Neil Road joins Tanjong Pagar Road.

Temple Street, Smith Street, Trengganu Street, Sago Lane and Neil Road

Shops in **Temple Street** sell a wide range of souvenirs that are worth browsing. Items on offer include cars made of paper. These – and other representations of earthly goods – are burnt after funerals in the belief that the genuine articles will accompany deceased relatives in the afterlife. Don't forget that, unlike many other shopping areas in Singapore, it is acceptable to bargain in Chinatown.

Smith Street is now primarily given over to food, with outside tables along one side of the road displaying many different kinds of local cuisine. On the other are small souvenir shops.

At the corner of **Smith Street** and **Trengganu Street** is a building that once held the famous **Lai Chun Yuen** Cantonese opera house. At the end of the 19th century this was the centre of entertainment in Chinatown, and it continued to be so until the arrival of the motion picture in Singapore in 1927. During the Japanese occupation, the bodies of those who had died from beriberi – a disease caused by vitamin deficiency – were stuffed under a staircase in the theatre. Fortunately the corpses were cleared out fairly regularly!

Sago Lane, named after the sago factories that once stood here, now has medical halls, rattan weavers, kite and mask shops and furniture restorers. The area used to have funeral parlours and the notorious death houses, where the terminally ill who had no family to care for them came to die (see box, page 17).

If you fancy a refreshing brew, try one of the tea houses on **Neil Road**. The Tea Chapter (9A Neil Road; tel: 6226 1917) can claim to have served a particularly special customer – Queen Elizabeth II. She dropped in towards the end of the 1980s and, for a fee, you can enjoy the privilege of parking yourself in the seat warmed by the royal behind. These tea houses offer a large range of teas, and frequently tea-appreciation talks and demonstrations. For more information, see *Tea houses*, pages 65–7.

Lau Pa Sat (formerly Telok Ayer Market)

When Telok Ayer Market opened in 1825, it extended in part over the sea and there were jetties for boats to load and unload their produce directly into and out of the market. In 1836 it was rebuilt in an octagonal shape devised by George Coleman before being demolished for land reclamation in 1879. However, it was resurrected once more on reclaimed land at its present site (19 Raffles Quay) in 1894. The municipal engineer, James MacRitchie (after whom the MacRitchie Reservoir was named), designed the new version, and this (though upgraded) is the building we see today. MacRitchie retained the octagonal shape and used beautiful ornamental cast-iron tracery from Glasgow to support the roof. In 1973 the market became a hawker centre. Dismantled while the MRT was being constructed in 1986, it rose yet again a couple of years later in its original position. It is now a thriving food centre – renamed Lau Pa Sat since 1991 – cooled by twirling fans, and busy with office workers during the lunch period and tourists and locals who can be persuaded away from Boat Quay in the evenings. Boon Tat Street, beside Lau Pa Sat, is closed to traffic in the evenings and, with smoke from the grills rising into the air, is always popular as a satay centre.

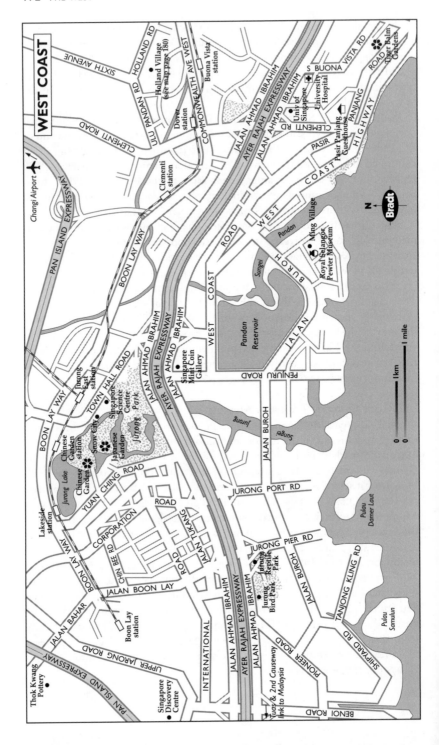

The West

As you travel to the west of Singapore Island, either by road or train, you will notice the housing developments and new towns that have sprung up along the route of the EW MRT line as far as Boon Lay. Beyond Boon Lay is the industrial region of Jurong, and at the far western end of the island is the area known as Tuas where there was once a fishing village, and where the new link bridge crossing the Johore Straits to southern Malaysia is now.

If you look at the island map in this region you realise how much land reclamation there has been – the coastline has conspicuously straight edges! In fact there are plans to reclaim yet more land around the many small islands off the Singapore coast between Singapore and Malaysia. This is causing some ill-feeling between the two countries, as the Malaysians feel their international boundary will be encroached as Singapore 'moves' nearer and nearer. Attractions in the west are largely dispersed, and you will usually need to use transport to travel between them.

GETTING THERE

The furthest west you can go on the MRT is to the Boon Lay terminus (EW line). By car, the Ayer Rajah Expressway (AYE) runs south of the MRT line, taking you as far as the second causeway crossing to Malaysia at Tuas, and the Pan Island Expressway (PIE) runs north of the MRT line, looping further inland. There are bus interchanges at Jurong East and Boon Lay.

WHERE TO STAY

Few people stay in the west, and accommodation is extremely scarce. One fairly cheap place is the **Pasir Panjang Guesthouse** 404 Pasir Panjang Rd, Singapore 118741; tel: 6778 8511; fax: 6779 1097/6872 4989. 54 rooms. Single S\$75, double S\$75. *Nearest MRT* Clementi (EW line) and taxi

WHERE TO EAT

African Heartbeat (The Aquarius, Science Park 2, #01-01, 21 Science Park Road; just off Pasir Panjang Road; tel: 6775 7988) can be difficult to find, but it is worth persevering. The air-conditioned restaurant (and alfresco area in front of it) nestles next to a romantic little lake, and is decorated with thatched huts, animal skins and other trappings of Africa. Run by the same people as Mama Africa in Chinatown (see page 166), it serves good African cuisine, including stews, soups and even dishes with crocodile for a mid-range price. Open Mon–Fri 12.00–14.30, and daily 18.30–22.00. Closed for lunch at weekends.

Just off Bukit Timah Road is **Brazil Churrascaria** (14–16 Sixth Avenue; tel: 6463 1923), a Brazilian barbecue restaurant where for a set price of S$37 (S$26 for salad only, S$26 for children under 12) you can work your way through a veritable mountain of meat. Make your selection of salad from the buffet-style counter, and then relax as the bubbly waiters bring meat dish after meat dish. Beef, sausage, chicken, pork, even fish – it's all here. Eat as much or as little as you like; those with larger appetites will enjoy a good-value feed. On Tuesdays seafood is also included on the menu. Open daily 18.30–22.30.

Michelangelo's (Block 44, Jalan Merah Saga, #01-60, Chip Bee Gardens; tel: 6475 9069) in Holland Village is a highly recommended Italian restaurant with an outdoor seating area, a warm Mediterranean feel, and helpful staff. Portions are hearty, and a meal costing S$40–50 will satisfy the most healthy of appetites. There is a very large selection of wines. The restaurant is very popular, and it is advisable to book your table, particularly in the evening. Lunch served 11.30–14.30 (excluding Sat), dinner 18.30–22.30. It is close to **Original Sin** (Block 43, Jalan Merah Saga, #01-62, Chip Bee Gardens; tel: 6475 5605), a good vegetarian restaurant, and **Sistina** (Block 44, Jalan Merah Saga, #01-58, Chip Bee Gardens; tel: 6476 7782), an Italian pizzeria, both of which are under the same management.

For very reasonably priced goulash, sauerkraut, pork knuckle, sausage, and other German fare, try **Baden-Baden** (42 Lorong Mambong, Holland Village; tel: 6468 5585). It is designed to capture the atmosphere of a pub, and you can sup on German beer. Open weekdays 11.30–24.00, Sat 11.30–01.00, Sun 12.30–24.00. The latest you can order food is 21.15.

There is a **hawker centre** at Boon Lay, which is due for refurbishment during 2002.

NIGHTLIFE

The west of Singapore is noted for its parks and other daylight attractions rather than for its pubs and bars. However, you will find places to have a drink in Holland Village (see pages 179–81), and in Pasir Panjang Village, which boasts a street nicknamed 'Pub Row'.

WHAT TO SEE AND DO
Parks and gardens

If you visit at the right time, the **Chinese and Japanese Gardens** (1 Chinese Garden Road, Singapore 619795; tel: 6264 3455; fax: 6265 8133) can be tranquil. The Chinese Garden apparently re-creates a classical, imperial garden of the Sung Dynasty. Its entrance gate is enormous, and stunningly beautiful, and inside there is a tea gallery, pagodas, pavilions and a stone boat. It is possible to climb the central pagoda for views of the housing blocks outside the gardens. It is claimed that the Suzhou Penjing garden – which contains thousands of bonsai trees – is the largest Suzhou-style bonsai garden outside China. The bonsai bougainvillaeas are lovely. Monitor lizards, turtles, egrets and a variety of fish are to be found in the lake (you can pay to fish in certain places), and it is pleasant to lie on the bank and watch birds in the branches of the trees above. In the Japanese Garden, a short walk away and designed according to traditional Japanese landscaping techniques, there is a Zen rock garden, summer houses and stone lanterns. Both gardens can be very peaceful as long as you are careful to visit early in the morning and during the week – they can be crowded at weekends. Open 09.00–19.00 every day. Admission (to both gardens) S$4.50 adult, S$2 children and senior citizens.

Getting there Chinese Garden MRT (EW line), and a short direct walk (the main pagoda is visible from the station).

The award-winning **Jurong Bird Park** (2 Jurong Hill, Singapore 628925; tel: 6265 0022; email: info@birdpark.com.sg; web: www.birdpark.com) has been one of the primary tourist attractions in Singapore for 30 years, and it is easy to see why. It is among the world's most extensive and impressive bird parks, and it exchanges breeding stock with reputable international collections. Covering 20 hectares, it holds 8,000 birds of hundreds of different species. There are three walk-in aviaries: the Waterfall Aviary, with the world's highest man-made waterfall; the Southeast Asian Birds Aviary, in which there is a simulated thunderstorm every day at noon; and the Jungle Jewels Aviary, with some

JURONG BIRD PARK SHOWS

Some of the shows on offer in the bird park are well worth watching. You should check times before arriving – and be aware that shows are subject to the weather conditions – but the following is the schedule of the main daily events at the time of going to press (2002):

Time	Show	Location
09.45	New Arrival Feeding	Main foyer
10.00	Fuji World of Hawks (birds of prey show)	Fuji Hawk Walk
11.00	All Star Bird Show	Pools Amphitheatre
12.00	Thunderstorm	Southeast Asian Birds Aviary
14.00	Hawk Show) (Sundays and public holidays only	Fuji Hawk Walk
15.00	All Star Bird Show	Pools Amphitheatre
16.00	Kings of the Skies (birds of prey show)	Fuji Hawk Walk

wonderfully colourful hummingbirds. There is a nocturnal house, a parrot display (where you can be photographed with one of the birds), twice-daily birds of prey shows (see *Jurong Bird Park Shows* box, page 175), and even a snow-filled penguin enclosure. Sit on the restaurant's veranda and watch flamingos and other waterbirds on the lake. You can tour the park by monorail, accompanied by a recorded commentary. Be sure to take your camera! Open daily 08.00–18.00. Admission S\$12 adult, S\$5 child, S\$8.40 senior citizens.

Getting there MRT to Boon Lay (EW line terminus) and then a bus (Nos 182, 194 or 251) from the bus station outside the terminus.

Adjacent to the bird park is **Jurong Reptile Park** (241 Jalan Ahmad Ibrahim, Singapore 629143; tel: 6261 8866). There are over 50 species of reptile kept in captivity here, the emphasis being on the more dangerous (and glamorous) of such animals. There are opportunities to have photographs taken holding snakes, along with live feeding demonstrations and other shows. Overall, though, this park is disappointing when compared with the bird park, and certainly does not merit a special trip. Open daily 09.00–18.00. Admission S\$7 adult, S\$3.50 child.

Getting there MRT to Boon Lay (EW line terminus), and a bus (182, 194 or 251) from the bus interchange beside the station.

Haw Par Villa (262 Pasir Panjang Road; tel: 6774 0300), also known as the **Tiger Balm Gardens**, tends to awaken very different reactions in those who enter. Some think it tacky and tasteless, others find the colour and sensationalism highly enjoyable and refreshingly memorable. Originally, this was the estate of the Boon brothers (Boon Haw and Boon Par), businessmen who made a fortune from the sale of an ointment invented by their father. This ointment – the enduringly popular Tiger Balm – provides fabulous relief from insect bites, blocked noses, arthritis and other ailments, and took off during the 1920s and 1930s. Damaged during the war, but restored shortly afterwards, the landscaped (and rather ghoulish) gardens were finally taken over by the government during the 1980s and transformed into the public attraction we see today.

The Tiger Balm Gardens are certainly not conventional. Much of the site – considerably larger than the original – is dotted with models of Chinese deities of various sizes enacting scenes from Chinese mythology. Many are very gory – rather like an oriental chamber of horrors – and serve as moral exempla. In the Ten Courts of Hell, for instance, sinners are punished in a series of gruesome and sadistically imaginative ways that include being eaten by dogs and impaled on spikes. Other sculptures are, frankly, confusing for tourists unversed in ancient tales of Chinese allegory. Walking among these strange figures you suddenly stumble across a monument to the Boon brothers, accentuating the air of surreality that permeates the gardens,

There is an indoor lecture hall, where you can watch traditional Chinese drama or learn about ancient custom and myth, and a small outdoor theatre where children can watch puppet plays. There are also fairground stalls, restaurants and shops. There has been some refurbishment as some of the statues were falling into disrepair, and certainly there were concerns four or five years ago that the gardens would be closed. Whether you think that this would have been a good or a bad thing depends entirely upon how you choose to face the experience. If you can allow yourself to revel in its gaudiness and eccentricity, and simply enjoy its very uniqueness, then it can blow away a few cobwebs. But if you crave elegance, refinement and tranquillity, this will be a hellish few hours. Open daily 09.00–17.00. Admission S$5 adult, S$2.50 child. It can take up to half a day to see everything.

Getting there Buona Vista MRT (EW line) and then bus 200; bus Nos 10, 30, or 188 from the World Trade Centre; bus No 143 from Orchard Road or Chinatown.

Museums and galleries

The **National University of Singapore Museums and Art Galleries** (NUS Museums Building, University Cultural Centre; tel: 6874 6917) run, as the name suggests, several exhibitions of art and historical artefacts in the NUS Museums Building, just off the Ayer Rajah Expressway (AYE). The **Lee Kong Chian Art Museum** displays Chinese art, much of it exquisite and some dating back over 7,000 years. There are 4,000 exhibits, including ceramics, painting, calligraphy, sculpture, jewellery, and works in jade and ivory. The **Ng Eng Teng Gallery** houses almost 1,000 works by Singaporean sculptor Ng Eng Teng. And the **South and Southeast Asian Art Collection** has a fair amount to see. Open Mon–Sat 09.30–16.30. Closed public holidays.

Getting there Clementi MRT, and then bus No 96 to the stop nearest the University Cultural Centre.

Within Singapore's mint is the **Singapore Mint Coin Gallery** (20 Teban Gardens Crescent; tel: 6566 2626) where there is a display of domestic coinage and medals, along with a limited number of foreign coins. Open Mon–Fri 09.00–17.00. Admission free.

Getting there Catch bus No 154 from Boon Lay MRT to Jalan Ahmad Ibrahim.

Other activities

The **Singapore Science Centre** (15 Science Centre Road, off Jurong Town Hall Road, Jurong; tel: 6425 2500) is said to be one of the best in the world, with over 650 interactive exhibits providing both lots of fun and educational insights into the mysteries of science. There's a talking statue of Einstein, as well as a Hall of Life Sciences, an Aviation Centre and a Virtual Science Centre. Open Tue–Sun 10.00–18.00, and bank holidays. Admission S$6 adults, S$3 children, S$2.50 senior citizens.

The **Omni-theatre** is next to the centre and shows Imax films on space travel or wildlife. Open Tue–Sun 10.00–21.00, and bank holidays. Admission S$10 adults, S$5 children.

Getting there Jurong East MRT (EW and NS interchange), then bus 66 or 335.

Next to the Singapore Science Centre is one of the island's newest attractions, **Snow City** (21 Jurong Town Hall Road, Snow City Building, Singapore 609433; tel: 6560 0179/6560 4773; fax: 6560 1297; email: contact_us@ snowventure.com.sg). Singaporeans are always looking for new things to see and do, and how often do you see snow near the Equator, never mind do anything on it? Once through the airlock you enter a snow chamber, where the temperature is kept at –5°C. You can snow-tube (slide down the slope in a round inflatable tube), ski or snowboard, explore an igloo, or just enjoy the snow and pelt your friends with snowballs. In fact, many Singaporeans regularly take winter sports holidays in places like Korea, so this is a good place to practise. Open Tue–Sun, and school and public holidays. The one-hour sessions commence at 09.45, 11.15, 12.45, 14.15, 15.45, 17.15, 18.45 and 20.15. Admission S$15 adult, S$9 child under 12, S$39 family (2 adults, 2 children). Entry fee includes the hire of jacket and boots.

Getting there Jurong East MRT (EW line and NS line interchange) and then bus 335 from the Jurong East Bus Interchange. Other buses 66, 198, 182, 178.

The **Singapore Discovery Centre** (510 Upper Jurong Road; tel: 6792 6188) is a delight for computer buffs. Explore the history of Singapore and the country's advanced technology with the aid of interactive computerised exhibits, realistic simulators, and a five-storey-high cinema screen. There are several military displays, including aircraft and other equipment, and even a shooting gallery. It is an impressive centre, and enjoyable for children and adults alike, but is also a slick and unashamed promotion of the country's technological and military expertise. Open Tue–Sun 09.00–18.00. Admission S$9 adult, S$5 child; some exhibits (including the motion simulator) attract additional charges.

Getting there MRT to Boon Lay (EW line), then bus Nos 192 or 193 from the interchange.

For a long time the **Thok Kwang Pottery** (85 Lorong Tawas, off Jalan Bahar, near Nanyong Technological University; tel: 6265 5808) was a well-kept secret among locals and a few expats. It certainly does seem isolated, and involves a longish walk from the bus stop up Lorong Tawas; however, it is now actively promoted as one of Singapore's tourist attractions. There is an amazing 'jungle' of Chinese and Taiwanese pottery and porcelain here, most of it laid out on the ground or in wooden shacks. You can see ranks of plant pots, elephant china stools of various sizes (for which you would pay considerably more in the stores in town), and, in several smaller rooms, the better quality china and jade. It also features the 'dragon kiln' – a long, tunnel-like kiln with fire glowing in its depths (hence the description) – which is in constant use. Open daily 09.00–17.00. Admission free.

Getting there Boon Lay MRT (EW line), then bus 172 or 199 to Nanyang Avenue (by the university), and a walk back to Lorong Tawas.

Ming Village (32 Pandan Road; tel: 6265 7711) is a faithful re-creation of a village from the Ming and Ping era of Chinese history. At the time China was renowned for the manufacture of porcelain, and the craftsmen here still use traditional techniques. In essence, this is a factory that is open to the public. Everything is housed under one roof, and you can watch the artists make not only original designs but replicas of historical masterpieces. The finished products can be purchased from the showroom (and shipped home for you if you wish). There are also guided tours available, as well as one-hour classes on painting porcelain. Open daily 09.00–17.30. Admission free (including guided tour).

Getting there Clementi MRT (EW line) and bus 78, or free pick-ups from Orchard Hotel, Mandarin Hotel, Raffles Hotel and Pan Pacific Hotel. Check with the concierges for details.

On the same site is the **Royal Selangor Pewter Museum** (32 Pandan Road, Ming Village, Singapore 609279; tel: 6265 7711; fax: 6266 2465). This houses antique pewter, from ordinary domestic utensils to elaborate ceremonial pieces, and a display of tools used to fashion the metal, and features a daily demonstration of the traditional processes used in pewter work. It is quite interesting and combines well with a visit to the Ming Village – but remember that both the village and the museum are really just factories and showcases for their wares. Open 09.00–17.30 daily. Admission free. Check for the time of the demonstrations – which usually coincide with visiting coach tours!

Getting there As for Ming Village, above.

HOLLAND VILLAGE

This is a small, self-contained area with narrow streets and old shop-houses which looks much as Singapore would have done before all the skyscraper offices and high-rise buildings were constructed. Now surrounded by blocks of Housing Development Board flats and private condominiums, it is very popular with Singaporeans and is a favourite haunt for expatriates. Here you will find a modest-sized, but good, wet-market and interesting shop-houses selling basketware, china, flowers and food (Madeleine's egg tarts are delicious). The **Holland Village Shopping Centre** has a Cold Storage supermarket on the ground floor and the two floors above are packed with stores full of Asian crafts, art, porcelain, clothes and furniture. There is also Lims, which is well known for its wide and fascinating range of Chinese goods. A bookshop here allows customers to 'hire' books; buy a book at the higher of the two prices listed inside the cover, read and return it within a month, and get the lower amount back (price depends on the age and popularity of the book).

At the corner of Holland Avenue and Lorong Liput, you will find a superb news-stand displaying an amazing selection of newspapers and magazines. There's an old-fashioned cobbler, a flower shop and several food courts, as

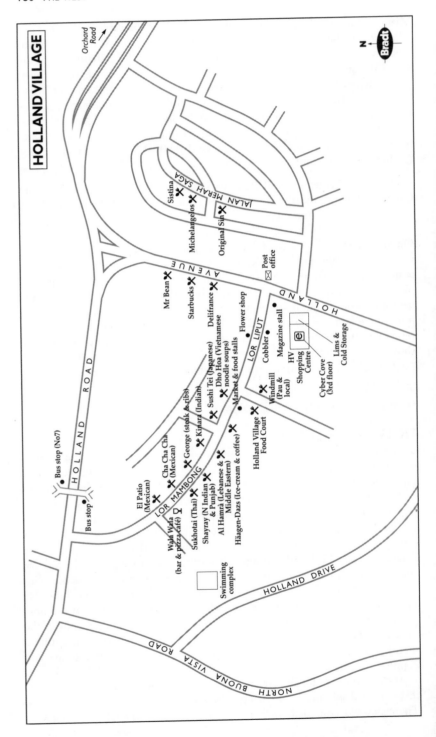

HOLLAND VILLAGE

well as numerous bars and restaurants cheek by jowl along Lorong Mambong. Most are worth a visit, but are fairly expensive. Buy curry puffs (pastry turnovers filled with curried meat or vegetables) or *pau* (Chinese white buns with a savoury or sweet red-bean paste filling, rather like a doughnut) at the food centres or cake shops.

Getting there Bus No 7 from Orchard Boulevard outside Orchard MRT station.

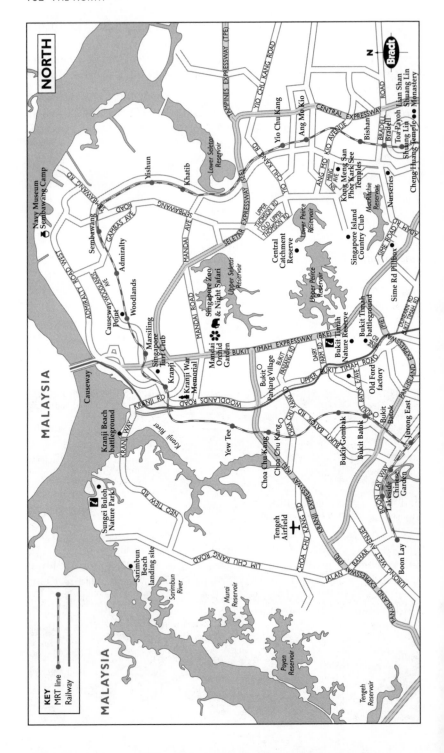

The North

Most of the nature parks, reserves and reservoirs are found to the north of the city, and consequently this is the greenest part of the island. However, there is little or no agriculture to be seen. A trip on the MRT (travelling west on the EW line to Jurong East interchange and then on the NS loop via Woodlands and back to Orchard Road) gives you a glimpse of what remains of the jungle that once covered the island. It also shows the new towns built by the Housing Development Board – places such as Bukit Batok, Choa Chu Kang, Woodlands, Yishun and Ang Mo Kio – that have replaced it.

Most Singaporeans live in these towns, which have busy shopping malls and community centres. They are well served by the MRT and by buses that run on a network of roads from the city, some of which were laid out by John Turnbull Thomson in the 19th century, but most of which have been constructed and extended considerably since independence.

Travelling by car, bus or taxi towards the north, the route follows Bukit Timah Road from the Little India junction with Serangoon Road, past Newton Circus and Bukit Timah to Woodlands Road, and on to the Causeway across the Straits to Johore.

By train, the rail line leaves Keppel Road Station in the south of the island and heads north towards Bukit Timah and then follows alongside the road to the Causeway crossing at Woodlands.

During the early 19th century, Bukit Timah was a rural and almost uninhabited area. When John Prince, the acting resident of the Incorporated Settlements, explored the possible route for a road in 1827, it took five hours to walk from the town to Bukit Timah. The road was extended to Kranji using convict labour in 1845, and Indian convicts were used in the early 1860s to hunt the tigers responsible for as many as 200 deaths a year in the area around Bukit Timah and Chua Chu Kong. Six animals were killed in one year alone. They were believed to have swum the Straits from Johore to Kranji, for several were found caught in fishermen's nets. The most famous story concerning a tiger is, of course, that of the tiger shot in the Billiard Room at Raffles (see page 6).

The Causeway across the Straits was constructed in 1919 and, although it was initially open only to goods trains, passenger trains began to run shortly afterwards. These provided an alternative to the ferry, which had been the only way for people to move to and from Johore. After World War II, rebuilding and reconstruction of the Causeway meant it also became possible to cross by road.

Because the Japanese invaded Singapore from the Malayan peninsula during World War II, the northern area's historical legacy mainly comprises gun emplacements like the Sime Road Pillbox (near the entrance to the Singapore Island Country Club) and battlefields such as those at Bukit Timah, Kranji Beach and Sarimbun Beach. The north also holds the site – the old Ford Motor Factory on Bukit Timah Road – where the British surrender was officially ratified.

The story of the Japanese invasion is largely one of military oversight on the part of the British. Lieutenant-General Percival, the British General Officer Commanding, Malaya, ignored all warnings that the island was vulnerable from the north. As a result, Singapore was only defended against invasion from the open sea to the south. Guns on the south coast and Sentosa were all directed seawards, and could not be swung around. The northern coastline from the Kranji River to Sarimbun River was too large an area for the few British and Indian troops based there to defend, and the mangrove swamps and jungle made the construction of fortifications almost impossible. In essence, the stretch of island facing the Malayan mainland and jungles across the Straits was utterly helpless. Winston Churchill said that 'the possibility of Singapore having no landward defences no more entered into my mind than that of a battleship being launched without a bottom'.

When the Japanese commander, Lieutenant-General Yamashita, established his headquarters in the Sultan's Palace in Johore Bahru at the southern tip of Malaya on February 6 1942, he had an excellent view of his key targets just a mile away across the Causeway. His aim was to capture the airfield at Tengah, head for the high ground at Bukit Timah, and take the Seletar, Peirce and MacRitchie reservoirs. By cutting off the water supply, he could force the British to surrender.

The Japanese crossed the Straits on February 7 and 8, and took Tengah airfield on February 9. They encountered a setback when troops became lost in mangrove swamps and suffered a major defeat at the Kranji River the following day. However, their tanks had been floated across the Straits to Lim Chu Kang Road and these proceeded along Choa Chu Kang Road to Bukit Panjang village. On February 12 there was a battle at Bukit Timah Road; the next day Yamashita moved his headquarters to the Ford Motor Factory. Percival, based in the Fort Canning Bunker (now restored as the Battle Box), struggled desperately to hold on to the island. By the afternoon of February 15, though, it was all over, and he signed an unconditional surrender to the Japanese in the boardroom of the Ford factory.

The Images of Singapore exhibition on Sentosa (see pages 206–7) and the Battle Box at Fort Canning (see page 137) cover the history of this period in fascinating detail and are well worth visiting.

There is no accommodation on offer in this region of the country.

GETTING THERE

The NS loop of the MRT leads to Woodlands, near the Causeway to Malaysia. By road, the Bukit Timah Expressway (BKE) and Bukit Timah Road from Newton Circus (which leads into Woodlands Road), will take you north as far as the Causeway. Bus No 170 goes from Bugis to Woodlands and the Causeway – and, indeed, on into Johore Bahru.

WHERE TO EAT

There are **food centres** in the shopping malls (such as the Woodlands Shopping Mall) which are found near most MRT stations.

WHAT TO SEE AND DO
Parks, reserves and open spaces
Bukit Timah Nature Reserve

Before its face was irrevocably altered through the effects of human 'progression', Singapore was covered in rainforest, with a fringe of mangrove forest around the coasts. The only remaining piece of such vegetation is to be found at the highest point of the island, 165m above sea level, in the Bukit Timah Nature Reserve (177 Hindhede Drive, off Upper Bukit Timah Road, Singapore 589333; tel: 6468 5736; fax: 6462 0723; web: www.nparks.gov.sg). While *bukit* and *timah* are Malaysian for 'hill' and 'tin' respectively, there is no tin here and the area is more probably named after the *pokok temak* tree which grew on the slopes.

The 164-hectare reserve was established in 1883. It offers a rare opportunity to experience such a landscape, is readily explored, with signposted pathways running through it that give access to a stunning array of wildlife, and gives a taste of what Singapore looked like before the arrival of Raffles in 1819. You can follow in the footsteps of biologists like Alfred Russel Wallace, who came here during the mid-19th century, and had such an influence upon evolutionary theory. The view from the summit is spectacular.

The forest contains over 800 species of plant, and a wide variety of animals (although to see the latter you will need patience, the capacity to sit still for long periods of time, and a tolerance of mosquitoes, which plague this terrain). During the 19th century, this area used to be a gutta percha tree plantation before the introduction of rubber trees. Some have diagonal scars on their trunks where they were tapped for latex. It is a good idea to cover up as, along with the danger of bites from mosquitoes, ants and hover flies, some of the foliage can cause skin irritation. Rengas saplings, for example, can give considerable discomfort to those with sensitive skin.

Of the fauna, invertebrates make up the largest proportion. You are likely to see different types of butterfly, beetle, ant and spider. The reserve is also home to the harmless, slow-moving giant millipede. In addition, you may come across snakes, including the venomous temple pit viper and the reticulate python (see page 8).

Troupes of long-tailed macaque monkeys (see page 6) are common sights here. They are best sought either at the bottom of the path just before the car-park or at the hill's summit. Please do not be tempted to feed them. They are wild animals, and handouts not only disrupt their natural diet but can make them aggressive.

The Bukit Timah World War II battleground, fought over by the Japanese and the British, is marked as one of Singapore's historic sites. Two war memorials, dedicated to the Japanese and Allied forces, and built by Allied prisoners-of-war, once stood at the top of the hill. However, these were demolished by the Japanese at the end of the war, and the only remains are a couple of pillars and a long flight of steps.

Early morning is the best time to visit. Take comfortable shoes, a camera, and plenty of liquids. The public relations department of Mobil Oil (tel: 7660 6110) produces a useful companion booklet called the *Guide to the Bukit Timah Nature Reserve* which can be ordered by phone or picked up at the Singapore Science Centre (see page 177). There is a visitor centre at the reserve. Open 08.30–18.30. Admission free.

Getting there Take bus No 171 from Scotts Road and alight at Bukit Timah Shopping Centre on Upper Bukit Timah Road. Bus Nos 5, 67, 75, 170, 172, 173, 182 and 852 also go here. Enter the reserve from Hindehede Drive. The journey takes about 20 minutes.

The reservoirs

The **MacRitchie**, **Upper** and **Lower Seletar**, and **Upper** and **Lower Peirce** reservoirs, isolated places off Thomson, Upper Thomson, and Mandai roads, are surrounded by secondary forests (secondary because the original land was cleared for rubber in the early 20th century) and broad areas of grassland rich in plants and animals. The Central Catchment Nature Reserve is made up of 2,000 hectares of these forests and is an important gene pool; it also provides the opportunity for long-distance trekking. Here there are nearly a thousand species of plant, and over 250 species of animal, some endangered like the Malayan pangolin and flying lemur (see page 6). The areas around the reservoirs are popular for walking and picnicking. People also come here to play golf. The MacRitchie Reservoir contains a park with a jogging track, exercise area and playground. There are monkeys to be seen here, although they can be aggressive, so exercise caution. To the north, in the Upper Seletar Reservoir (where the Singapore Zoological Gardens, Night Safari and Mandai Orchid Gardens are also to be found), you can go boating. Try your hand at fishing in the Lower Seletar Reservoir to the east. Alternatively, get away from everyone and sit quietly enjoying flowers reminiscent of those in an alpine meadow and watching small birds working the grasses for insects. Take food and drink as there are no real facilities.

Getting there If you are taking a taxi, agree a time and specific place for the driver to pick you up afterwards, as this is a large area. For MacRitchie Reservoir, take a bus (Nos 132 or 167) from Orchard Road/Orchard Boulevard. The nearest MRT stations are Novena (NS line), after which you take buses 166, 167 or

980, or Bishau (NS line), and bus No 156. For the Seletar reservoirs, go to Woodlands MRT (NS line), followed by bus No 156 and a long walk. For the Peirce reservoirs, take bus No 132 to Peirce Secondary School, and walk north to Old Thomson Road and Lower Peirce Reservoir Park.

Mandai Orchid Gardens

Situated next to the Singapore Zoological Gardens (see page 188) are the Mandai Orchid Gardens (Mandai Lake Road; tel: 6269 1036). Singapore exports a large quantity of orchids around the world, and this is the main centre for the commercial cultivation of the flowers. The gardens are stunning, although not extensive, and a visit should not take much more than an hour. There is a shop that offers a gift service, so that you can arrange for boxes of orchids to be sent anywhere in the world. Open daily 08.30–17.30. Admission S$2 adult, S$0.50 child.

Getting there MRT to Ang Mo Kio (NS line) and bus No 138; or MRT to Choa Chu (NS line) and bus No 927; or MRT to Woodlands (NS line) and bus No 926.

Sungei Buloh Nature Park

Overlooking the Straits of Johore, Sungei Buloh Nature Park (301 Neo Tiew Crescent; tel: 6794 1401) is the country's first wetland nature reserve. Almost 100 hectares of reserve hold prawn farms, mangrove swamps and freshwater ponds. There are good walking paths and ten observation points from which to spy upon 126 different types of bird, including waders and migratory species. For prime viewing, come early in the morning. Other creatures that inhabit this area are mudskippers, tree-climbing crabs, snakes and monitor lizards, as well as insects such as butterflies. The visitor centre also offers a ten-minute audio-visual show, running two-hourly from Monday to Saturday, and hourly on Sunday and holidays. Allow yourself three or four hours. Open weekdays 07.30–19.00, weekends and public holidays 07.00–19.00. Last entry 18.00. Admission S$1 adult, S$0.50 child and senior citizen.

Getting there MRT to Woodlands or Kranji, and then bus No 925. Note that the bus only stops at the entrance on Sundays and public holidays. On other days, get off at Kranji car park.

Thomson Road Nurseries

If you are a lover of horticulture, pay a visit to the Thomson Road Nurseries (Thomson Road, next to junction with Lornie Road) near the Singapore television studios. Here you can purchase a variety of startling plants that you are very unlikely to come across in the West. You may not find room in your luggage for a one-and-a-half-metre-high croton, or a standard bougainvillaea reaching two metres; however, there are rooted cuttings available. (Be aware, though, of restrictions on importing live plant material into your home country. Your local Ministry of Agriculture can offer advice on what you can and cannot take with you. See page 40.) It is best to combine a visit here with one to the MacRitchie Reservoir (see page 186).

Getting there Bus No 132 from Scotts Road or Orchard Road/Orchard Boulevard to MacRitchie Reservoir Park. Walk back under the flyover and you will see the nurseries on the right.

Singapore Zoological Gardens

Containing over 3,000 animals in 28 hectares of open enclosures relying on 'natural' barriers such as moats and stone walls rather than bars to prevent escape, the Singapore Zoological Gardens (80 Mandai Lake Road; tel: 6269 3411) are rightly lauded as one of the world's premier zoos. The zoo has won many awards for its approach, which is both caring towards the animals and entertaining for visitors, and is very different from the majority of animal parks in the Far East. The director studied in England, and was careful to learn from his experiences of zoos in other countries around the world in developing the strategy adopted here. The zoo points to its flourishing breeding programme as proof of the health and happiness of its animals, and the consequent success of its open concept. Certainly there is none of the endless pacing or staring common in caged mammals elsewhere. The lack of bars also breaks down any sense of separation from the animals, and makes for a thrilling and entrancing experience for the spectator.

Among the 200 species are the world's largest captive group of orang utans (for an additional cost you can take breakfast or afternoon tea with one of them), pygmy hippos and komodo dragons. There is a rainforest display and a trail among the treetops, running along a boardwalk six metres off the ground. Elephant rides, animal shows (daily at 10.30, 11.30, 12.30, 14.30 and 15.30), a children's zoo (where you can touch the farm animals), tram tours and an excellent gift shop round off a professional, impressive attraction. Open daily 08.30–18.00. Admission S$12 adult, S$5 child. You can purchase a ticket for both the zoo and Night Safari (see below) costing S$21.60 adult, S$12.80 child.

Getting there Bus No 138 from Ang Mo Kio MRT station (NS line), or bus No 927 from Choa Chu Kang MRT (NS line), or bus No 926 from Woodlands MRT (NS line)

Singapore Night Safari

After visiting the zoological gardens, have a bite to eat at one of the restaurants near the entrance, and wait for the Night Safari (80 Mandai Lake Road; tel: 6269 3411) to open. Located next door, the Night Safari is the world's only nocturnal zoo and has twice won the prestigious Leisure Attraction of the Year award. Over twice the size of the zoo, and with the Upper Seletar Reservoir on three sides, it is divided between geographical zones re-creating eight different habitats, and includes a Leopard Trail, a Mangrove Walk, and a free-flying bat enclosure. Explore several walking trails on foot, or hop aboard a 45-minute tram safari (last tram leaves at 23.15). Many animals are at their most active during the night, and the relative darkness gives the illusion of real closeness as walls and ditches become invisible. This, along with artificial moonlight that is both realistic and deeply romantic, makes for an unforgettable few hours. As well as pumas, otters, elephants and rhinos, you will come across less-familiar species such as binturongs and civets. Twice a night there is a Creatures of the Night show. Flash photography is prohibited. There is a restaurant at the Entrance Plaza, and refreshments on sale at the East Lodge, halfway around the East Loop route. Open daily 19.30–24.00. Admission S$15.45 adult, S$10.30 child. A combined zoo and Night Safari ticket available (see *Singapore Zoological Gardens*, opposite).

Getting there As for Singapore Zoological Gardens (see opposite).

Places of worship

One of the most flamboyant places of worship in Singapore, and the largest (covering over 10 hectares), the **Kong Meng San Phor Kark See Temple** (88 Bright Hill Road) is usually referred to as the Bright Hill Temple, and stands on a hill off Thomson Road. In the 1930s there were only two small shrines and a plot of farmland, but the temple now includes a cremation yard, the Hall of Great Compassion and the Hall of Great Virtues. Furthermore, a short walk within the temple area takes you to the golden, bell-shaped structure called the Ten Thousand Buddha Pagoda and the octagonal Precepts Hall.

Outside the temple you will find stalls selling statues, pictures and Buddhist rosaries. There is also a large terrapin pool. The area is always busy, but nevertheless has a distinct air of tranquillity, and the gardens are a pleasure. Open daily 07.00–18.00.

Getting there Bishan MRT station (NS line) and taxi. Alternatively, take bus No 130 from Ang Mo Kio (NS line) bus interchange to the stop opposite Tse Tho Aum Temple, walk right to Sin Ming Avenue, and left to first left and Bright Hill Road.

Kong Meng San Phor Kark See Monastery (88 Bright Hill Road; tel: 6453 4046), to the north of MacRitchie Reservoir (see page 186), is a lovely and architecturally interesting Buddhist temple.

Getting there Bus No 166 from outside the National Library in Stamford Road by the City Hall MRT. Alight before Thomson Plaza and walk north up Bright Hill Road.

Built between 1898 and 1908, the **Siong Lim Temple** (184E Jalan Toa Payoh) is now a national monument and commemorates Buddha's life and death. Inspiration for the temple came when a 19th-century Singaporean monk, Low Kim Pong, dreamt of 'a golden light rising in the west'. After discovering that his son had recently experienced a similar dream, he then had a chance meeting with a family of 12 Buddhist monks and nuns who had just landed after a pilgrimage to Sri Lanka, India and Burma. He persuaded them to stay, and donated S$500,000 of his own money towards the temple's construction. The temple was modelled on the famous Cong Lin Temple in Fizhou and was built by skilled Chinese craftsmen in various traditional Chinese styles reflecting the different communities in Singapore.

There is a colourful decorated gateway and the interior contains a statue of Buddha imported from Thailand. Another Buddha-like sculpted figure in the temple is not a representation of Buddha himself, but of a local Chinese man renowned for his pious and saintly character. The temple is noted for its rock garden.

Getting there Go to Toa Payoh MRT station (NS line) and walk across Toa Payoh Lorong 6, through Toa Payoh Town Garden to Jalan Toa Payoh. Turn left, pass under the interchange, and to the temple on the left.

Other places of interest
Ford Motor Factory
This motor car assembly plant (351 Upper Bukit Timah Road), built by Ford Motor Works in 1941, was the first of its kind in Southeast Asia. It was located on a hill on Bukit Timah Road and on the main route linking Singapore and Johore in Malaya.

It is of particular interest, however, as the site of the surrender of the British to the Japanese on February 15 1942; it was subsequently used to assemble Nissan trucks and as a depot for army vehicles during the Japanese occupation. After the war it continued as an assembly plant until its closure in 1980, when the buildings became warehouses. The boardroom where the surrender document was signed is still part of the factory, although the actual table and chairs used are now in the Australian War Museum and the Images of Singapore (see pages 206–7) respectively. The area is owned by a private company, and therefore is not a tourist attraction, but it nevertheless played a key role in the historical legacy of Singapore's involvement in World War II.

Kranji War Memorial and Cemetery
Close to the Causeway linking Singapore to the mainland of Malaysia, the Kranji War Memorial (9 Woodlands Road; tel: 6269 6158) pays tribute to the thousands of Allied troops who gave their lives throughout Southeast Asia during World War II. Some of these are buried on this hilltop overlooking the Straits. The graves of 4,000 servicemen who died during the Japanese occupation stand in neat rows, while the war memorial's 12 columns at the centre of the cemetery record the names of 24,346 others who died in the region but whose bodies were never recovered. The design of the memorial symbolises the three branches of the armed forces – army, navy and air force – whose members it commemorates. In the middle of the columns stands a 24-metre pylon surmounted by a star. At its base, written in Hindi, Urdu, Gurmukhi, Chinese and Malay (as well as English), are the words, 'To whom the fortune of war denied the customary rites accorded to their comrades in death', followed by 'They died for all free men'.

During the occupation, the war cemetery was a hospital burial ground, and only became a military cemetery after the war. Former presidents of Singapore are also laid to rest here. Quiet, peaceful and enormously evocative of a tragic period of the region's history, this is a moving place to visit. Open 24 hours daily. Admission free.

Getting there MRT to Kranji (NS line) or a long journey by bus (No 170) from the Queen Street depot.

The Navy Museum

Based on the north coast, in what used to be the HMS *Terror* barracks, the Navy Museum (Endurance Block, Sembawang Camp; tel: 6750 5585/5565) holds a fairly unimpressive collection of naval equipment and memorabilia, and has a distinctly propagandist feel to it. It merits a special visit only by those particularly interested in naval history. You will need to show your passport to gain admittance. Open Mon–Fri 08.30–16.30, Sat 08.30–12.00. Closed Sun. Admission free.

Getting there MRT to Sembawang, and then bus No 856 to Sembawang camp on Admiralty Road West. Ask at the gate for a pass to enable you to enter the camp.

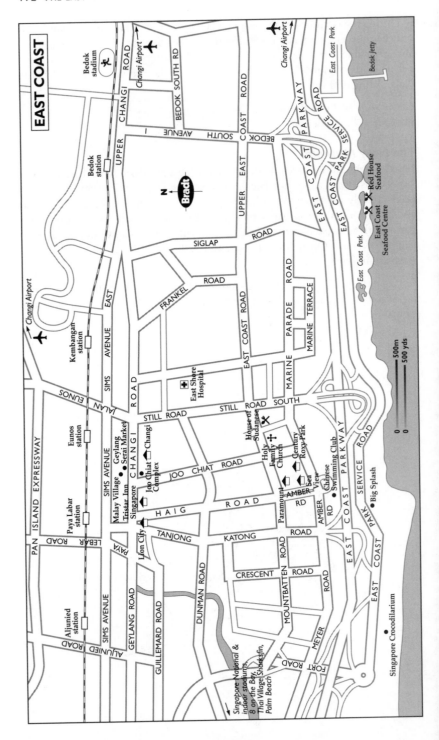

EAST COAST

The East

7

The eastern part of the island used to be home to Malay fishing communities, and the Malay quarter at Geylang Serai, on the Geylang Road, is to be found here, but it is now dominated by HDB blocks. This area is too large to explore wholly on foot – although some places, like Joo Chiat Road, are compact enough to wander around without transport. It can be pleasant to hire a bicycle and ride along the track running the length of the East Coast Park, which consists primarily of reclaimed land shaped into parks and beaches. There are numerous places to eat and drink along the way.

GETTING THERE
EW line on the MRT towards Pasir Ris and Changi Airport termini. By car, the East Coast Parkway (ECP) runs to the south of the MRT line, and the Pan Island Expressway (PIE) to the north. Bus No 2 goes from New Bridge Road in the city centre to Changi Village.

WHERE TO STAY
Luxury
Paramount Hotel 25 Marine Parade Rd, Singapore 449536; tel: 6340 2104; fax: 6447 2654; email: paramountsales@ytchotels.com.sg. Near Marine Parade and East Coast Park, 10 minutes' walk from beach. Clean, bright and airy, with friendly staff. Shuttle bus to SunTec City at 11.00 and 14.00, and hourly to airport. By taxi, 8 minutes from Singapore Expo and 10 minutes from Changi Airport and CBD. Rooms with balconies and sea views. Computer ports in deluxe rooms. Pool and business centre. Café Vanda in lobby (breakfast, and local and international food) is well known for the excellent value of its high teas (S$13.80) served at weekends. 250 rooms. Single S$220–85, double S$240–315, suite S$360–480. Recommended. *Nearest MRT* Paya Labar (EW line) and taxi
Century Roxy Park 50 East Coast Rd, Roxy Sq, Singapore 428769; tel: 6344 8000; fax: 6344 8010; email: resvn@roxypark.com.sg. Seventeen-storey hotel next to Roxy Sq Shopping Centre and 15-minute walk from East Coast Pk. Pool and fitness centre. Hourly shuttle bus (24 hours) to Changi Airport. Beads Bar (24-hour service), Feast@East coffee shop (buffet breakfast, lunch and dinner), Thai and international restaurant. 463 rooms. Single S$220–80, double S$240–300, suite S$380–480. Recommended. *Nearest MRT* Paya Labar (EW line) and taxi

Le Meridien Changi Singapore 1 Netheravon Rd, Singapore 508502; tel:6542 7700; fax: 6542 5295; email: meridien@singnet.com.sg. Near Changi Village, pier and beach, and useful as an overnight stop over from Changi Airport. 275 rooms. Single S$220–80, double S$250–300, suite S$380–750. *Nearest MRT* Tampines (EW line)

Mid-range

Lion City Hotel 15 Tanjong Katong Rd, Singapore 436950; tel: 6744 8111; fax: 6748 7622; email: lchotel@pacific.net.sg. Concrete block with 9 floors and unimpressive exterior, but pleasing reception area and clean, spacious en-suite rooms. TV and fridge in every room. Coffee house and restaurant on ground floor. 166 rooms. Single S$83–120, double S$83–120, suite S$210–460. *Nearest MRT* Paya Labar (EW line)

Tristar Inn Singapore 970 Geylang Rd, #01-01, Singapore 423492; tel: 6440 6696; fax: 6440 3343; email: tristarinn@pacific.net.sg. Opposite Malay Village and Geylang Serai market. Ten-minute taxi ride to Changi Airport. Good, clean budget hotel, used mainly by businessmen and a few tourists. Business centre with email (charge S$3 for 30 mins). Small pool. 112 rooms. Single S$92–150, double S$92–150, suite S$170–298. *Nearest MRT* Paya Labar (EW line)

Sea View Hotel Amber Close, Singapore 439984; tel: 6345 2222; fax: 6345 1741. Modern hotel, with helpful staff, near East Coast Pk (10–15-minute walk) and Seafood Centre (5 minutes by taxi). Clean bright rooms have views of sea, park or city skyscrapers in distance. Mainly business occupancy. Bleak and bare pool on ground floor behind Cold Storage supermarket (to be avoided!). Bali Hut restaurant (local and international breakfast, lunch and dinner buffets). 435 rooms. Single S$160–80, double S$180–230. Recommended. *Nearest MRT* Paya Labar (EW line) and taxi

Budget

Changi Hotel 80 Changi Rd, Singapore 479715; tel: 6346 3388; fax: 6345 7661; email: changihotel@pacific.net.sg. Renovated in March 2002, this is a clean and respectable hotel located on the busy Changi Rd. Tourist class, with friendly staff. Carpeted rooms with air conditioning and fridges. Coffee house, with breakfast S$5 (may be included in package). 61 rooms. Single S$80–90, double S$90–100, suite S$140. *Nearest MRT* Eunos (EW line)

WHERE TO EAT

The east coast is particularly renowned for its seafood, and there are many restaurants to choose from. For food so fresh it's still alive, head for the **East Coast Seafood Centre** (opposite East Coast Parkway) and hunt your own dinner (well, almost). Take a trolley and select your fish from those swimming in the large tanks of water. They are fished out, cooked, and brought to your table. The drunken prawns – so-called because they are tossed live into hot wine to cook – are particularly good. There is a large range of dishes, the ambience is thrilling and the view superb. Open daily 17.00–23.30. Within the East Coast Seafood Centre, **Red House Seafood** (Block 1204, #01-05, East Coast Seafood Centre, East Coast Parkway; tel: 6442 3112) offers a romantic setting.

The Olea (158 Upper East Coast Road; tel: 6449 3880) serves classic Greek food. The service is friendly and efficient, although the prices are a little on the high side. There is also a deli. Open 12.00–24.00 every day.

The **Al Forno East Coast** (400 East Coast Road; tel: 6348 8781) is a spacious restaurant serving good, traditional Italian cuisine. The food is mid-range in price, although the wine is expensive. Lunch served 12.00–1.45, dinner 18.30–22.15.

One of four outlets (others are to be found at SunTec City Mall, Boat Quay and Great World City), the **House of Sundanese Food** (218 East Coast Road; tel: 6345 5020) serves authentic – and cheap – dishes from West Java. The charcoal-grilled fish (*ikan bakar*) is excellent. Wine is not served here. Open for lunch 11.30–14.30 weekdays, 12.30–15.00 weekend; for dinner 18.00–22.00 weekdays, 17.30–21.30 weekend.

Near the National Stadium, on a pier jutting into the Kallang basin, is **8 On the Bay** (50 Stadium Boulevard, Oasis Complex; tel: 6346 8089). This octagonal restaurant serves Western cuisine, and has a 'light bite' menu targeted at those attending sports events. Budget for around S$50. Open daily 11.30–14.30, 18.30–22.30. Near by is **Thai Village Sharksfin** (50 Stadium Boulevard, #01-01, Oasis Building; tel: 6440 2292), a reasonably priced and lively restaurant specialising in shark's fin and other seafood. Open daily 11.30–15.00, 18.00–22.00.

Palm Beach (5 Stadium Walk, #02-16, Leisure Park; tel: 6344 3088) is a long-established seafood restaurant with a good reputation. It is large – spread over four floors – and the décor is simple but sophisticated. While chilli crab is a speciality, this restaurant is not afraid to experiment and it includes some unusual dishes on its menu. There is also a selection of non-seafood options. Expect to pay about S$40 each. Open daily 12.00–15.00 for lunch, 17.30–23.00 for dinner.

WHAT TO SEE AND DO

The **East Coast Park** (off East Coast Park Service Road), stretching along 20km of reclaimed coastland, is the city's most popular beach, and consists of sand imported from Indonesia. Behind the beach is a long, tree-filled park. It is here that the Singaporeans themselves come to relax, sitting on carpets of lalang, and sheltering from the sun beneath the coconut palms and rubber trees. There is also a range of more energetic activities in which to participate, either on the beach or in the park, including bowling, cycling, fishing, sailing, windsurfing, swimming, and rollerblading. The slightly less active can enjoy a picnic or a pleasant walk. At the time of writing, there was a pond teeming with tiny fish and often very large red-eared terrapins, each a popular species among Buddhists who buy them in order to release them from captivity and thereby gain credit in the next life (see page 9). The water would heave with the creatures as locals threw into the pool; however, it was on the verge of being tidied up, and it may be that this is no longer the case. There are many restaurants and bars to choose from, and the famous East Coast Seafood Centre is especially worthy of your attention (see opposite). The park is open from 07.00 to 19.00 daily, and admission is free.

Getting there Take a taxi or a bus (No 16) from Orchard Road to Marine Terrace and then pass through the underpass to get to the park and beach.

There are over a thousand crocodilians on display at the **Singapore Crocodilarium** (730 East Coast Parkway; tel: 6447 3722), varying from tiny hatchlings to huge monsters. The crocodilarium is a business venture rather than a zoo or conservation centre, and so it is worth remembering that the stars of the show will end up as handbags, boots and other fashion accessories; indeed, the souvenir shop sells items made from crocodile skin. Furthermore, it must be said that crocodiles are not readily tamed, and make poor performers; during the regular shows, handlers have to use a certain amount of force to cajole reptiles that are, at best, distinctly uninterested. As a consequence, this entertainment – while popular among locals – may leave a sour taste in the mouths of Westerners in the audience. The displays of hatchlings cannot hold the interest for too long either. Open daily, 09.00–17.00; feeding times are at 11.00 on Tue, Thu and Sat.

Getting there Bus No 36 from Orchard Road to Amber Road, or MRT to Paya Lebar (WE line) and bus No 76 to Amber Road. From here, go right, through the underpass by the Chinese Swimming Club, to the East Coast Park Service Road and into the park. Turn right and continue to the crocodile farm on the left.

On the northeastern coast of Singapore, **Pasir Ris Park** retains a flavour of the island's natural beauty before its aspect was altered in the quest for modernity. Unsurprisingly, as in most places here, it has not proved wholly resistant to the 'improving' hand of human intervention. An area of original mangrove forest, for instance, has been fitted with raised walkways and information boards so that it can be explored in relative comfort. You might be lucky enough to glimpse large monitor lizards, which frequent the muddy watercourses, and you should hear the sudden clatter of white-breasted waterhens taking flight from almost beneath your feet. Fiddler crabs and mudskippers fight, feed and breed along the bed of the river. Next to this is a beach of the whitest sand, and beyond that a small park containing a maze. The tranquillity of the protected park is unfortunately spoilt in a few places by diggers clearing adjacent land for further building programmes.

Pasir Ris is best visited when the heat is less oppressive, in the early morning or after 16.00 (although, if you choose the latter, remember that it will start to get dark from 18.30), and it is ideally covered by bike. There is a small stall to buy refreshments, but it is worth bringing liquids with you as the sun can be fierce and there is little shelter to be found.

Getting there MRT to Pasir Ris station (EW line), followed by a ten-minute bus ride (No 403).

A short walk from the mangrove swamp at Pasir Ris (see above), on the northeast coast, is **NTUC Lifestyle World** (1 Pasir Ris Close, Singapore

519599; tel: 6581 9113; fax: 6582 5875). This is a government-run holiday estate where Singaporeans unable to afford holidays elsewhere can come for cheap breaks. It is a depressing-looking place to take a vacation, having the air of a prison or barracks. However, there is a three-hectare theme park containing the Flume Ride (the highest water ride in Asia) and the 360° Cadbury Inverter. You can watch live music and theatre at Event Square, and there are over thirty eating places. Escape Theme Park open 17.00–22.30 weekdays, 10.00–22.30 weekends, public holidays and school holidays. Admission S\$5. A day pass, which includes four credit points which can be used against the cost of rides, varies from S\$15 to S\$28 depending on the season.

Getting there MRT to Pasir Ris (EW terminus), and bus No 21 for one stop from the Pasir Ris Bus Interchange, next to the station.

The **Sports Museum** (15 Stadium Road, west entrance of the National Stadium; tel: 6340 9516; fax: 6340 9834) celebrates Singapore's sporting achievements, past and present. Open weekdays 09.00–16.30, Sat 09.00–12.30. Closed Sun.

Getting there MRT to Kallang (EW line), then bus No 11.

JOO CHIAT

This area is named after Chew Joo Chiat, a rich Peranakan who bought land in the 1920s and 1930s and built shop-houses and homes for the Straits Chinese who moved into the area.

Telok Kuran English Primary School opened in 1923 (one famous ex-pupil is Lee Kuan Yew), and a Catholic Eurasian community established itself around the **Holy Family Church**, on East Coast Road, which was completed in the same year.

The **Seaview Hotel** and the **Singapore Swimming Club** appeared during the 1930s, and Changi Market (now **Joo Chiat Complex**, opposite the Malay Village and Geylang Serai Market on the corner of Joo Chiat Road) after the Japanese occupation. It became a well-known Malay trading station for food, flowers and spices.

In 1993, Joo Chiat was listed as a conservation area. As a result, the colourful rows of traditional Peranakan shop-houses and bungalows, and the narrow streets dating from the start of the 20th century, have been carefully preserved. It is a good place to get a taste of an older Singapore. It is also famous for its restaurants, which sell Peranakan food.

Getting there MRT to Paya Labar (WE line), and walk south towards Lion City Hotel before turning left on Changi Road to Joo Chiat Road.

GEYLANG SERAI

Geylang Serai holds a section of the population who called Singapore home long before either the Chinese or the Indians, for this is the Malay quarter.

Two hundred years ago there was a floating Malay village in the mouth of the river but, in 1840, the British dispersed it and the villagers moved to the Geylang area. During the 19th century, this part of the country used to be known as 'Geylang Konabra', but because lemon grass grew in profusion in the area, its name was changed to Geylang Serai – *serai* being the Malay name for lemon grass.

Geylang became the main centre for the Malay community in the 1920s when the competition for land in the Kampong Glam area became too great and families moved to join other Malaysians, Indonesians and Arabs who had already settled here. It still has a unique Malayan ambience and is the focus of events during many cultural celebrations, particularly in the 30 days leading up to Hari Raya Puasa (see page 97) at the end of the fasting month of Ramadan. The streets are lit with thousands of glittering lights and there is a colourful night bazaar of temporary stalls selling traditional cakes and delicacies.

What to see and do

Geylang Serai Market – a traditional, local market – is one of the largest in Singapore. Its cramped bazaar-like alleys are packed with stalls overlooked by high-rise housing blocks. In the 'dry' section you will find a vast range of goods from textiles, clothing and decorative household items to traditional Malay dress, prayer mats and pilgrimage paraphernalia. In the 'wet' section the stalls are laden with vegetables and fruit, *halal* meats, fresh seafood, herbs and ground spices.

There's also a food centre where you can take your pick from all kinds of Malay and Muslim foods. If you like banana fritters – a local speciality – keep a look out for the stall that sells them, or search in the surrounding street eateries. There are commonly three kinds of fritters, which vary according to the quality of the bananas used, and a fourth in which the banana is mashed with flour, shaped into a ball, and fried.

Getting there Take the MRT to Paya Labar on the EW line, walk south towards Geylang Road, and then through the site of the Malay Village to the opposite side.

The **Malay Village** (39 Geylang Serai; tel: 6748 4700) attempts to reproduce a Malay community at work. It is a smallish area (on a site of less than two hectares) which, although it tries hard to encourage tourists, and can be busier at weekends, is usually almost deserted during the week. You can see typical Malay buildings and shops specialising in art, Malay costumes and medicines, and a store selling caged birds. You can also watch – and take part in – kite making (Malay kites are truly unique), and see demonstrations of top spinning and batik painting. Unsurprisingly, batik fabrics, tops and kites are available to purchase. There is a 'floating restaurant', open only in the evenings, where you can eat Malay food – the fish curry dishes are excellent – while watching free performances of traditional music and dance. It should be stressed that it is worth checking to see what activities are taking place before visiting or the experience is likely to be a disappointing one. The village is at its best during festivals. Open every day 10.00–22.00. Admission S$10 adult or S$7 child to visit the museums and demonstrations, although you can walk through the site and visit the shops free of charge.

Getting there Nearest MRT is Paya Labar (EW line). Alight here and walk south towards Geylang Road.

CHANGI

To the far east of the island is Changi, well-known not only for its superb airport but also for its notorious prison, where the executioner enforces Singapore's strict system of laws. The **Changi Chapel and Museum** (1000 Upper Changi Road North; tel: 6214 2451; email: changi_museum@pacific.net.sg) used to be housed within the grounds of the prison itself. In February 2001, however, the museum and chapel were moved to their current location to allow redevelopment of the prison. The museum is dedicated to all those who were interned in Changi Prison during the Japanese occupation, and who suffered terribly there. It holds the sketches, paintings, photographs, letters and personal belongings of former prisoners-of-war and their families, and there is an audio-visual theatre showing films detailing the miserable life endured by such POWs.

The chapel is a replica of many of those built in Changi by prisoners during the war, and it displays a copy of the 'Changi Murals'. The original murals were painted in 1942 by Bombardier Stanley Warren while he was in the Changi Prison hospital, part of which (the dysentery wing) was converted into St Luke's Chapel. This has been restored, but it falls within the military camp at Changi and is thus out of bounds to the public. The murals were discovered under a coat of distemper in 1958. Open daily 09.30–16.30. Admission free.

Getting there MRT to Tanah Merah (EW line) and then bus No 2 to the stop after the Changi Women's Prison/Drug Rehabilitation Centre.

Three monster guns – the largest in the British empire to be used for coastal defence during World War II – were installed in the **Johore Battery** (Cosford Road). Each gun had underground magazines stashed three storeys deep, and lift shafts were used to bring the shells to the surface. The tunnels were uncovered in 1991 by representatives of the Prison Department. The Johore Battery is now part of the **Changi Experience**, where visitors can see a reconstructed gun and view the bunkers through a reverse periscope. Open Mon–Fri 09.00–17.00. Admission free.

Getting there MRT to Tanah Merah (WE line) and bus No 2 to the stop opposite Selarang Camp.

Changi Village is a favourite spot for fishermen and yachtsmen, with beaches and a jetty where you can catch a bumboat to ferry you across to

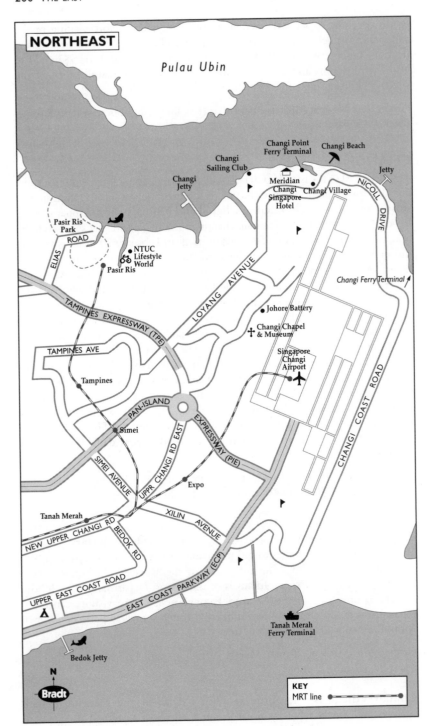

NORTHEAST

Pulau Ubin (see pages 208–9). There are no cinemas, fast-food centres or shopping malls.

Getting there MRT to Tampines (EW line), then bus No 29.

In 1942, **Changi Beach** was the scene of a terrible massacre. The Japanese lined up 66 Chinese men along the water's edge before shooting them. These were just a few of the thousands of Chinese who were executed on suspicion of having anti-Japanese sympathies. Tanah Merah was another of the killing grounds.

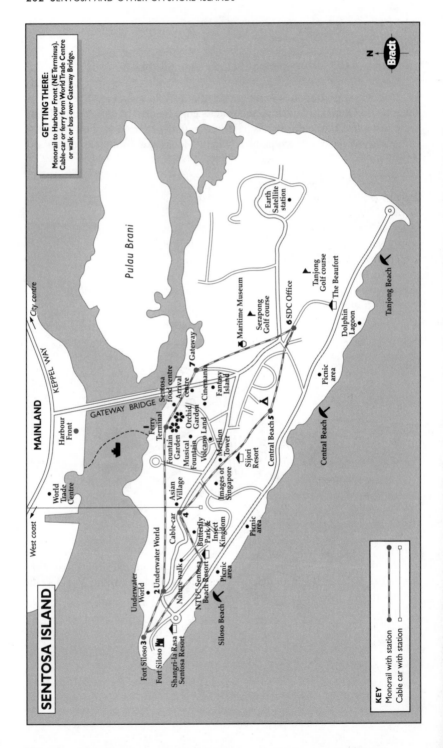

SENTOSA ISLAND

GETTING THERE:
Monorail to Harbour Front (NE Terminus).
Cable-car or ferry from World Trade Centre
or walk or bus over Gateway Bridge.

Pulau Brani

MAINLAND

City centre

KEPPEL WAY

West coast

World
Trade
Centre

Harbour
Front

GATEWAY BRIDGE

Underwater
World

2 Underwater World

Nature walk

Cable-car
4

Fort Siloso 3
Fort Siloso

Shangri-la Rasa
Sentosa Resort

NTUC Sentosa
Beach Resort

Butterfly
Park &
Insect
Kingdom

Picnic
area

Siloso Beach

Asian
Village

Ferry
Terminal

Fountain
Garden

Musical
Fountain

Volcano Land

Orchid
Garden

Images of
Singapore

Motion
Tower

Sijori
Resort

Central Beach 5

Sentosa
food centre

Arrival
centre

7 Gateway

Cinemania

Fantasy
Island

Picnic
area

Central Beach

Maritime Museum

Serapong
Golf course

6 SDC Office

Dolphin
Lagoon

Picnic
area

Earth
Satellite
station

Tanjong
Golf course

The Beaufort

Tanjong Beach

N

Bradt

KEY
Monorail with station
Cable car with station

Sentosa and Other Offshore Islands

SENTOSA

Just to the south of Singapore lies the island of Sentosa. While small in size, it is still the country's most successful tourist attraction, with over a million people a year trooping to experience its thrills. This was far from always the case. It is difficult to believe that just a few decades ago the island was entirely undeveloped, its inhabitants leading quiet, relatively unsophisticated lives. The British military took advantage of its solitude and position by manning an army base here until the early 1970s, and even 20 years back there were unspoilt, isolated areas to be found. Then, however, the government moved the locals into HDB housing on the mainland and set about creating an elaborate theme park and pleasure resort. Now you can travel around on free monorail or bus services, alighting to explore one of many carefully constructed sites. Alternatively, you can laze on manicured beaches of imported (and fairly hard) sand, or swim in lagoons roped off from the sea in full view of ships waiting to gain access to the harbour. On the eastern portion of the island there are also several golf courses.

The place is now entirely tamed – indeed it never pretends to be otherwise. Nevertheless, in parts it retains a certain beauty, and it definitely provides a day's entertainment for children and adults alike. It is popular with Singaporeans as well as foreign visitors so be warned: it can be extremely busy at weekends. Entrance to the island costs S$6 adult, S$4 child (unless the price is included in the fare you have paid to reach the island – see page 204). However, there are additional charges for many of the attractions on offer. You can cut down slightly on the cost by purchasing discounted tickets that allow access to several selected attractions. These are available from the World Trade Centre or the Mount Faber cable-car entrance.

At the southernmost tip of the mainland, next to the Causeway Bridge, stands the **World Trade Centre** (nearest MRT is Harbour Front, NE line terminus). From here you can board either a ferry or a cable-car to Sentosa (see *Getting there*, page 204). You can also catch the cable-car from the **Mount Faber Gardens** (Kampong Bahru Road, leading to Mount Faber Road), to the north of the World Trade Centre, where the 120m-high Mount Faber provides the focal point in some pretty parkland. The gardens are not extensive, and primarily serve as a pleasant and brief stopping point on the way to Sentosa. Visit early, when the gardens look beautiful, swathed in morning mist. From Mount Faber, visitors are rewarded with breathtaking views of the city skyline, the harbour and the islands off the coast. It is also a good location for birdwatching; during periods of migration, eagles and other birds of prey wheel on the thermals caused by the slopes of the hill. In addition, the determined will spot small passerine birds flitting through the abundant ornamental shrubs, looking for insects. To get there, take a bus from Orchard Boulevard/Orchard Road (Nos 65, 85, 124, 143). The nearest MRT is Redhill (EW line), after which you take bus No 145. Alternatively, you can take the MRT to Harbour Front (NE line terminus) and the cable-car from the World Trade Centre.

Getting there
By land
Take bus A from the World Trade Centre or bus C from Tiong Bahru MRT (EW line). The Sentosa E bus operates from Orchard Road, and its fare of S$7 adult (S$5 child) includes admission to the island.

There is a toll charge for taxis, and they will only drop off (or pick up) customers from one of Sentosa's hotels. It is possible to drive on to the island, but only after 18.30. Remember both that there is a bridge toll and that vehicles must leave by 03.00. The cost for a car containing up to five people is S$12.

You can also walk across the bridge – it takes about 20 minutes from the World Trade Centre. Admission S$6 adult, S$4 child.

By sea
There are ferries available from the World Trade Centre (1 Maritime Square; tel: 6270 7888). They depart Mon–Fri 09.30–22.00 (30-minute intervals), Sat and Sun 08.30–22.00 (20-minute intervals). Cost S$8.30 adult, S$5.30 child (includes admission).

By cable-car
You can board a cable-car – taking you at great height over the ship-filled harbour before dipping down to the island – either at Mount Faber (see above) or from the Cable Car Tower (3 Maritime Square; tel: 6270 8855) next to the World Trade Centre. These run daily 08.30–21.00. The fares are S$8.50 adult, S$3.90 child. For the brave, there is the option of a glass-bottomed car (S$15 adult, S$8 child). And at the weekends you can even have a meal (18.30–20.30; tel: 6277 9654), although the journey is not long and you risk indigestion. This costs S$120 per couple. Prices exclude admission to the island.

Where to stay
Luxury
Shangri-la Rasa Sentosa Resort 101 Siloso Rd, Sentosa, Singapore 098970; tel: 6275 0100; fax: 6275 0355; email: sen@shangri-la.com. Just below Fort Siloso, at

western end of island. On 'manicured' beach overlooking ships anchored outside harbour. Popular with locals at weekends, and a favoured venue for wedding parties. 459 rooms. Single S$280–360, double S$340–420, suite S$550–1,800.

The Beaufort 2 Bukit Manis Rd, Sentosa, Singapore 099891; tel: 6275 0331; fax: 6275 0228; email: beaufort@singnet.com.sg. In the centre of the island, near the Tanjong Golf Course, this hotel is quieter than others on Sentosa. Extensive grounds, pool, gym, tennis courts and other sports facilities. Restaurants and good service. 214 rooms. Single S$280–380, double S$280–380, suite S$450–1,500.

Mid-range

Sijori Resort 23 Beach View, Sentosa, Singapore 098679; tel: 6271 2002; fax: 6275 0220; email: reservation@sijoriresort.com.sg. Near the Merlion and all the main attractions. 61 rooms. Single S$180–245, double S$180–245, suite S$300–25.

Where to eat

There are various restaurants on Sentosa, and outlets selling fast food are particularly prevalent. You will also find a good food centre near the ferry terminal. The Mahalo Hawaiian Beach Bar offers snacks and lively music, and Sunset Bay is regarded as a popular hangout for yuppies and expats, and a place to indulge in beach games.

Sharkey's (Shangri-la's Rasa Sentosa Resort, 101 Siloso Road; tel: 6275 0100) is an alfresco restaurant offering good seafood. There is a wide selection of dishes featuring Sri Lankan crab, and an excellent grilled seafood platter. The cost should be approximately S$50 a head. Open daily 18.30–22.30.

What to see and do

The following attractions on Sentosa are listed in the order they are reached on the monorail circuit, from a starting point near the Visitors Arrival Centre (as you enter the island by the road bridge or from the ferry terminal). If you arrive by cable-car, your nearest site of interest will be the Butterfly Park.

Fountain Gardens and Musical Fountain

Said to be the world's most complicated display of its kind, the fountain spouts streams of water to the accompaniment of vivid lights and an eclectic selection of music. There is also a dragon in a pool periodically spraying water from its mouth. There are free shows daily at 17.00, 17.30, 19.30, 20.30 and 21.30. Monorail stations 1 and 4.

The Merlion

Towering over the Musical Fountain, and immediately conspicuous as you arrive on the island, the 37m statue of Singapore's national symbol – half-lion, half-fish – can be climbed, and offers magnificent views from the vantage points of either its mouth or the top of its head. It is also illuminated as part of the Rise of Merlion and Musical Fountain shows at 19.30, 20.30 and 21.30 (free). Open daily 09.00–22.00. Admission S$3 adult, S$2 child. Monorail stations 1 and 4.

Asian Village

A fairly uninspiring collection of buildings aimed at simulating the architecture and culture of villages in different regions of Asian. Set around a small lake, there are craft shops selling souvenirs, themed restaurants, and an adjacent funfair (Adventure Asia) offering 'joy rides'. Village open daily 10.00–21.00 (admission free). Adventure Asia open 10.00–19.00 (unlimited rides cost S$10). Monorail station 4.

Nature Walk

The free Nature Walk – also known as the Dragon Trail because of the sculptures of mythical beasts that you encounter on the way – follows a 1.5km trail through secondary forest. Among the wildlife are long-tailed macaques (as elsewhere, these animals have been emboldened by frequent human contact and should be treated with caution). Monorail station 4.

Underwater World

This splendid, cutting-edge oceanarium features a broad range of saltwater species, including sea cucumbers, sea dragons, beautiful tropical fish, stingrays and sharks. There are thousands of fish, many of them breathtakingly colourful. A transparent underwater tunnel, measuring 80m and complete with moving walkway, brings you within inches of the creatures. The complex has links with Singapore Zoo (see page 188), which is a strong recommendation in itself, and it is arguably the highlight of Sentosa. One of the more recent attractions is Dolphin Lagoon (see opposite), where you can watch shows featuring marine mammals. Open daily 09.00–21.00. Admission S$17 adult, S$11 child (includes Dolphin Lagoon). Monorail station 2.

Fort Siloso

Located at the very western end of the island, the fort was originally constructed by the British in order to defend the approach to Singapore harbour. It was manned with three seven-inch and two 64-pound guns. There are exhibits showing its development between the late 19th century (when it was built) and the time of the Battle for Singapore in 1942. You can tour the bunkers and tunnels, and tackle an assault course. Allow just under an hour. Open daily 09.00–19.00. Admission S$3 adult, S$2 child. Monorail station 3.

Butterfly Park and Insect Kingdom Museum

Walk among 2,500 live butterflies – featuring species found across Southeast Asia – in a specially designed enclosure containing spectacular beds of flowering plants. There is also a collection of over 4,000 mounted insects, including scorpions, and another of live insects such as stick insects and beetles. Open daily 09.00–18.30. Admission S$6 adult, S$3 child. Monorail station 4.

Images of Singapore

A well-presented museum tracing the history of Singapore from the 14th century to World War II. Wax figures and film presentations are used to re-create the lives of the early settlers, to re-enact the signing of the treaty by Sir Stamford Raffles, and to detail the two surrenders during World War II (of the British in 1942 and the Japanese in 1945). There are also exhibits explaining the traditions and festivals of the Chinese, Indian, Malay and Peranakan peoples of Singapore. Allow an hour. Open 09.00–21.00 (latest entry 20.30). Admission S\$8 adult, S\$5 child. Monorail station 4.

Sijori Wondergolf

An alternative to the golf courses to the east of the island, which cater to the more 'serious' golfers, the 45 holes here are targeted at exponents of the crazy version of the game. Open 09.00–21.00. Admission S\$8 adult, S\$4 child. Monorail station 4.

Dolphin Lagoon

To be found at the point where Central and Tanjong beaches meet, the dolphins perform daily shows at 11.00, 13.30, 15.30 and 17.30. Open 11.00–18.00. Admission S\$11 adult, S\$6 child. Tickets to Underwater World (see opposite) include entry to the Dolphin Lagoon. Monorail station 5. There is also a swimming and recreation area at Central Beach, where you can splash around, sun yourself and hire canoes.

Maritime Museum

Standing outside the monorail loop, this museum explores the history of Singapore's mariners (and its bustling port), charting the developments in technology and design surrounding boats and other related equipment. Exhibits include some intricate models and a 100-year-old steam crane. Open Wed–Sun 10.00–18.00. Closed Mon and Tue. Monorail station 7.

Fantasy Island

A must for children, this aqua-park contains 13 thrilling rides and 32 chutes, among them the longest elevated water ride in Asia. The slides are graded according to difficulty (and scariness), and there are areas for young children. Open Mon–Thu 10.30–18.00, Fri, Sat and public holidays 10.30–22.00. Admission S\$16 adult, S\$10 child. Monorail station 7.

Volcano Land

Considerably less exciting than one might imagine, Volcano Land boasts the world's largest man-made volcano – although just how many rival man-made volcanoes there are is anybody's guess. Visitors descend inside the cone to learn about evolutionary theory before experiencing the climactic eruption (which takes place every 30 minutes and is visible from outside). Open daily 11.00–19.00. Admission S\$12 adult, S\$6 child. Monorail stations 1 and 7.

Cinemania

A 3-D movie experience, complete with roaring sound and moving seats. Screenings are every half-hour. Open 11.00–20.00. Admission S\$10 adult, S\$6 child. Monorail stations 1 and 7.

A TRIP TO SENTOSA

Andrew Rudd

We bumped into a Catholic priest in the courtyard of a church on Queen Street. Having discussed our trip so far, we were informed that if we did nothing else while in Singapore, we had to go to Sentosa Island. Why? Because it's what tourists do!

In fairness, we hadn't read that much about Sentosa. We anticipated that it would be easy to get to as we boarded the MRT to a station we were certain would be close to our intended destination. Unfortunately, it turned out to be a 45-minute walk away, in the mid-afternoon heat.

There are several ways to reach the island itself – by road, by ferry, or, the method recommended to us, by cable-car (see page 204). As we neared the towers, with the flimsy-looking wire and bouncing gondolas extending in either direction from it, we made the mistake of ambling into a building where everyone was wearing suits. Looking out of place in our shorts and T-shirts, we had stumbled into the World Trade Centre.

After locating the cable-cars at our second attempt, we were soon winging our way across the sea, enjoying a fantastic gondola trip and ignoring the grimy windows. The 360° views were amazing, along the coast to the dominating skyscrapers of the CBD that stood out in the distance, while ahead of us the green of Sentosa grew ever larger. Before we knew it we were venturing into the not-quite-Disney-like world.

Sentosa has it all. There are places to stay, restaurants to eat in (including

Orchid Gardens

These contain a large variety of beautiful orchids, with over 200 species on display. You will also find a flower clock, a Japanese tea-house, a carp pond, and a restaurant. Open 09.30–18.00. Admission S$3.50 adult, S$2 child. Monorail stations 1 and 7.

PULAU UBIN

If you fancy getting away from the crowds, you could do worse than spend a day on Pulau Ubin (*pulau* means 'island'), off the northeastern corner of Singapore. A greater contrast with the thrills and spills of Sentosa is difficult to imagine. Here, as you sit by the sea and admire the traditional fishing huts (known locally as *kelongs*), or visit one of several Ma Chor temples, it is easy to convince yourself that you have stepped back in time. The island is dotted with quarries, which provided stone for many of the buildings on the mainland, and prawns are farmed here, lifted in nets from ponds that trap the shellfish at high tide. The island's mangroves and forests are rich sources of wildlife, and the diverse terrain has made it popular with mountain bikers (there are several places to hire bikes as you alight from the bumboat). There is a visitor centre a short walk from the jetty.

a McDonalds, if you wish), and attractions galore, all linked by a nifty monorail shuttling people to and fro. There is no mistaking that this island is designed to lure the tourists.

We toured the island on the monorail, although walking around would have enabled us to study the many statues and sculptures in more detail, or at least given us the chance to lounge on the beach for a bit! Of the attractions we visited, I would heartily recommend Underwater World, even to those with no particular interest in marine life. It was truly spectacular, with colourful displays of rare species to investigate. Our money was definitely well spent there.

As night fell we made our way back to the mainland, the return journey in the gondola being even more striking than before, the tiny lights of people at work in office buildings littering the landscape. In our insignificant pod, soaring high above the ground, we were separated from the hustle and bustle of the world below, able to revel in the fact that we were in such a fantastic place.

Sentosa does not represent the culture and variety of Singapore as much as it perhaps should. The history of the island is partially covered by some of the attractions, but far more could be made of it. On the other hand it's not meant to be that serious. It's a fun place and worth a visit. Incidentally, when we left the cable-car towers we caught a bus back to the centre. It cost the same price as the MRT and dropped us within 20m of the hotel doors. How typical! Always check the best way to get to and from a place beforehand!

Getting there

Bumboats leave regularly (once each has enough customers aboard) from the jetty at Changi Point, and the crossing costs about S$1.50. To get to Changi Point, take bus No 2 from Tanah Merah MRT.

Where to stay and eat

There are few places to stay or to eat on the island. The **Ubin Lagoon Resort** (1000 Pulau Ubin, Singapore 508419; tel: 6542 9590; fax: 6542 9591; email: ulr@pacific.net.sg) has 106 rooms (double S$170–90, suite S$210–50), and includes sporting and adventure facilities (also open to non-residents). The ferry takes 20 minutes to reach the resort jetty from Ponggol Marina. The **Pulau Ubin Seafood Restaurant** (on the northeast coast; tel: 6545 8202) serves very good fish, but is expensive. Open 11.30–21.00.

ST JOHN'S, KUSU AND SISTERS ISLANDS

To the south of Sentosa lies a cluster of smaller islands. **St John's** has become a popular camping destination for weekend visitors, although it is quieter during the week. The birdlife is fascinating, several species having established themselves here after escaping from dealers when the animal trade was a thriving business in Singapore. The greater hill mynah and sulphur-crested cockatoo are two such escapees. You may also see the rare magpie robin, as well as bulbuls, sunbirds, flowerpeckers and coppersmith barbets (whose name derives from their clinking call, which sounds like a smith working copper). There is a healthy colony of monitor lizards, too. Other than opportunities for wildlife watching, there are picnic areas and lagoons for swimming. There are no hotels on St John's, although some magnificent colonial bungalows are available to rent. Details are available from the booking counter at the World Trade Centre, or from the Sentosa Development Corporation (tel: 6275 0388).

Kusu is smaller, and takes little time to explore. Legend states that it was once a huge marine turtle that transformed itself into a rock in order to save some shipwrecked sailors. It is sacred to Taoists, who make an annual pilgrimage to the Tua Pekong Temple (see *Chapter 3, Holidays, Festivals and Events*, page 96). There is also a Muslim shrine, Kramat Kusu, and places to picnic and to swim. There is no accommodation.

Getting there Ferries to both islands can be taken from the World Trade Centre (tel: 6862 8322/ 6275 0388), leaving twice daily during the week, and six times on Sundays and public holidays. They travel first to Kusu (about 30 minutes) and then to St John's (one hour). See *Chapter 2*, page 37, for ferry times, or contact the World Trade Centre (tel: 6275 0661). Be wary of becoming stranded overnight by missing the last return ferry. Cost S$9 adult, S$6 child.

The **Sisters Islands** have reefs that make for good snorkelling or scuba-diving. Locals also picnic here. There are no hotels or places to eat.

Getting there There are no ferries. A water taxi from Jardine Steps or Clifford Pier (70 Collyer Quay; tel: 6532 7441) will cost about S$50 an hour, and takes between six and 12 passengers. If you are being dropped off, be sure to make arrangements for the return journey – and pack some insect repellent!

Trips into Malaysia

Singapore provides a good base from which to visit other countries in the region. Most convenient is Malaysia because of the short causeway linking it to Singapore. However, Indonesia is only half an hour away by air, Thailand just an hour, and neither Brunei nor the Philippines is much further. You will require a passport valid for at least six months in order to enter any of these countries. Most visitors are issued with a permit entitling them to one- or two-month stays, and a visa is not usually necessary.

Malaysia is accessible by ferry, bus, and coach, and you can take a train or plane if you wish to travel further than Johore Bahru, the nearest city to Singapore. For information on these, see the *Getting there and away* section on pages 43–7. In addition, there are various organised tours to the country, including day and half-day trips by coach or taxi. Ask the concierge at your hotel or scan the *Straits Times* for details. It is also worth contacting the Malaysian Tourist Board (tel: 6532 6351).

Malaysia is divided between the main peninsula, and the two states of Sabah and Sarawak on the island of Borneo. The independent country of Brunei sits between Sabah and Sarawak, and the rest of Borneo, the greater part, belongs to Indonesia. Malaysia is noted for its expanses of rainforest, and is rich in wildlife (although the commercial exploitation of the country's timber is progressing at an alarming rate).

On crossing the Causeway which links Malaysia and Singapore, and after completing the simple immigration formalities, you will find yourself in **Johore Bahru**, the most southerly region and capital of the state of Johore. Although the countries are very close together, Johore Bahru lacks the sanitised feel of Singapore and, while much of the city is developed, it retains more of the atmosphere familiar to readers of Joseph Conrad. The food – and the seafood in particular – is excellent, and prices are cheaper than across the water. There are many bargains to be found in the night markets here.

Also within easy reach is **Desaru** (or the 'village of casuarinas'). This is a haven of relaxation and watersports, and boasts 25km of white, sandy beach fringed with graceful casuarina trees imported from Australia.

Malacca (or **Melaka**), up the western coast of peninsular Malaysia, has a history spanning over 600 years, and was at various times populated by the Portuguese, the Dutch and the British. The town square holds a church of vivid red, still containing its original pews (now over 300 years old), and there are many other well-preserved architectural testaments to the diverse cultures

TICKETS PLEASE!
Hannah Postgate

For something a little different, try the night train from Singapore to Kuala Lumpur. For those of us who possess an adventurous spirit, this is still the way to travel across the continent. Reminiscent of the days of steam trains and panamas, this makes an otherwise uninspiring journey something of a memorable trip. It's comfortable, civilised and a whole lot safer than the bus.

The overnight sleeper train takes around nine hours and leaves and arrives at a reasonable hour – unlike so many night trains that just dump you, bleary-eyed and barely conscious, on a deserted platform during the early hours of the morning.

The train, and indeed my bed for the night, turned out to be remarkably comfortable. (That's coming from the breed of traveller who is not too proud to admit that she can't sleep just anywhere. I don't believe the seasoned traveller who tells you, 'Oh, I can sleep anywhere...', as you bounce down a dirt-track, on a hard bench, on the journey to which there seems no end!)

There are three classes: first (private compartments that sleep two people), second (still with beds, but less luxurious and shared by more people), and

the area has entertained. Malacca is strongly associated with the Nonya (or Peranakan), the Chinese who married Malaysians, and fashioned a unique blend of cultures which differentiates them from other Chinese people found in Singapore and elsewhere.

Off the east coast is **Tioman**, where you can enjoy the Berjaya Tioman Beach Resort, a five-star hotel, a golf course and all sorts of watersports and diving facilities.

Further inland is Malaysia's capital, **Kuala Lumpur**, which can be reached by air (or train; see box above). Like Singapore, it has made a concerted effort to compete as a force in the modern global economy, and it is characterised by concrete and skyscrapers. The thrusting Petronas Twin Towers are the tallest in the world, and symbolise the country's claim to significant economic power. However, the city lacks the order of Singapore, and has a 'shabbiness' that would not be tolerated by its cousin. Pubs, karaoke clubs, discos, cinemas and cigar bars can all be found here, along with a fantastic market.

From Kuala Lumpur, you can visit the **Genting Highlands**, a playground of relaxation standing 2,000 metres above sea level, where you will find Malaysia's only casino, a huge artificial lake, the inevitable golf course and a theme park packed with modern rides. In contrast, however, this part of the country is also famed for its expanse of rainforest, its fruit farms and its tea plantations (the higher altitudes are cool enough to grow tea). Butterflies proliferate in the **Cameron Highlands**.

If you are in search of a tropical paradise, there are some stunning places close to Malaysia's shoreline. Head for the 104-island archipelago off the northwest coast. The largest is **Langkawi**, with its palm-fringed beaches, blue

third (just seats – and hard seats at that). I do not recommend the latter, but either of the other two is fine. Some subscribe to the theory that you meet more people by avoiding first-class travel, so feel free to give second class a go.

As you come to expect in Singapore, the train is clean and runs on time – more than can be said for many European trains nowadays. The beds are not really designed for long, gangly Westerners, though, and anyone approaching six feet tall will feel the squeeze. However, they come with clean linen and (provided you are unaffected by the length) are very comfortable. The rocking motion and 'clackety-clack' sends even the travel-insomniac to sleep. The only snag on this overnight trip is being woken up to clear immigration at the crack of dawn.

Normal rules apply – stash your stuff and watch your valuables, especially in second class. Other advice would be to bring your own food as they can charge the earth to hungry passengers on a long trip like this one.

This train currently leaves from the Tanjong Pagar station at Keppel Road, which is on land owned by Malaysia. There is, however, ongoing discussion about opening a new station at Woodlands, and reclaiming the track and the land for Singapore.

waters, abundant wildlife, and lovely thatched houses built on stilts to prevent flood damage. The best-known tourist resort is **Penang**. While much of the island has been developed to cater for visitors, the capital, **George Town**, preserves a certain old-world charm.

The two offshore states of **Sarawak** and **Sabah**, on the island of Borneo to the east, are excellent places for anyone interested in flora and fauna, and are less developed than parts of the mainland. Sarawak was once the home of an Englishman named James Brooke, who landed here at about the time Stamford Raffles was establishing Singapore as a major port. Brooke admired Raffles' enterprise, and determined to emulate him. Arriving in a ship called the *Royalist*, he found himself in the middle of a fierce rebellion by the Malays, the local people, the Dyaks, and the Chinese against the rulers of the area who lived in Brunei. The rebels begged Brooke to assist them, and he was so successful that the Sultan of Brunei appointed him Rajah of Sarawak. Known as the 'white rajah', he and his successors ruled Sarawak until 1946 when it became part of Malaysia. Now the area's forest is home to a magnificent butterfly, resplendent in black, red and blue, called Rajah Brooke's birdwing. Unfortunately, its numbers are dwindling because of deforestation and over-collection, and you are more likely to come across a dead specimen in a glass case than in the wild.

Gliding frogs

Appendix 1

THE SINGLISH LANGUAGE

While various languages are found in Singapore, including Mandarin, Chinese dialects, Malay and Tamil, English is spoken everywhere. The version used, however, is characterised by colloquialisms unique to Singapore, and has become known as 'Singlish'. While this form rarely forms a significant barrier to communication for English speakers, below are some of the more baffling terms you might encounter:

Action	To show off, as in 'He always likes to *action*'.
Arrow	To be required to do something you would rather not, as in 'He was *arrowed* to meet his mother-in-law at the airport'.
Aahyah	An exclamation whose meaning depends on the situation in which it is used, usually expressing surprise or dismay. Examples include, 'Oh, no!', 'Is that so?', 'Goodness gracious!'.
Blur	Related to the English meaning, but used in a different context. 'At the conference he should have known all the facts, but he was very *blur*.'
Boh-chup	From the Hokkien, meaning 'could not care less'. 'Ah, *boh-chup*, I'm not going to work today.'
Can	OK, as in 'We'll go shopping later, *can*?', to which the response would be '*Can*'.
Chim	Hokkien word meaning 'deep' or 'profound', and pronounced 'cheem'. 'Her ideas were very *chim*.'
Chope	To reserve, as in 'We'll have to get there soon to *chope* seats for everyone'.
Gostum	Derives from the English 'go astern' (reverse). 'He missed his turning so he had to *gostum* until he could turn off.'
Havoc	Chaotic or wild, as in English, but can be used as an adjective. 'My girl is so *havoc*. She is at a disco every night!'
Kayu	From the Malay, meaning 'stupid', and pronounced 'kah-yoo'. 'He has failed his exams again. He is so *kayu*.'
Kiasu	From the Hokkien, meaning 'afraid to lose face'. 'He is so *kiasu*, he won't admit his watch is not a genuine Gucci.'
Lah	No particular meaning, but often used to complete sentences. Especially common is 'OK, *lah*?' or 'Very funny, *lah*'.
Langgar	From the Malay, meaning 'to collide with'. 'I'm afraid I might *langgar* another car'.
Obiang	From the Hokkien word for 'ugly'. 'These fashions are so *obiang*.'

215

Pai she	Hokkien for 'shy' or 'embarrassed'. 'She's a teenager, and very *pai she*.'
Shiok	Malay word meaning 'wonderful'. 'I'm full up. That meal was *shiok*.'
Skarly	Suddenly, as in 'I thought I was on my own, but then he *skarly* appeared'.
Solid	Used as an exclamation, as we might use the word 'great'. 'Look at that car! That's *solid*!'
Sotong	Malay word for 'octopus', a creature that has the ability to squirt black ink to bewilder predators – thus 'confused' in Singlish. 'Didn't you know about it? You must be *sotong*.'
Suaku	Hokkien word for 'village idiot' or 'bumpkin'. 'You must know about the latest computer! Don't be so *suaku*!'
Terok	Malay word for 'difficult' or 'troublesome'. 'He really is a *terok* person to work with.'
Tompang	From the Malay, meaning 'to ask a favour'. 'If you're going to the letter box, can I *tompang* this letter to be posted?'
Ulu	Deserted or empty. 'This place is absolutely *ulu*.'
Uwee	A U-turn – presumably derived from Australian slang. 'I'm going to do a *Uwee*.'

Appendix

FURTHER INFORMATION
Books
General

The Singapore Tourist Board publishes numerous free leaflets, several of which are included in the list below. The US company called Longitude can also offer suggestions for further reading, and provide a mail-order service. Visit their website at www.longitudebooks.com.

An Insider's Guide to Singapore, Singapore Tourism Board, 2002
Cruising Singapore, Singapore Tourism Board, 2002
Festivals and Events in Singapore, Singapore Tourism Board, 2002
Official Guide to Singapore, Singapore Tourism Board, 2002
Singapore and Malaysia Map, Bartholomew Maps
Singapore River, Singapore Tourism Board, 2002
Yours to Explore: Orchard Road, Singapore Tourism Board, 2002
Singapore Film and TV Handbook, Singapore Economic Development Board
Singapore in Colour, Singapore, Sing Wah, 1967

Wildlife and conservation

Briffett, Clive *A Guide to the Common Birds of Singapore*, Singapore Science Centre, 1986
Chin, Wee Yeow and Briffett, Clive *A Guide to the Bukit Timah Nature Reserve*, Nature Society of Singapore
Cubit, Gerald and Payne, Junaidi *Wild Malaysia*, MIT Press, 1990
Cox, Merel *A Photographic Guide to Snakes and Other Reptiles of Peninsular Malaysia, Singapore and Thailand*, Ralph Curtis Publishing, 1998
Francis, Charles M *A Photographic Guide to the Mammals of South-East Asia*, Ralph Curtis Publishing, 2001
Hails, Christopher and Jarvis, Frank *Birds of Singapore*, Times Editions, 1987
Kiam, Chua Ee *Ours to Protect*, Nature Society Singapore, 1993
Kiat, Tan Wee and Fook, Chew Yen *Naturally Yours, Singapore* The [Singapore] National Parks Board, 1992
Layton, Lesley, *Songbirds in Singapore*, Oxford University Press, 1991
Polunin, Ivan *Plants and Flowers of Singapore*, Times Editions, 1987
Robson, Craig *A Guide to the Birds of Southeast Asia*, Princeton University Press, 2000
Trees and Nature Areas in Singapore, Singapore Tourism Board, 2002
Williams, Winston *Singapore's Fabulous Jurong Birdpark*, The Jurong Birdpark, 1989

Economics and finance

Expatriate Living Costs in Singapore, Singapore International Chamber of Commerce, 1999/2000

Murray, Geoffrey and Perrera, Audrey *Singapore: The Global City-State*, St Martin's Press, 1995

Regnier, Philippe *Singapore: City-State in South East Asia*, University of Hawaii Press, 1992

Singapore Investment News, Singapore Economic Development Board, 1999

The Investor's Guide to Singapore, Singapore International Chamber of Commerce, 2000

History and politics

Barber, Noel *Sinister Twilight: The Fall of Singapore*, 1968

Barber, Noel *The War of the Running Dogs: Malaya, 1948–1960*, 1971

Chinese Customs and Festivals in Singapore, Singapore Federation of Chinese Clan Associations, 1989

Flower, Raymond *Raffles: The Story of Singapore*, Croom Helm, 1984

Hua, Siow Jin *Ray Tyer's Singapore Then and Now*, 1993

Liu, Gretchen *Singapore: A Pictorial Survey, 1819–2000*, Charles E Tuttle, 2001

Maya, Jayapal *Old Kuala Lumpur*, Oxford University Press, 1994

Maya, Jayapal *Old Singapore*, Oxford University Press, 1994

Nicol, Gladys *Malaysia and Singapore*, B T Batsford, 1977

Singapore's 100 Historic Places, National Heritage Board, 2002

Yew, Lee Kuan *The Singapore Story*, 1998

Yew, Lee Kuan *From Third World to First: The Singapore Story, 1965–2000*, 2000

Yong, Yap Siang *Fortress Singapore: The Battlefield Guide*, Romen Bose and Pang, Ministry of Defence, 1992

Health

Wilson-Howarth, Jane *Healthy Travel: Bugs, Bites & Bowels*, Cadogan, 1995

Wilson-Howarth, Jane *Your Child's Health Abroad*, Bradt, 1998

Fiction

Barber, Noel *Tanamera: A Novel of Singapore*, 1981

Clavell, James *King Rat*, Dell, 1962

Conrad, Joseph *Lord Jim*, Penguin Putnam, 1991

Elphic, Peter and Smith, Michael *Odd Man Out: The Story of the Singapore Traitor*, 1993

Gay, Jenny *Sweet and Sour Singapore*, 1992

Lim, Catherine *The Teardrop Story Woman*, 1998

Maugham, W Somerset, *Collected Short Stories: Volume 4*, Viking, 1995

Shelley, Rex *Sounds and Sins of Singlish, and Other Nonsense*, 1995

Websites
Travel advice

Canadian traveller www.singapore-ca.com

Chinese traveller www.singapore.com.tw

German traveller www.new-asia-singapore.de

Japanese traveller www.newasia-singapore.or.jp
Nordic traveller www.newasia-singapore.nu
UK traveller www.newasia-singapore.com
US traveller www.singapore-usa.com

Government

IT in Education www.moe.edu.sg/iteducation
Ministry of Education www.moe.edu.sg
Ministry of Manpower www.gov.sg/mom
National Computer Board www.ncb.gov.sg
Singapore Broadcasting Authority www.sba.gov.sg
Singapore E-commerce Hotbed www.ech.ncb.gov.sg
Singapore Economic Development Board www.sedb.com
Singapore ONE www.s-one.net.sg
Telecommunication Authority of Singapore www.tas.gov.sg

220

KEY TO STANDARD SYMBOLS

—·—·—	International boundary			Historic building
······	District boundary		✝	Church or cathedral
— — —	National park boundary			Buddhist temple
✈	Airport (international)			Buddhist monastery
✈	Airport (other)			Hindu temple
✛	Airstrip		୯	Mosque
	Helicopter service		▶	Golf course
▬▬	Railway			Stadium
·········	Footpath		▲	Summit
— —	Car ferry		△	Boundary beacon
— —	Passenger ferry		◉	Outpost
	Petrol station or garage		✕—✕	Border post
ᴾ	Car park			Rock shelter
	Bus station etc			Cable car, funicular
✑	Cycle hire		▬▬	Mountain pass
M	Underground station		o	Waterhole
	Hotel, inn etc		✳	Scenic viewpoint
▲	Campsite			Botanical site
	Hut			Specific woodland feature
♀	Wine bar			Lighthouse
✕	Restaurant, café etc			Marsh
✉	Post office			Mangrove
☏	Telephone			Bird nesting site
e	Internet café			Turtle nesting site
	Hospital, clinic etc			Coral reef
	Museum			Beach
	Zoo			Scuba diving
i	Tourist information			Fishing sites
$	Bank			
	Statue or monument			
	Archaeological or historic site			

Other map symbols are sometimes shown in separate key boxes with individual explanations for their meanings.

Index

Page numbers in bold indicate major entries, those in italics indicate maps.